CANADIAN SPIRITS

CANADIAN SPIRITS

The Essential Cross-Country
Guide to Distilleries, Their
Spirits, and Where to
Imbibe Them

STEPHEN BEAUMONT & CHRISTINE SISMONDO

NIMBUS
PUBLISHING
— NIMBUS.CA —

Nimbus Publishing Limited
3660 Strawberry Hill Street, Halifax, NS, B3K 5A9
(902) 455-4286 nimbus.ca

Printed and bound in Canada
NB1442

Cover Design: Alex MacAskill, Midnight Oil Print & Design House
Interior Design: Peggy Issenman, Peggy & Co.
Editor: Whitney Moran
Proofreader: Angela Mombourquette
Photo research: Ian Gibb and Alexandra Harrington
All photos provided and owned by distilleries except where noted.

Library and Archives Canada Cataloguing in Publication

Title: Canadian spirits : the essential cross-country guide to distilleries, their spirits, and
where to imbibe them / Stephen Beaumont & Christine Sismondo.
Names: Beaumont, Stephen, 1964- author. | Sismondo, Christine, author.
Description: Includes bibliographical references.
Identifiers: Canadiana 20190156694 | ISBN 9781771087681 (hardcover)
Subjects: LCSH: Distilleries—Canada—Guidebooks. | LCSH: Microdistilleries—
Canada—Guidebooks. | LCSH: Liquors—Canada. | LCSH: Canada—Guidebooks. | LCGFT:
Guidebooks.
Classification: LCC TP590.C2 B43 2019 | DDC 641.2/50971—dc23

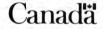

Nimbus Publishing acknowledges the financial support for its publishing activities from
the Government of Canada, the Canada Council for the Arts, and from the Province of
Nova Scotia. We are pleased to work in partnership with the Province of Nova Scotia to
develop and promote our creative industries for the benefit of all Nova Scotians.

Dedicated to the memory of Richard Beaumont, a wonderful and endlessly supportive man who was my friend as well as my father. This one's for you, Dad!
— SB

This book is for Allan, who does a lot more than most people will ever know. Thank you, from the bottom of my heart, for all of it.
— CS

Alert

Kauujitoq
(Resolute)

• Inuvik

Cambridge Bay

Igaluit
(Frobisher Bay)

• Dawson

YUKON
TERRITORY

Whitehorse •

NORTHWEST
TERRITORIES

NUNAVUT

NEWFOUNDLAND
& LABRADOR

Watson
Lake

Echo Bay

• Inujivik

Yellowknife

Gander

Kangiqcliniq
(Rankin Inlet)

Fort
Nelson

Hay River

Fort Smith

Schefferville

Happy Valley-
Goose Bay

St. John's

Prince
Rupert

Churchill •

Prince
George •

BRITISH
COLUMBIA

ALBERTA

Edmonton •

SASKATCHEWAN

MANITOBA

Chisasibi
(Fort George)

QUEBEC

Sept-Iles

PRINCE
EDWARD
ISLAND

Sydney

Flin Flon •

Chibougamau

Victoria •

Calgary •

Vancouver •

Saskatoon •

Lethbridge •

Regina •

Winnipeg •

ONTARIO

Moosonee •

NEW
BRUNSWICK

Charlottetown

Quebec •

Fredericton •

Saint John •

Sherbrooke •

Halifax •

NOVA SCOTIA

Thunder Bay •

Montreal •

Sudbury •

Ottawa ★

Toronto
Hamilton •
London •

Windsor •

CONTENTS

FOREWORD

t wasn't too long ago that, in the eyes of most of the world, Canadian distilling was, to be quite honest, a bit of a joke. Not that many Canadians were aware of this fact, as we sipped proudly away on our rye whiskies, blissfully unaware of how precious little of their namesake grain they contained. But if you travelled beyond our borders, you'd not find much in the way of respect.

Which is not to say that Canadian spirits didn't sell well, especially Canadian whisky. South of the border, for the longest time, our whisky significantly outsold bourbon and Tennessee whiskeys combined! But what made it so popular was the same characteristic that diminished it in the eyes of whisky experts around the globe, namely its mild, borderline bland flavour. Because Canadian whisky laws allow for the addition of a small percentage of what's known as "flavouring spirits"—usually a more boldly flavourful whisky, but also sometimes other spirits or even wine—wags of the spirits world would deride our whisky as "flavoured vodka."

Some tried to counter this image, most notably Corby Distillers in the mid-1990s with a range of high-end whiskies that took only a few short years to fail, but most attempts by the big distilleries to "premiumize"

Canadian spirits were lacklustre at best. As for craft distilling, even as small-batch distilleries were popping up all over the United States, there were none in Canada save for a small and scattered handful.

Change came, but as is typical for Canada, with our patchwork of provincial laws and regulations, it arrived at different times and at a different pace across the country. Thanks to its "BC Craft" legislation, the product of some effective lobbying work on the part of the province's handful of pioneering small distilleries, British Columbia arrived first to the craft spirits party in 2013. The Maritimes followed shortly thereafter, Nova Scotia—which, in fact, had led the way a couple of decades earlier with its Glenora Distillery— taking the lead alongside Prince Edward Island, while Québec and Ontario lagged for another couple of years before finally picking up speed. With Newfoundland and Labrador and the Yukon, the Prairie provinces brought up the rear of the craft distilling boom and are, at the time of writing, still very much in development.

What it all adds up to is a national craft spirits market that is quite literally growing by the week. And that takes us to a Toronto bar on a mid-February evening in 2018.

Between that snowy day and the commencement of our work, the number of distilleries in Canada swelled by no fewer than fifty, a growth of some 40 percent, with new ones being discovered regularly even as others were found to still be in the planning stages or, in some unfortunate instances, already defunct. Keeping on top of it all, and defining a point at which we would stop adding and subtracting, became our full-time job.

All of which ultimately led to the book you hold in your hands. It is a snapshot of what is an astoundingly vibrant, changeable, and now internationally respected industry, one of which all Canadians can be justly proud. Canadian whisky has retained its place among the pantheon of great global whiskies, joined today by world-class gins, vodkas, rums, and many other assorted spirits. It's an industry worthy of celebration, and this is our way of celebrating it.

Whether you are a seasoned spirits expert, a curious newcomer, or just someone wanting to add a distillery tour or two to your next Canadian vacation, we believe you'll find plenty in the following pages to set you to thinking—and make you at least a little bit thirsty. So please sit back, pour yourself a glass of something soothing or fortifying, and join us on a spirited romp across Canada.

As we sipped paradoxically tropical cocktails, Christine and I discussed the need to bring order to what was then the chaos of the Canadian distillery scene. Both being writers, the best means to that end, we thought, would be a conclusive guidebook, and both being drinks writers, we figured that we were the ones to do it! What we didn't anticipate at the time was the magnitude of the task we had just assigned ourselves.

Cheers!
Stephen Beaumont

INTRODUCTION

My co-author and fellow spirits aficionado, Stephen Beaumont, calls this book a "snapshot."

I couldn't have said it better, which is one of the many reasons he's such a tough act to follow. Indeed, much of our time chronicling this dynamic scene was spent figuratively "herding cats"—keeping track of new developments, launches, and the many renovation, relocation, and re-branding projects underway. It's a young industry, in more ways than one, since not only is craft distilling new in Canada but a lot of the people involved in it are young. And, young or old, there's no shortage of committed and enthusiastic characters with a lot of energy and openness in this business.

That energy is what makes this such an exciting scene. Although most distilleries share a few common threads, such as making the most of local ingredients, no two philosophies or motivations are really the same. Everybody had a different story to tell and a dream they were following and, quite sincerely, it was hard not to fall a little bit in love with each of them and their projects. Some were working on telling the story of their homeland and ancestral traditions with Canadian ingredients; others were trying to revive the story of spirits in their region. We met a whole lot of people with a firm commitment to zero-waste distillation and sustainability and others who were working to promote stronger, more diverse communities with their practices. It was nothing short of life-changing to meet so many iconoclasts with their own unique visions for the future of Canada's terroir.

As with anything worth doing, though, these are people facing significant obstacles. Some obstacles come from government regulations, taxes, and provincial control boards that are only slowly adjusting to the new world of small-scale distilling; others have to do with inter-provincial trade barriers and the limitations of small markets. Craft distillers also face stiff competition from big brands, who can provide incentives and discounts that they simply aren't in a position to offer. That's especially a problem when it comes to selling to bars and restaurants, which have their own problems with tight margins and often have little choice but to buy more affordable big brands over craft spirits, even if they'd really love to be able to support local independents.

Each region presents its own challenges and, outside of British Columbia and a couple of Atlantic provinces, nearly everybody had a convincing story as to why their province was the toughest place in which to do business. And, surely, the proliferation of craft start-ups in certain areas—BC and Alberta in particular—suggests that some regions have conditions that are more friendly to craft spirits than others. We're not here to settle that debate, of course, but the one problem that nearly everyone shared was that the public was still a little unsure as to what, exactly, craft spirits were. Several different distillers, for example, told me that one of the top questions they get from visitors is: "So, what kind of beer do you make here?"

That's not really surprising, given that, until recently, Canadian distilleries have been closed to the public and, as a result, people have a very unclear idea about the process which, to a novice, might appear complicated or magical. The basic principles, in fact, are pretty simple; getting it right is trickier. The devil is truly in the details. It can take a while to learn the secrets behind making a truly world-class gin, whisky, or rum and how to elevate the craft of making spirits into an art.

Two or three years ago, I might have guessed that we were a decade away from this happening in Canada on a wide scale. Some of the early outliers had made remarkable products, but they were few and far between. I'm very happy to say I was wrong about that. Prepared for a lot of uneven product, I embarked on my journey with a healthy degree of skepticism and was, instead, confronted with

some remarkable and memorable spirits. Somewhere along the way—in most regions—craft distillation has hit critical mass and, together, Canadian products are getting better every day.

I'm hoping that with this book, readers will learn a little more about craft distillation in general and the Canadian scene in particular, and come away with even a fraction of the amount of enthusiasm I've come to have for this nation's craft spirits industry.

Santé!
Christine Sismondo

A HISTORY OF
DISTILLING
IN
Canada

If you've ever spent time in a bar, which, we imagine, most reading this book have, then you've probably heard a few stories about the history of spirits in Canada—from bootleggers to whisky barons and temperance leagues to moonshiners. And some of them might even be true.

No question, Canadian alcohol history is a fascinating story—complicated, yes, and with more than its share of tall tales and misinformation. One of the more interesting recent developments, though, is about how the current craft spirits movement echoes the past and is beginning to revive a distillation culture that, only a dozen years ago, was considered permanently lost to big business.

So, how did we get here? Well, in the beginning, there was rum. Even though Canada is associated with whisky around the world, in early colonial days, its most important spirit would have been rum, just as it was everywhere else in North America. Invented largely to deal with another problem—namely, how to get rid of all the molasses (a by-product of the sugar industry)—rum was used by settlers as medicine, currency, and, of course, for recreational drinking.

However, rum wasn't actually the very first alcohol in the country—only the first spirit. Before the Europeans arrived, Indigenous peoples all over the Americas would have been familiar with fermented beverages—beer made from corn, agave, or spruce. What the colonial settlers did introduce, though, were *distilled* spirits, commonly produced in Europe for medicinal and recreational use starting around the twelfth century. At first, most of the rum in Atlantic Canada and New France would have been imported from the Caribbean but, by the end of the eighteenth century, rum was being made (with imported molasses) in Québec City and elsewhere.

OUR FAVOURITE RUMS

Barrelling Tide 5 Fathom Rum (p. 33)
Ironworks Bluenose Rum (p. 40)
Yongehurst Harbour Rum (p. 119)
North of 7 Leatherback Rum (p. 135)
Capital K Tall Grass Oaked Rhumb (p. 140)

Rum distillation started to fall off as settlers moved farther west and established farms, since it doesn't make much sense to import other people's waste for distillation when you have your own to deal with. As Québec and Ontario began to be populated and farmed by European settlers, farmers, who sometimes had bumper crops for which they had neither market nor storage space, would often build a still to turn surplus grain into liquor.

Spirits can be made from just about any agricultural product and, once distilled, don't go bad, no longer attract rodents or other pests, and can be easily transported. As a result of these advantages, farms and spirits grew in lockstep in Canada, essentially for the same reason rum was invented—to reduce and eliminate waste. Turn your trash into cash.

These weren't big operations. Some would have been started by the Loyalists who migrated to Canada from the United States after the American Revolution. Others were

German, Irish, Scottish, English, French, and, later on, Ukrainian settlers, who brought regional distilling practices and traditions with them. Because most worked with tiny pot stills, they had no choice but to make small batches. What they could and did do, however, was work their stills hard and long, pumping out a whole lot of whisky. So much, in fact, that prices dropped to about ten pence a gallon in the 1830s, roughly the equivalent of five dollars per litre in modern terms. Since it was so cheap and readily available, people started to use it for everything—to guard against the cold, to celebrate with, to ward off bad spirits, to wake themselves up, to put themselves to sleep. Whisky was consumed day and night, whenever the taverns were open—which was pretty well all day and all night.

Located on every corner, taverns were as ubiquitous as today's coffee shops. In Ontario, for example, there was one tavern for roughly every three hundred people. Many of these were open at all hours and almost always full of folks socializing, working, holding meetings, or trading goods. And, instead of coffee, people drank spirits—roughly twenty-five litres of *absolute alcohol* per adult per year— over twice as much as we drink now.

Even the most liberal among us can see that such excessive alcohol consumption was likely going to cause problems. Which it did. In response to the alcohol-related rise in violence (both domestic and in tavern brawls)

One half mile of barmen along Yonge Street during Prohibition parade, March 8, 1916. (John Boyd / Library and Archives Canada / PA-072525)

Gooderham and Worts Ltd., Toronto Canada, Canadian Rye Whiskey by Arthur H. Hider and published by the Toronto Lithograph Company. (Library and Archives Canada, Acc. No. R9266-1617 Peter Winkworth Collection of Canadiana)

and the growing number of impoverished and/or neglected children, temperance groups would eventually become a serious political force, especially in southern Ontario and the Atlantic provinces. New Brunswick, for example, attempted to go entirely dry with its 1855 Prohibition Act but, largely because nobody enforced it, the experiment failed and the law was soon repealed.

In the 1860s, the spirits industry started to transform from one dominated by small farm-stills into big business. The US Civil War (1861–1865) was a major factor here, driving up the export market, since Canadian farmers, manufacturers, and distillers were suddenly needed to help supply basics to the States, particularly whisky, which doctors and medics used as an antiseptic, painkiller, and disinfectant for the wounded. Whisky had become an important commodity, increasingly dominated by larger operations whose owners had invested in efficient column stills. By 1870, Toronto's Gooderham & Worts distillery (established in 1837) had become the most valuable industrial

business—of any kind—in the entire province of Ontario.

Gooderham & Worts would soon be joined by four other distillers— Henry Corby, Hiram Walker, J. P. Wiser, and Joseph Seagram, established in the mid-1800s, the last having taken over William Hespeler's massively successful rye whisky operation in Berlin (now Kitchener). Each of these had his own grand plans and visions and, together, the group would come to be known as the "Big Five." By the end of the nineteenth century, many of the small stills had been shuttered, no longer able

OUR FAVOURITE SINGLE MALT WHISKIES

Glen Breton Ice 12 Year Old (p. 37)
Lucky Bastard Single Malt (p. 148)
Eau Claire Single Malt Whisky (p. 161)
Shelter Point Artisanal Single Malt Whisky (p. 197)
Yukon Spirits Two Brewers Release No. 12: Peated (p. 260)

to compete, and a decade after the Civil War ended, only some twenty licences remained, down from nearly two hundred.

In 1890, a new law would come into play that would make it even harder for the little guys to compete—all whisky had to undergo two years of barrel-aging to be sold as "Canadian whisky." Between that and the blending practice that became common in that era, our whisky underwent a serious quality revolution around this time and its reputation internationally shot up, especially since Canada was the first country in the world, in 1887, to introduce mandatory minimum aging requirements., which, at first was only one year.

Despite the value of this industry and the wealth and power big distillers had, temperance talk wasn't going away. Nor were the endless raging debates over prohibition laws, which, in many regions, led counties and townships to opt for going dry—something made possible under the Canada Temperance Act of 1878.

In 1898, Canadians went to the polls to vote on a nationwide prohibition law. Despite the fact that 51 percent voted in favour, Prime Minister Wilfrid Laurier felt the slim majority wasn't enough to justify it. Since there were regions—Québec and some more urban areas—where a majority were wildly opposed to it, it seemed unreasonable to force them to live under the anti-modernist feelings of what was, in their communities, but a small minority. Regions that wanted

to go dry were welcome to do so—there just seemed to Laurier no need to force the wishes of a small majority on the rest of the country.

In response to this, activists turned their attention to getting as many towns and counties as possible to go dry. Prince Edward Island was the lone province that went fully dry, until the First World War prompted Manitoba, Nova Scotia, Alberta, and Ontario to hop on the water wagon in 1916. Four more provinces followed suit in 1917, and the following year the War Measures Act prohibited all alcohol—a ban that lasted until 1920. By then, most distilleries were making industrial alcohol, anyway, which was needed for the war effort.

At war's end, it was up to each province to repeal its legislation and open up the liquor stores and bars again. We borrow the information in the table on the next page from *Booze: A Distilled History*, Craig Heron's brilliant history of this subject—and thank him for it, since we know he did a lot of research assembling these dates.

Even this table doesn't fully convey how long it took for the true "modernization" of the alcohol industry in Canada, since the re-establishment of public drinking didn't necessarily mean bars were allowed to serve spirits or cocktails. In 1934 Ontario for example, public drinking was limited to beer parlours, and it wasn't until 1947 that bars could apply for "cocktail tavern" licences.

Most people think Canadian spirits got a big boost during American

PROVINCE	ENACTED PROHIBITION	REPEALED TO ALLOW RETAIL SALES	ALLOWED PUBLIC DRINKING
PEI	1901	1948	1964
Manitoba	1916	1923	1928
Nova Scotia	1916	1930	1948
Alberta	1916	1924	1924
Ontario	1916	1927	1934
Saskatchewan	1917	1925	1935
New Brunswick	1917	1927	1961
British Columbia	1917	1921	1925
Newfoundland	1917	1925	1925
Yukon	1918	1921	1925
Québec	1919	1919	1921

Prohibition. But as you can see, it was a complicated situation, since provincial prohibitions were still in force for most of the fourteen years that all of America went dry. Québec was the outlier, which is why Samuel Bronfman set up the Distillers Corporation in 1924 in the town of LaSalle, located south of Montréal (though now a city borough). Unlike in the United States, alcohol prohibition was never particularly strongly enforced and there were a great number of legal loopholes, including mail-order booze, sacramental wine, and prescriptions for medicinal alcohol. Pharmacies were busy.

Some whisky definitely *did* make it across the Detroit/Windsor "funnel" and through the export houses at the southern border of Saskatchewan. And there were a good number of Maritime "rum-runners" sending boats with supplies south to "Rum Row" off the Jersey Shore to help the thirsty Americans. But the majority of smuggled liquor went through St. Pierre and Miquelon, two islands in the Atlantic that are still a part of France, and, while some of that particular contraband came from Bronfman's enterprises, much more actually came from Europe and never even touched Canadian soil before making its way to America's east coast.

Although more Canadian distilleries survived prohibition (per capita) than did American ones, these were still hard times and the value of many

OUR FAVOURITE VODKAS
Cirka Vodka (p. 69)
Rheault Loon Vodka (p. 125)
Sperling Silver French Laundry Vodka (p. 152)
Troubled Monk Vodka (p. 181)
Stillhead Vodka (p. 200)

The sixty-plus years between Canada's various prohibitions and the establishment of its first small distillery—Nova Scotia's Glenora—belonged to Big Whisky. Flush with cash from from exports, Seagram's bought up a large number of competing distilleries and even expanded into the United States with its 5 Crown and 7 Crown brands after Prohibition. And for the large part, these whiskies were smooth, light, and to our more adventurous palates, kind of bland. It was mixing whisky, destined to be served in the extremely popular "7 and 7" (7 Crown and 7-Up).

distilleries plummeted. Some businessmen bought them up at fire-sale prices, gambling that the tides would turn eventually, which led to a consolidation of the Canadian distillation industries during the late 1920s. The gamble paid off in 1933, when the United States repealed its nationwide Prohibition but had nothing to celebrate with since American stills had been shuttered for fourteen years. Bronfman came to the rescue here, with barrel after barrel of aged whisky stocks ready to roll. Anticipating the legal changes in the US, and being ready to meet a surge in demand, helped make his business phenomenally successful. It also helped establish Canadian whisky as a favourite in the United States, a status it continues to hold today. Until about fifteen years ago, Canadian whisky was America's bestseller, managing to outsell even bourbon south of the border.

Although there was no prohibition during the Second World War, most distilleries slowed down production to, once again, make industrial alcohol for the war effort. Postwar, though, Canadian facilities redoubled their efforts by expanding with new facilities, especially in the west. Most notable were Frank McMahon and George H. Reifel, who in 1946 founded Alberta Distillers, where they would revive the tradition of 100 percent rye whisky, and the then-state-of-the-art Seagram's distillery in Gimli, Manitoba, which opened its doors in 1968 and also opened people's eyes to the great potential for spirits production in the bread basket of Canada. We'll pick up on some of that history when we turn our attention to the International Giants.

Glenora Distillery in Cape Breton, Nova Scotia.

NOTE

Bibliographical sources for this section can be found on page 269, along with suggestions for further reading.

WHY CANADIAN CRAFT DISTILLING AND WHY NOW?

n Canada, as in the United States, craft distilling followed the path, and the pattern of evolution, laid out by craft brewing. So to understand the former, it helps to first take a quick look at the latter.

While the first few of what were then called "microbreweries" opened in the US several years before they did in Canada, the growth of a handful of small breweries into a legitimate microbrewery movement occurred more-or-less simultaneously in the two countries, beginning around the mid-1980s and really taking off five to ten years later. The reason they rallied so quickly was simple: these new breweries provided alternatives to the less flavourful, mass-produced lagers of the dominant breweries of the time.

Fast-forward, now, to the present century and the craft distilling movement, which gained traction south of the border significantly before it did in Canada. Some of those earlier small-scale distillers did try to follow the microbrewery lead by disparaging the massive, multinational distilling companies, but there was one problem: those big distilleries didn't make

uninteresting and largely homogenous products, but instead produced many, if not most, of the world's great spirits!

And so, like the explosive second wave of craft breweries, craft distillers instead followed the mantra set up by the adherents of the "100-mile diet" and emphasized the benefits to be found in "drinking local." It worked, sort of.

In the United States in the early twenty-first century and in Canada a decade or so later, craft distillers were challenged on several fronts, but none so much as the per-bottle cost of making spirits on a small, rather than massive, scale. As a result, "drinking

OUR FAVOURITE LIQUEURS

Avril Amaretto (p. 81)
Hansen Morning Glory Chocolate
Hazelnut Cream Liqueur (p. 165)
Victoria Cacao Chocolate Liqueur (p. 204)
Gillespie's Lemoncello (p. 217)
Okanagan Spirits Blackcurrant Liqueur (p. 251)

local" also frequently meant paying more—sometimes much more.

This consumers proved themselves prepared to do, but only to a point. And for many, that point centred on quality and taste.

Plainly stated, while some early craft distillers on both sides of the border were putting out great spirits from Day One, others were decidedly more hit-and-miss. This resulted in a situation where a potential buyer could be looking at three brands on a liquor store shelf: one at a good price from a known, international distillery; another, more expensive label from a recognized local champion; and a third option at an even higher price from a distillery known to make products that can be phenomenally good or astoundingly mediocre. Or worse.

As the novelty of having a distillery down the road began to vanish, or the "local distillery" was joined by several others, the pressure on craft distillers to turn out consistent and consistently good products—pressure that, quite frankly, should have been there all along—grew quickly and significantly. Some rose to meet that challenge and thrived, while others did not and ultimately faded away. And still some others managed to hang on without changing to any great degree in terms of either quality or consistency—although we suspect that members of this last cohort will ultimately be forced to choose between the first two camps.

Which brings us back to the present day, when only a scattering of small-scale distillers still try to demonize the big companies; "drink local" still has some sway, but not nearly the sort of appeal it once had; and craft distilling in Canada is growing at an almost exponential rate. While the first two assertions might at first blush appear to be quite at odds with the last, craft distilling has proved to have not just one, but several tricks still up its sleeve.

OUR FAVOURITE ESOTERIC SPIRITS

Compass Distillers Aquavit (p. 36)
Sivo Valkyrie Aquavit (p. 67)
Bruinwood Advocaat (p. 209)
Dragon Mist Baijiu (p. 215)
Woods Pacific Northwest Amaro (p. 237)

As with modern craft brewing, one of the advantages small-scale distilling has over large-scale is the flexibility to create and innovate at a rapid pace. It can take months or even years for a multinational company to develop, package, and market a new product, whereas a small operation that sells most of what it makes out its front door can do the same in days or weeks. This means that new distilling techniques that tease out different and unique flavours, unusual fermentable ingredients, and odd or offbeat flavourings can be used, assessed, and kept or discarded quickly and with relative ease, thus allowing small distilleries to maintain the consumer's interest in a way that large distilleries simply cannot.

Environmentalism is another arrow that craft distilling keeps in it quiver. As sustainability goes increasingly mainstream, many Canadian distillers are making it part of their mandate, to the extent that zero-waste distillation is no longer a pie-in-the-sky concept but considered a legitimately attainable goal. (In fact, such goals often march hand-in-hand with the innovation movement noted above.) Consumers who share the concerns these distillers express over climate change and humankind's impact upon nature will inevitably be drawn to their brands.

Finally, unlike a multinational distillery that buys grain and other raw materials by the railcar load, small distilleries are able to make enterprising and effective use of local ingredients in a way that only their lack of scale allows. Whether it is buying their grain or fruit from a farmer a kilometre or two down the road or personally foraging for the botanicals to be used in their gin, Canadian craft distillers are connecting drinkers to the land in a way that no large spirits company ever could. The stories these sort of initiatives allow the company to tell don't hurt, either.

All of which adds up to fertile ground for small-batch Canadian distillers. And so long as the federal and provincial governments continue to make legislative adjustments that recognize the unique challenges facing craft distillers, and those distillers continue to strive towards excellence, it is reasonable to expect that these glory days of Canadian spirits will continue for some time to come. The revolution in Canadian distilling has only just begun!

OUR FAVOURITE GINS

Distillerie du St. Laurent Dry Gin (p. 84)
Black's Gin (p. 129)
Wild Life Gin (p. 183)
Long Table London Dry Gin (p. 219)
Legend Black Moon Gin (p. 247)

HOW TO USE THE CANADIAN SPIRITS GUIDE

① Name, address, and phone number. This is fairly self-explanatory but, since distilleries do *occasionally* move—albeit rarely, and generally either in search of more square footage or a more central location—we encourage you to double-check this information before you set out for a visit.

② Almost all the distilleries have websites, but not all websites are created equal. Our experience is that using an "info@distilleryname.com" email address or web-based inquiry form yields about a 50 percent response rate, so questions are best delivered by phone or, even better, in person. Many if not most of Canada's small-scale distillers are operated by too few people with too little time, so we advise patience when awaiting a response to an inquiry.

Barrelling Tide Distillery

164 Parkway Dr, Port Williams, NS B0P 1T0
(902) 542-1627
www.barrellingtidedistillery.com

When Russell Murphy met his soon-to-be wife while they were both working on a Holland America cruise ship, he already had an interest in distilling, but the then chef had no plans to make a career out of it. As Murphy describes it, however, his interest soon developed into an obsession and it wasn't long before the pair were travelling to visit and work in distilleries rather than taking more ordinary vacations.

The obsession came to fruition in 2016, when Barrelling Tide opened as the first distillery in Nova Scotia's Annapolis Valley fruit belt.

The company's first products were a vodka, a gin, and, thanks to the availability of local fruit, a raspberry liqueur. These were soon joined by numerous other liqueurs, each produced only when the fruit is in season locally, and a rum distilled out of molasses purchased from the New Brunswick-based Crosby's. The "Barrelling" side of the distillery will make itself apparent as the years pass, with barrel-aged rum already on the market and whiskies and brandies in maturation.

Although tours are not on offer, except for groups, the entire distillery is viewable through the large shop windows and anyone working at the store is able to talk visitors through the process, ending with a sample of the products, of course.

TIDE GIN (40%)
An immensely attractive aroma of slightly minty, slightly citrusy herbs introduces this classic New World gin, defined not by its juniper but by the aromatic character that continues through the soft, alluring palate to the peppery, spruce-y finish.

5 FATHOM RUM (42%)
Salted oak barrels contribute to an aroma that combines a molasses-y caramel with notes of the seashore. On the palate, it's rich, round, and sweet, with chocolate taking the place of the caramel and lingering licorice candy on the finish. Sip neat and keep away from cola.

**CHERRY LIQUEUR (20%)
& CRANBERRY LIQUEUR (24%)**
From an extensive line of fruit liqueurs, these are, like the others, distilled from Annapolis Valley fruit and then blended with juice from the same fruit, with no sugar added. The Cherry both smells and tastes like candy dark cherries, not too sweet and with a bit of flavourful tanginess to balance, while the Cranberry has all the tartness you might expect from the fruit, accompanied by soft herbal notes and a lightly warming finish.

33

③ This is, to the best of our knowledge at the time of writing, the basics on what each distillery offers in the way of tours, tastings, on-site sales, and hospitality. Tours and tastings particularly vary widely in terms of price and timing—some are free and available at almost any time the distillery is open, while others come with a price tag and are scheduled according to the season. We strongly advise confirming this information before planning a visit.

| Tours | Samples | On-site sales | Bar |

④ Every distillery has a story, usually a compelling one, and we have done our best to present those here. Nothing can compare, however, with getting the scoop in person and from the horse's mouth, as it were.

⑤ We have done our very best to present a cross-section of the best or most distillery-defining brands from each operation, although for the most part the selection of specific spirits was left to the distillers or distillery owners themselves, and owing to space limitations, each distillery was limited to a maximum of four product reviews. If you come across a style or type of spirit with which you are unfamiliar, please consult the glossary at the end of the book.

A WORD ABOUT NGS

What is NGS?, we hear you ask. Well, it's quite common within the craft distilling world and is really a fairly simple matter, except when it's not. Allow us to explain.

On the simple side, NGS is Neutral Grain Spirit, meaning very high strength alcohol that is created from grain and bought in bulk by distillers for further processing, or rectification, on site. The sources of NGS are many and varied, but principally it is purchased from very large distilleries interested in keeping a quick and easy flow of cash into their coffers.

What happens after the NGS gets to the smaller distillery is what makes it a more complicated matter.

Since NGS is ultra-pure alcohol, some distillers will merely add water to lower the strength, possibly redistill it one last time, then package it as their own vodka. This, in our view, is a bit of a cheat, as it works out to essentially buying someone else's spirit and selling it as your own.

For other distilleries, however, the receipt of the NGS is just the start of an extended process. Some will combine it with many and varied botanicals, steep and redistill once or twice, and in so doing create their own gin. (This is quite commonplace in the EU, where regulations dictate that the base alcohol used for what they define as distilled gin be a minimum of 96 percent alcohol.) Others will use it as a base spirit for fruit liqueurs or in-house barrel aging, whether as a gin, high-proof whisky, or other spirit, and still others will flavour and rectify it in different ways to make any of a variety of spirits.

In *Canadian Spirits*, we have tried as much as possible to identify where NGS is involved and have not included vodkas made exclusively from purchased NGS. We must confess, however, that it is sometimes difficult to get to the facts of the matter, and as such we cannot guarantee that all NGS spirits have been so identified.

THE LARGE LEGACY DISTILLERS

n the nineteenth century, we had the whisky barons. Now, we have a half-dozen or so big distillers in Canada who produce on a scale that most craft distillers can't even fathom. A distillery like Hiram Walker & Sons, for instance, makes more whisky by the first morning coffee break than a small producer can make all year. We shouldn't drive past the big distilleries' contributions, however, since craft distillers have drawn ample inspiration and occasional technical advice from some of these giants, many of which make some truly excellent products.

The vast majority of what the nation's largest distillers produce is, of course, whisky, since that's Canada's signature spirit, and as an important export to the massive American market, is also what pays the bills. You might be surprised to know, however, that some products you'd never suspect were made in Canada at all—such as Gordon's Gin, Russian Prince Vodka, even Malibu Rum—are distilled alongside the whisky at some of the country's large production facilities. In part, that's because they

are part of massive foreign-owned, multinational corporations, who contract out the distillation of certain brands to outposts, based on proximity to the markets and natural resources. Sometimes it's cheaper to ship a finished product, sometimes it isn't.

And, since mergers, acquisitions, and takeover bids seem to be never-ending, this network of giant multinational liquor companies is fluid and often in the process of changing hands, making it practically a full-time job, involving a nine-page flowchart, to keep track of who owns, makes, and/or distributes what. (We cannot even guarantee that every association we make within these pages will still exist by the time you read this!) As such, it makes more sense to focus on the general traditions of these distilleries, which, despite all the changes, tend to be built upon their core lines, alongside innovative new products that typically still honour the historical character of the distillery.

One of the largest producers and exporters in Canada is the Gimli Distillery in Manitoba, about an hour's drive north of Winnipeg. Owned by global giant Diageo since 2001, Gimli pumps out more than 200,000 litres of whisky every day, much of which becomes Crown Royal. It was established on this five-acre site a little over a half-century ago by Sam Bronfman, when he realized it was one of the best places in all of Canada to make whisky. The logic behind building a massive alcohol factory in a town with fewer than 2,500 people—and away from the major markets—becomes clear when you visit: Aside from the relatively cheap land, it's next to a large freshwater lake (Winnipeg) and borders a region populated with hundreds of farms that provide a significant portion of the country's wheat, rye, corn, and barley. Possibly even more important is the fact that it's almost smack-dab in the middle of the country and conveniently located near trans-Canada train and truck shipping routes to the United States. All roads actually do lead to Winnipeg.

OUR FAVOURITE CANADIAN WHISKIES

Hiram Walker Lot No. 40 (p. 28)
Crown Royal XO (p. 27)
Forty Creek Confederation Oak Reserve (p. 28)
Still Waters Stalk & Barrel 100% Rye (p. 117)
Goodridge&Williams Northern Grains
Canadian Whisky (p. 218)

Its influence shouldn't be understated either. Aside from proving that making whisky in the prairies was a smart move, some of the earliest interesting special releases of Canadian whisky came from Crown Royal, which was anticipating a demand for premium whisky as far back as the 1980s and 1990s. It's also kept Americans interested in Canadian whisky for many years, since Crown Royal is phenomenally popular south of the border, especially so in Texas, strangely enough.

Speaking of exports, that's what keeps the lights on at the second-largest producer in the Prairie provinces, Black Velvet, in Lethbridge, Alberta. Originally called the Palliser Distillery, it was opened in October 1973 to produce vodka, light rum, and gin, including Gilbey's, at one time Palliser's sister company. Black Velvet whisky is made there now, but it's worth noting that it wasn't always. The instantly recognizable smooth, light, and heavily marketed whisky was originally made in Québec at the Schenley distillery in Valleyfield, just southwest of Montréal, on an island in the St. Lawrence River. After various acquisitions and mergers, it eventually happened that the people who owned Black Velvet came to own Palliser, and so moved all production to Alberta and renamed it. Although it's easy to lose track of this value brand here in Canada, it's an important export, with about 10 million litres shipped to bottling facilities in California and Kentucky every year.

Slightly smaller in scale, but still very impressive, are Alberta's Highwood and Alberta Distillers. These are both exceedingly high-quality distilleries, which, in some ways, should also be given a fair share of credit for boosting Canadian whisky's fortunes, given that they're responsible for some of the most interesting aged whisky experiments in the country, as well as some influential early single-grain expressions. Alberta Distillers, for example, which was established in Calgary in 1946, owned the 100 percent rye whisky category for many years with its Alberta Premium, a whisky that won international acclaim year after year. Many eventually followed Alberta Premium's lead, but it took some time for other distillers to catch on to the promise of Canadian rye. At the time of this writing, Alberta Distillers is owned by Beam Suntory and, over the years, has made several different premium or special release whiskies, including Dark Horse and Tangle Ridge, a double-casked blended rye. Strangely enough, Alberta Distillers doesn't make Beam Suntory's Canadian Club Premium, which instead hails from Windsor's Hiram Walker—more about that later.

Highwood straddles the fence between a big guy and a craft distillery, since it's still independently owned and family-run, unlike any other distillery in this section. Established as the Sunnyvale Distillery in 1974 in High River, just south of Calgary, this facility was renamed Highwood a decade later and, now with thirty-five employees, has grown substantially since, in part thanks to its acquisition of Potter's Distillers, an Okanagan producer. Since the distillery doubles as a contract packager *and* sources some of its blending spirit, it's hard to pin down exactly how much it is producing each year, but we know it's in the hundreds of thousands of cases, much of it vodka, gin, and rum. One of Highwood's most recognizable products is White Owl—a whisky that's been aged and filtered to become white again—but it's starting to become well known for its long-aged Centennial and Ninety whiskies, which are often released after two decades in the barrel.

Ontario distilleries have also had super-aged releases. Take Collingwood's Canadian Mist, for instance, which offers whiskies like Collingwood 21, which came out in 2016 and added to a range of core products that includes its regular expression, Collingwood Double Barrelled and, of course, Canadian Mist. It opened in 1967, when Barton, a Kentucky company, decided to invest in a Canadian venture, and four years later it was sold to Brown-Forman, which still owns the behemoth plant that's in the same ballpark, production-wise, as Black Velvet.

As big as it is, however, Canadian Mist is dwarfed by the Hiram Walker distillery in Windsor, Ontario, which has the largest distillery capacity in North America. Operating literally twenty-four hours a day, seven days a week, the facility has thirty-seven fermenters and stills producing 48 million litres of alcohol per year. Some of this winds up becoming whiskies such as J. P. Wiser's, Lot No. 40, and Pike Creek, but the distillery is also responsible for Malibu Rum, Polar Ice Vodka, and the McGuinness line of liqueurs. As well, it makes buckets of whisky for its competitors, including rival Canadian Club, one of Canada's best-known brands. Perhaps fitting, given that it was Hiram Walker himself who established the "Club" brand shortly after he founded the distillery in 1858 in Walkerville (now Windsor).

As of the fall of 2017, consumers could finally tour the Hiram Walker site, making this giant operation the first major Canadian distillery to offer the public a glimpse of its inner workings. Hours for the "J. P. Wiser's Experience" are limited and, sadly, the tour doesn't include all areas of the facility or the legendary whisky workshop that master blender Dr. Don Livermore offers to students and whisky writers. Instead of downplaying the blending tradition in Canada—which often confuses American consumers, since Canadians are allowed, according to federal regulations, to add 9.09 percent of other spirits and wines to the blend—Livermore makes a virtue of it. He'll refer to a row of other spirits and wines, for instance, as his "painter's palate" that gives him the flexibility to create an infinite number of blends, using tiny portions of sherry wine, rum, cognac, or even other whiskies

to create new expressions. Certain Wiser's bottlings, Gooderham & Worts expressions, and the super-popular Lot No. 40 rye whisky are testament to the ability of the man known as "Dr. Don" to know exactly when to blend, how much to play around with, and, in some cases, when to just leave a good thing alone.

If you were to name a single person who helped raise the bar for Canadian spirits, Livermore would most certainly be a candidate. But so, too, would be John K. Hall, who founded Grimsby, Ontario's Forty Creek in 1992, when all but a few distilleries were concentrating almost exclusively on making light, smooth, mixing whisky—much of it destined for the export market. Hall, also a winemaker bucked that trend when he started distilling at his winery, Kittling Ridge, and decided to painstakingly revive and reinvent the Canadian blending tradition by fermenting, distilling, and aging each grain separately. That was a departure from Big Whisky's practice of relying on massive streams of Neutral Grain Spirit (NGS) as a base for Canadian "rye" whisky.

It took Hall a decade to release his first batch, but when he did, in 2002, it was a hit—Ontario was ready for a fresh approach to whisky. He also released special editions, some of which grew into year-round fan favourites, and experimented extensively with different blends and aging—even going so far as to make his own port and sherry wine, just so he could use their casks to make

special expressions, and harvesting damaged Canadian oaks to make special barrels. By 2014, Forty Creek was the fastest-growing brand in Canadian whisky, a fact that helped convince the Italian spirits multinational, Gruppo Campari, to buy the comparatively small distillery and take it to the next level.

And whatever happened to the old Schenley distillery, where Black Velvet, one of Canada's most successful exports ever, was invented? It's still there, now known as Valleyfield, and pumps out some 30 million litres of alcohol per year, some destined for Seagram's, Smirnoff and Captain Morgan products, including ready-to-drink cocktails. It's been the most

significant distillery producing whisky in Québec since it was established in the 1940s, but it looks as if it might get some competition soon, now that the US–based Sazerac Company has bought the old Corby Distillery in Montréal. Once the source of De Kuyper "Geneva" Gin (made in the style of Dutch genever) and Peachtree Schnapps, the American whisky giant has refurbished the site, rechristened it the "Old Montreal Distillery," and, as of 2018, started making Canadian whisky there once again.

Since Sazerac has a pretty good batting average for great whisky, we can hardly wait.

TASTING NOTES

ALBERTA DISTILLERS (BEAM SUNTORY)

Alberta Premium (40%)

For many years the standard-bearer for 100% rye whiskies, inside and outside of Canada, this stands the test of time. Smooth and approachable, yet with a good amount of grain-based spiciness, it makes a solid Manhattan or a superior Rye and Ginger.

BLACK VELVET DISTILLERY (HEAVEN HILL)

Black Velvet (40%)

An archetypal Canadian whisky from the mid- to late 1900s, this has a very caramelly nose and a soft palate that continues the caramel theme, supplementing it with hints of cooked stone fruit. Over the years, the base of millions of mixed drinks with cola or ginger ale.

CANADIAN CLUB (BEAM SUNTORY)

Chairman's Select 100% Rye (40%)

We're thankful that, after years of mastering blends, Canadian Club finally turned its attention over to making pure rye whisky—Chairman's Select is cascading with caramel and tropical fruit, with a little sprinkling of baking spice at the finish. Ideal for Old Fashioned cocktails.

Premium (40%)

The label might say "Premium," but to generations of Canadians this is simply "CC." The nose leans more to fruity caramel than rich toffee, while the flavour adds notes of vanilla to a spicy body, making this the base spirit for an archetypal Rye and Ginger.

Small Batch Classic 12 Year Old (40%)

This liquid certainly hit a sweet spot at the 12-year mark, with its deep toffee and vanilla flavours mingling together with burnt orange and a buttery oak ending. Enjoy neat.

COLLINGWOOD (BROWN-FORMAN)

Collingwood (40%)

Not particularly evocative of its grains, this is a solid and serviceable whisky with herbal butterscotch on the nose and a round and rich palate of roasted caramel, vanilla, hints of tannin and herbs, and an oaky finish. A dependable mixing whisky.

Collingwood Double Barrelled (45%)

Aged in once-used oak barrels and finished in new charred oak, this shows well its char on the nose and follows with a fruity, almost smoky palate with hints of roasted banana and a dry, oaky finish. Try it in a Canadian Sazerac.

CROWN ROYAL (DIAGEO)

Fine De Luxe (40%)

The main brand of Crown Royal is known and respected for its combination of softness and flavour, with apple, oak, roasted sugar, and a whiff of fireplace on the nose and a mild, silky, caramelly body that ends in warmth and a bit of smoke.

Northern Harvest Rye (40%)

Famous as one critic's pick for whisky of the year in 2016, this substitutes balanced spice for Deluxe's trademark sweetness on the nose and an oaky mix of dried apple and stone fruit and peppery spices on the palate. Sip with one cube of ice or mix in a Manhattan.

XO (40%)

This cognac barrel–finished whisky offers great depth on the nose, with muted spice, a perfumey mix of apple notes, and a subtle, caramelly oak, while the body is round and soft, but also complex with a mix of vanilla and spice. Eschew the ice and enjoy neat.

XR (40%)

Crown's highest-end blends, this features the last whiskies from the LaSalle distillery in Montréal. The nose has hints of pepper, caraway, and coriander, along with caramel and vanilla, while the round, full, and rich body is the ultimate expression of the Crown style. After dinner or with a good book, no ice.

FORTY CREEK (CAMPARI)

Barrel Select (40%)

The flagship of the distillery that led the way in the Canadian whisky revival, this rich gold whisky has a floral-spicy-caramelly-vanilla nose and a body that has enough sweetness and spice to mix, but also sufficient character to drink on the rocks.

Copper Pot (43%)

Darker and much fruitier than its Barrel Select kin, this has stewed fruit and baking spice on the nose and a very full and round, somewhat winey body that evokes port wine and intense orange liqueur. The makings of a fine Manhattan or après-ski quaff.

Confederation Oak Reserve (40%)

The first Canadian whisky to be aged in Canadian oak, this has a superbly balanced nose of spice and oak and fruit, with a body that speaks equally to spicy rye and sweet corn, with a bonus of drying oak. Sip on its own or, if you must, a cube of ice.

Double Barrel Reserve (40%)

The bourbon barrels in which this undergoes its second aging, or finishing, show easily in the vanilla, butterscotch aroma, with charred oak notes, while the body has an almost smoky edge within all its richness. For after dinner and in a solid Whisky Sour.

HIGHWOOD DISTILLERS

Centennial 10 Year Old (40%)

The bourbon barrels in which this whisky, made from a mix of rye and wheat, is aged are immediately apparent on Centennial's soft, vanilla-laced nose, while the body takes the spiciness of rye and softens it to fruity richness. Try in a Manhattan with an assertive vermouth.

White Owl Whisky (40%)

Don't confuse this bourbon barrel-aged and filtered spirit with white dog, as it is styled quite differently. Despite its colour, there is a whiff of caramel on the nose and an appealing viscosity on the palate, with some stone-fruit notes and a quick finish. Try in a white Old Fashioned.

HIRAM WALKER (PERNOD RICARD)

Gooderham & Worts Four Grain (44.4%)

Rye, wheat, barley, and corn are combined in this whisky with a refined and complex nose, highlighting rye spice and oak, and a rich but also reserved palate offering baking spice, caramel, and dried fruit. An aperitif whisky.

J. P. Wiser's 15 Years Old (40%)

An elegant and fruity whisky, this offers dry toffee notes and a hint of cocoa in its aroma, fruity banana and green apple in the body, and a dry finish that hints at Mexican spiced chocolate. For sipping neat or with an ice cube at the day's end.

Pike Creek Canadian Whisky (42%)

Now aged in used rum barrels—it was port barrels when it was first released—this has an unsurprisingly rum-influenced aroma and a sweet, round, fruity molasses body with allspice and nutmeg notes in the finish. Serve with dessert.

Lot No. 40 Rye Whisky (43%)

The champion of the Northern Border Collection, this is Canadian whisky for all reasons: full-bodied and rich enough for a whisky and cola; sufficiently spicy for a Manhattan; with a complexity suited to solitary sipping, on its own or with ice.

WHITE DOG VS. NEW MAKE VS. MOONSHINE

Throughout these pages, you will find various references to "white dog," "new make whisky," and "moonshine," and you might wonder whether there is a difference between them. Well, the answer is that there is, or maybe there isn't.

As with the correct way to make a Martini, there is little consensus as to how each term is defined, even among the experts. In his book *Tasting Whiskey*, American spirits writer Lew Bryson employs the expressions pretty much interchangeably, whereas Scotland's Dave Broom, in *The World Atlas of Whisky*, ignores "moonshine" but notes the continental divide by suggesting that "white dog" is an American term for "new make." Canadian Davin de Kergommeaux, on the other hand, in his *Canadian Whisky*, disregards all three and notes only "white whisky."

For our purposes, however, there is a difference. We view "white dog" as, quite specifically, an unaged whisky made from a mix of grains that may include, but is not necessarily limited to, corn, rye, and wheat. "New make," on the other hand, is in our opinion an expression best reserved for single malt (ie: barley malt–based) whisky that has yet to hit the barrel, and "moonshine" is a spirit made from practically anything, but formulated to be sold as is rather than crafted to see the inside of an oak barrel. De Kergommeaux's "white whisky" is by definition an American exclusive, since it is illegal to use the term in Canada, where anything bearing the name "whisky" must be aged at least three years, an anathema in tradition-bound Scotland.

ATLANTIC CANADA

Well before there was any other craft distilling activity in Canada, before Victoria Spirits or Dillon's Distillers or Myriad View, there was the Glenora Distillery, founded in Cape Breton in 1990. So it can rightly and honestly be stated that modern, small-scale distilling got its start in Nova Scotia.

Of course, with two bankruptcies and the untimely death of its founder within its first decade, before any of its whisky had even come to market, Glenora didn't exactly set a stellar example for other Canadian entrepreneurs who might have been inclined to follow its lead.

Fortunately, Canada's eastern coast tends to foster resolute spirits, so despite Glenora's early trials and tribulations, the distillery not only survived, but thrived, growing better and better with each passing year. And rather than discouraging others from following in its steps, the ultimate success of the operation sparked the creation of many of Canada's earliest craft distilleries, making Atlantic Canada a sort of birthplace for this country's modern distillery movement.

Not that this should come at all as a surprise. With plenty of open space and an abundance of fermentable materials, from PEI potatoes to Annapolis fruit and fields of grain in between, the country's eastern provinces have long been home to a distilling culture, as anyone who has ever attended a Maritime kitchen party will know. The rise of craft distilleries first in Nova Scotia and Prince Edward Island, then in New Brunswick and Newfoundland and Labrador, simply marked the legitimization of a practice that has been a part of eastern Canadian life for generations.

And while those latter two provinces still lag behind PEI and Nova Scotia in terms of distillery development, the recent arrival of such impressive start-ups as Sussex Craft and Devil's Keep bodes well for the future of Atlantic Canadian spirits.

Authentic Seacoast Distillery & Brewery

75 Ferry Road, Guysborough, NS, B0H 1N0
(902) 533-3904
authenticseacoast.com

Authentic Seacoast might be the most ambitious alcohol producer in Atlantic Canada, incorporating as it does a brewery, distillery, and, newly planted in 2018, winery. Add in the company's Full Steam coffee roaster, Harbour Belle Bakery, and historic DesBarres Manor Inn and it all begins to look more like a mini-empire than a mere business concern.

For all of the overall enterprise's many faces, however, the distillery is still a relatively new facet, established in 2012 but existing principally as a blender and ager of other people's spirits until 2017, which owner Glynn Williams says was the "year of mastering the scale-up from a small blended to a larger concern."

That "larger concern" involves housing the distillery and brewery—the latter born in a Guysborough pub—in the same expansive warehouse just outside the town centre and scaling up production to fill barrels with what will eventually replace the Atlantic-aged but western Canadian–distilled spirit in the company's rye-forward GLYNNEVAN line of whiskies. For the time being, Authentic Seacoast's number one product remains the full and fruity Fortress Rum, composed of Caribbean rum aged at the Fortress Louisbourg in Cape Breton, while a single vodka, Virga, is the distillery's only fully in-house creation.

This does nothing to diminish the appeal of the distillery as either a prime tourist attraction or a solid up-and-comer on the Canadian craft distilling stage. With ample experience in blending and aging, and solid distilling chops evident in the vodka, there is every reason to believe that the future is bright for this aspiring Atlantic powerhouse.

VIRGA HANDCRAFTED VODKA (46%)

Made from 100% Nova Scotia spring wheat, this has a hint of seashore in its otherwise fresh and clean aroma and an impressive, creamy fullness in its lightly sweet, softly spicy finishing body. Evocative of new-make whisky.

Barrelling Tide Distillery

1164 Parkway Drive, Port Williams, NS, B0P 1T0
(902) 542-1627
barrellingtidedistillery.com

When Russell Murphy met his soon-to-be wife while they were both working on a Holland America cruise ship, he already had an interest in distilling, but the then-chef had no plans to make a career out of it. As Murphy describes it, however, his interest soon developed into an obsession and it wasn't long before the pair were travelling to visit and work in distilleries rather than taking more ordinary vacations.

The obsession came to fruition in 2016, when Barrelling Tide opened as the first distillery in Nova Scotia's Annapolis Valley fruit belt.

The company's first products were a vodka, a gin, and, thanks to the availability of local fruit, a raspberry liqueur. These were soon joined by numerous other liqueurs, each produced only when the fruit is in season locally, and a rum distilled out of molasses purchased from the New Brunswick–based Crosby's. The "Barrelling" side of the distillery will make itself apparent as the years pass, with barrel-aged rum already on the market and whiskies and brandies in maturation.

Although tours are not on offer, except for groups, the entire distillery is viewable through the large shop windows and anyone working at the store is able to talk visitors through the process, ending with a sample of the products, of course.

TIDE GIN (40%)

An immensely attractive aroma of slightly minty, slightly citrusy herbs introduces this classic New World gin, defined not by its juniper but by the aromatic character that continues through the soft, alluring palate to the peppery, spruce-y finish.

5 FATHOM RUM (42%)

Salted oak barrels contribute to an aroma that combines a molasses-y caramel with notes of the seashore. On the palate, it's rich, round, and sweet, with chocolate taking the place of the caramel and lingering licorice candy on the finish. Sip neat and keep away from cola.

CHERRY LIQUEUR (20%) & CRANBERRY LIQUEUR (24%)

From an extensive line of fruit liqueurs, these are, like the others, distilled from Annapolis Valley fruit and then blended with juice from the same fruit, with no sugar added. The Cherry both smells and tastes like quality dark cherries, not too sweet and with a bit of flavourful tanginess to balance, while the Cranberry has all the tartness you might expect from the fruit, accompanied by soft herbal notes and a lightly warming finish.

Caldera Distilling

65 River John Road, River John, NS, B0K 1N0
(902) 456-7348
caldera.ca

When Tracy Stuart retired from competitive rowing shortly before the London Olympics, she and husband Jarret decided they needed a new direction in their lives. As the ex-Olympian and displaced Nova Scotian told the magazine *At Home* in a 2016 interview, "We were sitting on my parents' deck, sipping Scotch, and said for fun 'we could make this.'"

And so they did, or sort of. The pair bought a 170-acre farm on Nova Scotia's north shore, built themselves a home, then turned the existing barn into a visitors' centre and erected another building to house the still. Tracy's father joined Jarret in Colorado for distillers' training, and with Scotch as their inspiration, the making of whiskies became their focus.

As of the fall of 2018, Caldera was distilling about 35 to 40 percent of their own farm-grown grain, with the remainder being purchased and a goal of raising their own crop content to 65 to 70 percent. While their own whiskies continue to age, purchased whisky from western Canada makes up part or all of their two products, Champlain Cognac Blended Whisky and Hurricane 5 Whisky, although exact percentages are unknown.

HURRICANE 5 WHISKY (40%)

This is perhaps best described as a classic Canadian whisky updated for a more modern palate, with all the softness and approachability that made Canadian whiskies popular, but bolder and more full-bodied, with ample caramel, vanilla and orange notes. Sip alone or in an Old Fashioned or Manhattan.

CHAMPLAIN COGNAC BLENDED WHISKY (48.5%)

To our knowledge the only Canadian whisky blended with cognac, this has a suitably intriguing nose with orange, vanilla, and spice notes, plus a body that offers depth, complex and dry fruitiness, and extraordinary length. Sip alone, despite its strength, or with a single ice cube if you must.

Coldstream Clear Distillery

87 Main Street West, Stewiacke, NS, B0N 2J0
(902) 956-3393
coldstreamclear.com

Born as an idea when Riley Giffen was in his second year of university studying organic chemistry and using distilling techniques to separate citrus oils, Coldstream Clear became a reality when Riley's father, Robert, joined him in his hobby distilling experiments a year or two later. By the time the student was in his final year, it was agreed that the time had come to go legit, and so father, son, and mother, Elaine, made it official with licensing in January of 2015 and the distillery's grand opening in the fall of that year.

Coldstream Clear quickly outgrew its original location on the family property, however, and a new (if rather unlikely) premises was found in a mall at the intersection of Main Street and Highway 162, in central Nova Scotia roughly midway between Truro and Halifax. Distilling takes place in the back of the retail store and cocktail bar, and sourced spirit supplements what is produced on premises.

We are told that NGS is sourced for some of the distillery's products, particularly the Canned Collection of ready-to-drink cocktails, and some Caribbean rum is also bulk purchased for blending—although the single barrel rum is made entirely at the distillery. Some of the more innovative products, such as the Hopped Vodka, are also 100 percent distilled in-house.

PREMIUM HOPPED VODKA (40%)

Anyone familiar with the dry-hopping of beer will recognize that technique in the fresh, leafy, and lightly citrusy aroma of this vodka, not to mention the lightly grassy and lemony palate. Over-chilling loses the hop effect, so serve cool or at room temperature.

1749 SINGLE BARREL RUM, BARREL #10 (40%)

Light amber in colour, this rum aged in a single malt whisky barrel has a mix of soft caramel, vanilla, and tropical fruit on the nose, with a correspondingly soft and sweetish palate that lends itself far more to sipping than it does mixing.

CLASSIC COFFEE (20%)

With a nose of well-roasted and coarsely ground coffee beans, this liqueur announces its provenance with a bold voice. On the palate, the coffee turns out to be well-sweetened, suiting this to after-dinner White Russians, or perhaps even pouring over ice cream.

Compass Distillers

2533 Agricola Street, Halifax, NS, B3K 4C4
(902) 446-0467
compassdistillers.ca

The casual imbiber could be forgiven for not even realizing that the swish cocktail bar at the corner of Agricola and Charles Streets is also home to a distillery. But make your way to the back of the stylish yet cozy and comfortable room and a glass wall reveals Tess, the Vendome still that produces the spirits on offer at the bar, to be enjoyed straight or in classic or more inventive and modernist cocktails.

(Tess might also be the only still in Canada with an Instagram account, @tessthestill.)

Created by three partners fascinated with spirits, Compass Distillers is housed in what used to be the Nauss bicycle shop—discovered by accident when the partners were having dinner at a restaurant across the street. After effectively gutting the place, the trio then discovered their distiller, Ezra Edelstien—the hobby-distilling son of the contractor they hired to build their bar and distillery.

It all came together in the late fall of 2017, resulting in what local indie weekly *The Coast* called the area's "tower of boozy power," or what might be less grandiosely described as a lovely distillery with an equally delightful bar in front. For those desiring the fully immersive experience, there is also an Airbnb apartment on the top floor.

VODKA (40%)

None of that "odourless and tasteless vodka" stuff here; this is a spirit crafted to proclaim its origins in wheat. A dry graininess defines the aroma while the almost chewy body speaks to dry cereal and faint citrus notes. A whisky drinker's vodka.

GIN WILD (45%)

Like juniper? Well, then you'll love this gin! The nose edges more to the floral than peppery side of things, but the flavour is full-on juniper, with just enough grainy sweetness to balance it out. Bold and flavourful and well-suited to a Martini.

AGED GIN (40%)

Gin and oak can be a most unpleasant combination, but here it works. The new American oak is most evident on the nose, but not obnoxiously so, while the body deftly combines notes of juniper, vanilla, oak, and toasted caraway spice in the finish. A sipper.

AQUAVIT (40%)

The anise on the nose of this traditionally formulated aquavit lies somewhere between fennel and liquorice candy, while the typical caraway seed dominates the flavour, but with a gentle nudge rather than a punch. A lovely Maritime take on a Scandinavian classic.

Glenora Distillery

13727 Route 19, Glenville, NS, B0E 1N0
(902) 258-2662
glenoradistillery.com

Canada's oldest craft distillery, and North America's first single malt distiller, is Glenora. But the road from its creation in 1990 to its first whisky release a decade later was not a particularly smooth one.

Founded by Bruce Jardine, and assisted during its start-up by no less than the experts at Scotland's Bowmore Distillery, Glenora hadn't been around long before it experienced the first of the two bankruptcies that would plague it in the early years. The resulting layoffs were followed by ownership changes, all while the whisky rested and aged. Sadly, Jardine did not live to see the distillery's initial product launch in November of 2000.

Even the joy of finally launching a whisky was dampened by the Scotch Whisky Association (SWA) of Scotland, which almost immediately challenged the distillery's use of the word "Glen" in its name. (See sidebar on page 38 for details.)

Thankfully, the first decade of the new century was much better to Glenora, with whisky production continuing apace, the SWA's lawsuit ultimately dismissed, and numerous awards bestowed upon its wares. By 2018, production was up to more than 150 barrels per year, and as high as

GLEN BRETON RARE 10 YEAR OLD (43%)

Floral and slightly lemony on the nose, this soft and approachable single malt is an excellent introduction to the distillery. Enjoy pre-dinner with a cube of ice.

GLEN BRETON RARE 14 YEAR OLD (43%)

Despite limited availability, this is the distillery's bestseller, and no wonder. Floral notes of yellow stone fruit and vanilla define the nose, while the body adds lemon curd and hints of coconut before a dry finish. A satisfying sipper for any time.

GLEN BRETON ICE 12 YEAR OLD (43%)

Aged in icewine barrels from Malagash, Nova Scotia's Jost Vineyards, this deep golden spirit has a fruity, honey-ish richnes on the nose and a silken body that boasts an almost confectionary appeal without being sweet. An after-dinner dram.

GHLEANN DUBH 13 YEAR OLD (43%)

The distillery's lone peated whisky, and also the only one to feature Scottish malt. Powerfully smoky in its aroma, the peatiness is tamed somewhat in the body by the whisky's typical fruitiness, finishing with a dry oak char.

190 barrels in 2017, and renovations and expansions had been made to the on-premises Inn, the Washback Pub (featuring daily ceilidhs and stylish Warehouse restaurant). A Culinary Whisky Package includes tour and tasting, three-course dinner, and overnight accommodations.

Though it might have had a shaky beginning, the "grand old man" of Canadian craft distilling would seem to have a very bright future.

THE SWA VS. GLENORA

Although it is a comparatively young industry, Canadian craft distilling has not been without its moments of notoriety, the most significant and dramatic of which was the nine-year battle between Nova Scotia's Glenora Distillery and the Edinburgh-based Scotch Whisky Association (SWA).

Well-known for traversing the globe to protect the interests of Scottish whisky producers, the SWA took issue with Glenora's intended use of the Glen Breton Rare name long before the distillery had even a drop of spirit on the market. Claiming that the Glenville, Cape Breton–based operation was trying to unfairly take advantage of the positive global reputation of Scotch whisky by "adopting a Scottish-sounding name," the SWA launched a legal challenge in 1990 that wound up lasting nineteen years and making it all the way to the Supreme Court of Canada.

In the end, however, the court ruled that Glenora had the right to use the name and, in the summer of 2009, put an end to it once and for all by denying the SWA grounds for appeal. The distillery celebrated its hard-fought victory with the release of a new whisky, a 15 year old fittingly called Battle of the Glen.

Halifax Distilling Company

1668 Lower Water Street, Halifax, NS, B3J 1S4
(902) 431-0505
halifaxdistillingco.ca

Perhaps surprisingly, the roots of Halifax Distilling are found in North Carolina, where partners Julie Shore and Arla Johnson have their roots, and run through Prince Edward Island, where the duo founded their first Canadian businesses, an inn and the Prince Edward Distillery.

The development of a wind farm nearby prompted the couple to look elsewhere, however, and having sold the inn and shuttered the distillery—which at time of writing was inactive and for sale—re-established themselves as distillers on the downtown Halifax waterfront.

When visited in the fall of 2018, the Halifax operation was still young enough that most of its own products were yet aging in barrels in back of the large bar, store, and tasting room space, but we were told that the J. D. Shore Reserve Rum and J. D. Shore Canadian Rum Cream each contained significant amounts of the new distillery's spirits. Other rums were at the time composed mostly of sourced Caribbean rum and the whiskies on offer at the time were brought in barrels from the PEI operation.

During the summer tourism season, the bar swarms with visitors and locals alike and tours are regularly scheduled, although passers-by are also welcome to simply enjoy a drink or a tasting flight at the bar. For those seeking a longer experience, a food menu is also available and live music is regularly scheduled at night.

J. D. SHORE LIMITED RESERVE RUM (40%)

Primarily aged in new charred oak, this amber-hued rum shows considerable woodiness on the nose and offers a mix of fruity—peach jam, apricot—and faintly spicy notes in the body. An afternoon sipper.

J. D. SHORE CANADIAN RUM CREAM (17%)

Said to be composed entirely of the distillery's own rum aged for two years in ex-bourbon barrels with Madagascar vanilla beans, this very creamy liqueur is appealingly sweet with vanilla and coconut notes to go along with the rum flavours.

Ironworks Distillery

The Blacksmith's Shop, 2 Kempt Street, Lunenburg, NS, B0J 2C0
(902) 640-2424
ironworksdistillery.com

I t all began with a story in Air Canada's *enRoute* magazine. Although he says that he almost never looks at in-flight magazines when he flies, it was during a short trip to Halifax in the fall of 2008 that Pierre Guevremont found in *enRoute* a story about two new distilleries on Prince Edward Island and the growing craft distilling movement in the United States. He was intrigued.

Returning home with the magazine in hand, Guevremont consulted with his wife, Lynn MacKay, and the pair began planning. Two weeks later they were enrolled in a distilling course in the United States and seven months after that they had secured the historic Walters Blacksmith's Shop building to house their distillery in Lunenburg.

Following about a year of renovation, the Ironworks Distillery opened its doors with an apple-based vodka, a pear eau-de-vie, and a pair of fruit liqueurs, all true to the couple's vision of making the best use of local produce. Rum distilled from imported molasses came later, as did a gin built on an NGS base, and, unusually, a marc—a spirit made from the seeds, skins, and stems of grapes grown in Windsor, about one hour away.

MARC (42%)

Marc is the French equivalent of grappa, and this one is very true to those roots. The nose is fruity-herbal-grassy with light floral notes, while the body is full and captivating, with herbal grape notes and a lingering, lightly spicy finish. Doubles as a lovely aperitif or digestif.

BLUENOSE RUM (42%)

Deep and dark, this is arguably the quintessential East Coast rum, with coffee and sassafras on the nose and a very rich body that combines hints of espresso with a robust but not overly sweet molasses flavour. A great rum for almost any occasion.

PEAR EAU DE VIE (40%)

Baked and fresh pear, backed with a hint of baking spice, introduces this impressive Nova Scotia take on Poire Williams, and the body delivers on that promise with boozy dried pear notes and a faintly phenolic finish. A tremendous after-dinner tipple.

APPLE BRANDY (42%)

There is no question as to the apple-ness of this brandy, which in France they would call calvados, notable in the baked apple and apple skin nose and full, round, apple-fuelled body. The Nova Scotia equal of its French peers.

Aside from the distilling operation, the couple also owns the Liquid Assets store in the Halifax airport, located after security and selling exclusively Nova Scotia–produced wines, beers, ciders, and spirits.

Pears being grown for Ironworks's "Pear In Bottle" Pear Eau-De-Vie .

Steinhart Distillery

5963 Highway 245, Arisaig, NS, B2G 2L1
(902) 863-5530
steinhartdistillery.com

In planning for fall 2019

As explained on the distillery website, Thomas Steinhart still remembers helping his grandfather stoke their wood-fired still at their home in Germany's Black Forest. What is not mentioned on the site, however,

ORGANIC VODKA (40%)

Light and floral on the nose, this is perhaps best described as a refreshing vodka, with hints of orange blossom and a mild, spring-y perfume that runs from the nose right through to the finish. Chill, pour, sip, repeat.

GIN (47.5%)

If you are looking for a classic London Dry gin with a bit of a twist, look no further. The nose is more fragrant and appealing than the big British brands, while the body offers a richness with impressive botanical complexity. Perfect for Martinis or G&Ts.

WILD BLUEBERRY GIN (47.5%)

Dry and full-flavoured, this has a subtle blueberry character, with the fruit melding nicely with the typical London Dry gin characteristics, ending in a finish that is half eau-de-vie and half flavoured spirit. For solo sipping.

MAPLE VODKA (40%)

The distillery's very first product, this has a nose that is identifiably maple without being overly sweet and sugary, more the essence of maple, and a rich and round body that again speaks to syrup without being cloying. Enjoy chilled or experiment with in cocktails.

is that he distilled with his father as well. So when he eventually grew weary of all the business travel his work required, it was only natural that he would settle down to open a distillery of his own.

The Steinhart Distillery was purpose built beginning in 2012, with the grand opening taking place in October of 2014. Although he takes pride in his iconoclastic personality, Steinhart also recognized that there might be a benefit to fitting right in with his Canadian environment, so he launched his business with a Maple Vodka.

The distillery has since expanded to over a dozen products, with everything but the gins fully produced in-house. (Steinhart argues that the great gins of England also begin with sourced spirit, which is true to a large degree.) All the flavourings he employs in his gins and vodka are natural and steeped into the spirit.

A recent addition has been a brewery that Steinhart uses to make beers principally in classic German styles. A German community favourite is the distillery's Schnitzel Shack, where beer, wine, cider, and cocktails are available to enjoy alongside pasta dishes and, of course, schnitzel. The tasting room is licenced and pours the beers as well as the spirits.

Still Fired Distilleries

9548 Highway 8, Annapolis Royal, NS, B0S 1A0
(902) 471-7083
stillfireddistilleries.com

It was while swapping stories and sharing drinks around a campfire in late 2015 that it dawned on partners Andrew Cameron and Owen Ritchie that their hobby distillery–turned-part-time business had morphed again into something more. Having displayed their wares to significant acclaim some days earlier at a Halifax hunting and sports trade show, the two underwater welders recognized that it was time to leave their jobs and devote themselves full-time to the distillery trade.

While Still Fired Distilleries had existed as a concept since summer 2014, when Cameron put together a business plan, and as a small-scale commercial operation catering almost exclusively to local residents since June of 2015, Cameron says that campfire moment was when the business truly got its start.

Upon Owen Ritchie and Andrew Cameron's first meeting in 2011, neither man had anticipated that their friendship might ultimately lead them into the distilling business. But the long periods of time that their jobs forced the two to spend away from home revealed a mutual interest in spirits, which in 2013 spawned the idea of operating a small hobby still.

As sometimes happens in such situations, the friends and family with whom the pair shared their spirits responded with positive and enthusiastic feedback, which led to Still Fired opening its doors with a corn-based vodka and its now-signature Granny's Apple Pie Moonshine.

PREMIUM VODKA (40%)

Its corn base shows in a slight perfume of canned creamed corn on the nose and a creamy, sweet body. A slight showing of heat on the finish suggests that this would be ideal for Vodka Soda or Vodka Tonic highballs.

FUNDY GIN (40%)

The sea and the seaweed, or dulse, included among the botanicals are immediately evident in the slightly saline nose, while the body tends more towards peppery juniper mixed with umami. Lightly chilled, this is lovely just as it is.

GRANNY'S APPLE PIE MOONSHINE (20%)

This mix of cider, spices, and spirit delivers a full and robust aroma with notes of baked apple and spice—even a whiff of crispy crust. The body is lightly sweet and, again, very dessert-like. Serve at room temperature in place of dessert.

RAPTURE OF THE DEEP DARK MOLASSES MOONSHINE (45%)

One of three molasses- and cane sugar–based moonshines—read: under-aged rum—this is steeped with vanilla, coffee, and maple syrup to a smooth, round, almost chocolaty body that belies its strength. Mix equally with cola.

Deep Roots Distillery

2100 North York River Road, Route 248,
Warren Grove, PE, C0A 1H5
(902) 620-1085
deeprootsdistillery.com

Mike Beamish might have been working for the federal government in Ottawa during the 1980s, but his heart resided in the Maritimes. So when he sought an escape from the civil service, he found it in a teaching job on Prince Edward Island in 1987, where shortly thereafter he also found what he describes as a "hobby farm," located about ten minutes outside of Charlottetown.

APPLE BRANDY (40%)

After two years in Hungarian oak barrels, this sweet brandy made from the distillery's own orchards offers vanilla, oak, and apple core notes in the aroma, while the body is soft, sweetly fruity, and drying on the slightly spicy finish. Still in its early days, this is already good and bound to improve.

MAPLE LIQUEUR (25%)

Fermented cane sugar is distilled on site, then blended with syrup from PEI, Nova Scotia, and New Brunswick to make a liqueur that is pleasantly and fragrantly maple-y on the nose and more evocative of dark maple syrup in the body.

ABSINTHE (72.5%)

Infused with herbs, then distilled, then infused again, this is no shy spirit, bursting as it is with anise and a wide assortment of other botanicals. Blended with water—via an absinthe fountain if possible—it makes a wonderful, palate-coating aperitif or nightcap.

Of course, as with many such enterprises, the apple orchard he planted as a "hobby" soon began to consume not just his, but his entire family's time. And one of the problems that vexed him was the issue of "fallen apples," perfectly good fruit that fell to the ground before it could be picked and thus was unmarketable. The answer he arrived at in the early 2010s was distillation.

After taking a distilling course in 2013, the now-retired Beamish set up the distillery with his son in November of that year, with their first products ready slightly less than a year later. Apples were soon joined by cane sugar as fermentable materials, and an absinthe joined the Apple Brandy as the company's flagship products.

Visitors are not only able to sample a wide variety of products, including several liqueurs, but can also take a tour Beamish describes as "roots to bottle," which begins in the orchard and ends in the tasting room.

Matos Winery & Distillery

3156 West River Road, Route 9
St. Catherines, PE, C0A 1H1
(902) 675-WINE (9463)
matoswinery.com

As per the order of its name, and evidenced by the tiny still that spends much of its time stuck in a corner, Matos is primarily a winery rather than a distillery. And indeed, Jaime and Heather Matos, both emigrants from the Azores off the coast of Portugal, began planning their business in 2006 as a winery, with the notion of adding a distillery—to make the Portuguese version of grappa—arriving only later.

That Portuguese spirit, called Bagaço, was the reason Jaime decided to add a distillery component in 2012, one year after the winery was finally born. It's not a huge seller, he admits, but forms the base for all the other products the company produces, save for occasional releases of American oak–aged PEI Apple Brandy.

Although it is located not far from either the Confederation Bridge or Charlottetown, Matos is nonetheless rather out of the way, making a visit a pleasant, scenic day trip for residents and visitors alike.

BAGAÇO (40%)

A traditional Portuguese interpretation of grappa, this has a yeasty, fruity, bread dough-y nose and a round, grapey, lightly herbal body that fades quickly in the aftertaste. A straightforward spirit with much to recommend it as an early evening sipper.

ANGELICA (17%)

The Bagaço is blended with must from chardonnay and gamay grapes to create this light, sweet, and floral sipper that serves as a fairly simple and straightforward alternative to port or Madeira.

ORANGE LIQUEUR (23.5%)

Aficionados of more famous orange liqueurs might be taken aback by the fresh orange aroma of this Bagaço-based alternative. Sugar is added to spirit that has sat on orange zest, creating a fairly aggressive sweetness that begs mixing with straight spirits.

ANISETTE (31.8%)

Aniseed and fennel are cooked down and blended with Bagaço to create this soft, quite sweet, and very anise-accented spirit with just a hint of grassy herbalness. Well-suited to late night sipping.

Confederation Bridge, which connects Prince Edward Island to Nova Scotia.

1336 Route 2
Rollo Bay, PE
C0A 2B0
(902) 687-1281
straitshine.com

Myriad View Artisan Distillery

When Ken Mill and his wife befriended the newly arrived Dr. Paul Bellow and his wife, in part to encourage the family physician to remain in their rural PEI locale, he never imagined that the frequent appearances of illicit Island moonshine at parties might lead the pair into a new business. But when challenged by Bellow to create a business based on the legal production of 'shine, the pair opened the doors of Myriad View on July 2, 2007, after helping to literally create the law that made distilling legal in the province.

If there is a more suitably named distillery in the Maritimes, we know not what it might be. For the views from the distillery are indeed myriad, with the shoreline to the south and forest and farmland to the east, west, and north. A prettier location on the Island would be hard to imagine.

The first two products were Strait Shine and Strait Lightning, both distilled from cane sugar and molasses fermented on the premises, and differing mainly in strength. As both of the partners' wives are gin drinkers, gin and vodka followed two years later, both composed of sourced and redistilled grain-based NGS, plus cane- and molasses-based rum, NGS-based whisky and pastis, and a brandy made from the grapes grown on-premises and aged in oak for a minimum of five years.

The goal at Myriad View is to represent everything in its proper historical Island context, so the rum is at "boat strength," or the potency it would have shown when Islanders smuggled it off the rum transport ships, the gin is close to genever, and the 'shine is strong.

STRAIT VODKA (40%)

Fans of Bloody Caesars will welcome this vodka to their drink, as it boasts a thinnish body that lets the mixers come through on top of its solid alcoholic warmth and boozy finish.

STRAIT SHINE (50%)

If you're familiar with Island moonshine, you'll know what to expect from this. If not, rough rum-like notes define the nose, while the body is on the sweet side, slightly apple-y and warming on the finish. Perhaps just what the doctor ordered?

STRAIT GIN (51%)

Slightly minty on the nose, with faint baking-spice notes, this is a sweetish, vaguely sugary gin that invites mixing, with a citrusy front and a sweet, cinnamony finish. The base spirit for countless potential cocktails.

STRAIT BRANDY (40%)

Billed a V.S.O.P., this brandy has a very attractive, orange-y nose with the faintest of spice notes and a vague hint of red wine grapes. The body is sophisticated, round, balanced in its fruitiness and spiciness, and delightfully warming on the finish.

Blue Roof Distillers

4144 Route 16, Malden, NB, E4M 2G1
(506) 538-7767
blueroofdistillers.com

t's likely that Blue Roof isn't the only Canadian distillery born of a university project, but it's probable that it is the only such business based on a sixth-generation potato farm.

Operated by the Strang family, growers of potatoes since 1855 and a commercial family farm since Devon and Richard Strang's father expanded operations in the mid-twentieth century, it was Devon's idea in his second year at Sackville, New Brunswick's Mount Allison University to create a business plan around finding a creative use for the unmarketable "small potatoes" that inevitably turned up in the harvest. Distilling them, he thought, could provide an effective hobby business.

According to Richard Strang, the idea was that the distillery would be a "downtime" project, pursued only when the farm was quiet. In such a vision, however, the family did not figure in the effect of the highly visible farm—with landmark vivid blue roofs—being located on a highway that annually transports 1.6 million or more cars to Prince Edward Island, not to mention the draw of the oversized "Tater Nate" statue in front of the distillery. Initial estimates of selling perhaps seven thousand to eight thousand bottles in the first

year quickly skyrocketed to over eighteen thousand!

In their second year, a gin has been added to the lineup of vodkas and the cars continue to stop on their way to and from the Island while the Strangs' "hobby project" continues to grow.

PREMIUM VODKA (40%)

There is a sweet earthiness to the aroma of this all-potato vodka, which translates into the flavour as well. A palate-entry sweetness develops a more rustic and drier character as it progresses to a faintly herbal finish. A fine base vodka for cocktails.

100 VODKA (50%)

The extra strength contained in this more potent version lends it very well to straight-up sipping, with a creamier, richer aroma than the Premium and a correspondingly bigger, fuller palate. To be savoured slowly over ice.

STRANG'S ORIGINAL POTATO SPIRIT (70%)

Made from Russet potatoes rather than the yellow ones used for the Premium and 100, this has a notably sharper nose—principally because of the extra potency—and a spicy, still creamy body with considerable heft on the finish. A good base for fruit-based drinks.

HANDCRAFTED GIN (43%)

Built on the potato vodka base, there is considerable perfumey citrus on the nose of this somewhat reserved gin, with more citrus and some second-half juniper in the flavour. A gin for vodka drinkers making the crossover.

Devil's Keep Distillery

2492 Route 640, Hanwell, NB, E3E 2C2
(506) 292-4679
devilskeepdistillery.ca

 ay Fitzpatrick and Joe Allen are friends who work in the venture capital field, and as such found themselves travelling together quite a bit and, at the ends of their long days, drinking beer together. So perhaps it was only natural that the duo eventually began discussing the possibility of opening a brewery of their own in their hometown.

As they pondered the matter further, however, they realized that Fredericton was already rather replete with breweries considering its modest population. So instead of jumping on the back end of a trend, they decided to get on "the front end of a new wave," as Allen put it. That new wave was distilling.

After about a year of planning, some rather intensive training, and a most helpful connection with the local community college, Devil's Keep opened its doors in December of 2018. While the Vodka is all that is available at the time of writing, plans are in place for a gin release in late 2019, whiskies much further down the road, and the eventual establishment of a showcase distillery and tasting room in the heart of Fredericton.

Hopewell Rocks Park, just across the border from Nova Scotia.

VODKA (40%)

A somewhat curious aroma of earthy grain with a whisper of cherry pie filling introduces this spirit, but doesn't do justice to the round, rich, almost chewy body with a lively complexity that mixes fruit and grain with spice and depth. For sipping or mixing—your choice.

Distillerie Fils du Roy

599 Chemin Principale, Petit-Paquetville
NB, E8R 1G7
(506) 764-2046
distilleriefilsduroy.com

Established in 2012, the Distillerie Fils du Roy was New Brunswick's first modern small-scale distillery and, on top of that, one of Canada's most-awarded, with accolades coming in from almost the moment it opened. And it's tempting to attribute some of that success to the fact that Sébastien Roy, its founder, had a healthy fascination with the science of alcohol from a young age.

"When I was young, before we had computers or the internet, my parents had a deep collection of books that I would look through and I was fascinated by these articles on alcohol production in fermentation," recalls Roy. "So when I was fourteen, I mixed sugar and water and yeast in a container and hid it in my closet. And when I saw the bubbles, in my head, it was like a Nobel Prize for me since I thought I had created life."

Much later, he developed an obsession with absinthe whilst on a trip to Europe and, when he returned home, had a fateful conversation with his mother, who was concerned about the future of her industry (printing), since a lot of businesses were closing down. Roy suggested she finally go into business for herself, half in jest adding that maybe they could open a

distillery together. The next day, she was looking at properties and making appointments at the bank.

Despite the rest of the family's concerns that this business was a crazy idea, the pair opened up a tiny grain-to-bottle operation together, which, over several years, has expanded and become an important Canadian distillery and tourist attraction—despite its remote location, it averages between 250 and 400 visitors per day in high season. Fils Du Roy even has a second location, in Saint-Arsène, Québec, making it the only craft distillery we're aware of that straddles two provinces.

Sébastien Roy.

GIN THUYA (45%)

We first tried this punchy and simple juniper-forward gin back in 2014, when not every craft gin in Canada had perfectly mastered its botanical mix. Thuya stood out back then for its spicy vision, which was infused into a clean and clear corn spirit with a hint of boreal forest. Way ahead of its time and still a top pick for one of the better gins in Canada.

Gagetown Distilling & Cidery

30 Court House Road, Gagetown, NB, E5M 1E4
(506) 488-2286
gagetowndistillingcidery.ca

As a seventh-generation farmer, Matthew Estabrooks was no stranger to the ups and downs of the agriculture market. But as sales from the family apple farm began to lag owing to decreased demand, he took a different route than had his parents and grandparents.

VODKA (40%)

The sweetish, fruity aroma is your first indication that this is no grainy and forgettable white spirit, and the first sip confirms it. Creamy, sweet in front but spicy in the mid-palate and dry-finishing, this is a vodka for enjoying on its own at any temperature.

MOONSHINE (50%)

Distinctly different from the vodka, although also made from corn, the moonshine offers sweet creamed corn on the nose and peppery, faintly phenolic body that belies its strength right up until its somewhat fiery finish. Appealing in its strength.

UNFILTERED GIN 7 (45%)

Apple-based spirit and seven botanicals team up to create this aromatically spruce-forward gin with a foresty-floral body that turns decidedly citrusy in the finish. A wise choice for a G&T or a distinctive Tom Collins.

He pivoted from selling the fresh commodity to retailing a processed product, in his case first cider and then spirits.

Cider sales came first, in 2011, with his interest in distilling forged not long after. Estabrooks began, he says, with a tea kettle and some copper pipe in the barn, graduated to using a pressure cooker and then a barrel, and eventually decided to scale into full commercial production. Beginning with a week-long course in distilling at Urban Distilleries (see page 257) in Kelowna, BC, he and business partner Heather Rhymes received their federal licence in the late spring of 2017 and their provincial credentials that September. By July of the following year, retail sales had begun.

"I was surprised at first by how simple it was," Estabrooks recalls. "But the bigger it gets, definitely the more complicated it gets."

Things got a bit more complicated in the summer of 2019 when the distillery added a long-anticipated tasting room and cocktail bar, which locals and visitors have reportedly taken to with enthusiasm.

Moonshine Creek Distillery

11377 Route 130, Waterville, NB, E7P 0A5
(506) 375-9014
moonshinecreek.ca

When Jeremiah Clark's wife became pregnant, he says he started to think about doing something bigger with his life. And being a bartender who loved his job, that 'something bigger' was almost certain to revolve in some way around alcohol.

So he and his brother, Joshua, already experienced homebrewers and winemakers, decided to look into the viability of creating a local craft distillery. Hailing from a rural, blue-collar part of New Brunswick, they found a similar, "straightforward" vibe in southern Tennessee, and so spent a couple of weeks touring distilleries and speaking with the people behind them, people who Jeremiah says were remarkably open with them.

"I guess with us being from so far away, they really didn't see us as potential competitors," he says.

After supplementing his Tennessee knowledge with a course taught by the Washington-based Artisan Craft Distilling Institute in PEI, Jeremiah set to work developing a business plan, which he says went through "about twenty revisions" before becoming investor-ready. It worked. In August of 2018, four years after the idea was first formed, Moonshine Creek opened with two products: Apple Crumble Moonshine, their tribute to Tennessee's ubiquitous apple pie moonshines, but with a Canadian "crumble," and White Pup, an unaged whisky.

Rounding out 2019, the brothers have big plans, including a distilled maple spirit called Canadiana, which they liken to white rum, and several potential co-brandings. Having exceeded their first-year projections by a considerable degree, however, the first goal is to simply keep the store's shelves stocked through the busy tourist season.

GET'N PICKLED (40%)

When the second ingredient listed—after grain spirits—is white vinegar, you know that you have something for other than straight sipping. Briny, acidic, and, yes, even garlicky, this is for Bloody Marys and Caesars, or perhaps a "pickleback," if you like that sort of thing.

APPLE CRUMBLE (25%)

Cloudy from the apple cider that is blended with the grain spirits, this is absolutely true to its name, with both a nose and flavour that is precisely evocative not of apple pie, but specifically apple crumble. Sip over ice on a summer day or after dinner in winter.

DOUBLE DOUBLE (25%)

With the colour and aroma of freshly brewed coffee, French-pressed to account for the slight haziness, this liqueur has a well-sweetened flavour of coffee, brown sugar, and an undercurrent of dark chocolate. Drink with, or instead of, after-dinner coffee.

Sussex Craft Distillery

119 Cougle Road, Sussex Corner, NB, E4E 2S5
(506) 433-2800
sussexcraftdistillery.com

The story of the Sussex Craft Distillery is not quite the *Full Monty* of the spirits world, but neither is it entirely dissimilar. When PotashCorp shut down the mine in Sussex in 2016, it threw over four hundred people out of work and severely depressed the town. Recognizing that Sussex had an agricultural history as well, a group of nine investors who had long been friends decided to pool their resources on a project that would, in the words of John Dunfield, one of the nine, "bring a bit of pride back to the community."

And so, with the help of a hobbyist distiller and a training program in western Canada, Dunfield became a part-time distiller and Sussex Craft was born.

Although its main products are rums, the idea of Sussex Craft is to use local ingredients as much as possible. So the rums are aged in stainless steel tanks with charred wooden staves cut from Acadian oaks, and local fruits and herbs are steeped in NGS to make the company's range of liqueurs. By far the distillery's best-seller is the Northern Comfort, aged with sugar maple staves and blended with spices and New Brunswick maple syrup.

While the still-young operations remains a side project for Dunfield, he is heartened by both the reaction he gets from repeat buyers and the three medals the company won in its first Canadian Artisan Spirit Competition. They may be a bit behind their Maritime distilling peers, but Dunfield is betting they can catch up soon.

WARDS CREEK PLATINUM (44%)

This white rum is billed as "a little more traditional," and if that means clean, crystal clear, and refined, we agree. Slightly fruity on the nose, the palate is softly sweet with notes of roasted sugar cane and a dryly spicy finish. The base of an excellent Mojito.

DUTCH VALLEY LIQUEUR (22%)

There is a strong presence of anise on the nose, but also hints of orange zest and other citrus, plus an earthiness. The body is quite sweet and not nearly so liquorice-like, but still accented by liquorice and spice. Chill and enjoy after dinner.

CRANBERRY LIQUEUR (20%)

Local cranberries and not too much sugar go into this naturally bright red liqueur, resulting in a dryly berry-ish nose and a more tart than sweet body that screams fresh cranberries. Sip chilled or add a drop to a glass of Nova Scotia sparkling wine.

NORTHERN COMFORT (30%)

The aroma serves notice that there is more to this than just maple, like charred wood, baked fruit, and hints of baking spices. On the palate, the maple syrup assumes prominence, but with the support of spice and charred wood. Drink warm in winter and chilled in summer.

Winegarden Estate

851 Route 970, Baie Verte, NB, E4M 1Z7
(506) 538-7405
winegardenestate.com

Travelling around Maritime distilleries, you hear a lot of people talking about "firsts." But when Elke Muessle tells you that Winegarden was the first distiller of fruit-based spirits in Atlantic Canada, you can believe her.

Started in 1992 by Elke's and distiller Steffen's father, Werner Rosswog, a German immigrant from the Black Forest, Winegarden was intended to be what common parlance would deem a "hobby distillery," using local apples that were unsuitable for market to make a schnapps. One thing led to another, though, and by 1997 the family had branched out into fruit wines, adding conventional grape wines to the portfolio three years later.

Quite naturally, the fruit wines also led to fruit liqueurs, followed by various eaux-de-vie and, eventually, an apple brandy, released at five and ten years of age. Today, while the winery has assumed the mantle of principle business, the distillery's portfolio has expanded to well over two-dozen spirits and liqueurs, the former uniformly named for Werner's great-grandfather, German distiller Johann Ziegler Sr.

JOHNNY ZIEGLER APPLE SCHNAPS (40%)

The only distillate that the Rosswogs still refer to as "schnaps"—they discovered that eau-de-vie was a more marketable term for Canada—this clear spirit has an unmistakably apple-ish aroma and a slight sweetness up front leading to a smooth, spicy, and dryly fruity finish.

JOHNNY ZIEGLER 5 YEAR OLD FRUIT BRANDY (36%)

One of two brandies the distillery makes—the other is a 10 year old—this is remarkably refined for a spirit so relatively young, with vanilla, brown spice, and dark dried fruit on the nose and a pillowy, slightly over-woody body that mixes oak, herbal, and very soft fruit notes. A lovely late-night sipper.

JOHNNY ZIEGLER EAU DE VIE ANIS (38%)

Not for the anise-phobic, this clear spirit states its intent early with a full and fragrant aniseed and star anise aroma and follows through with a very clean, dry, crisp, and boozy anise body. Aperitif or digestif, it's your choice.

BLUE HILL BLUEBERRY LIQUEUR (23%)

While unquestionably blueberry-ish, this moderately sweet liqueur is actually fairly reserved in its fruitiness, with a mix of fruit and soft alcohol notes on the nose and a fairly sweet, moderately fruity body that finishes with the flavour of fresh blueberry skins.

The Newfoundland Distilling Company

97 Conception Bay Highway
Clarke's Beach, NL, A0A 1W0
(709) 786-0234
thenewfoundlanddistillery.com

CLOUDBERRY GIN (40%)

The slight colour may come from the included cloudberry or savoury, but both are present in the fragrant aroma. On the palate, there is a complexity of berry and piney-peppery juniper, with herbal notes in the background. A unique and intriguing spirit.

SEAWEED GIN (40%)

Seaweed in the name, but not the aroma, which is more typically London Dry. That seaweed does, however, provide an abundance of umami, making it rich, round, sweet, and full, with a peppery finish. Avoid mixers and drink on its own.

When Chef Bill Carter returned home to Newfoundland intent on becoming a whisky distiller, international artist Peter Wilkins, who knew Carter from before the chef had left to work in Ottawa, was all ears. As he bashfully admits today, Wilkins figured that combining the running of a distillery with the creation of art would be easy. And was it?

"I haven't made any art since we opened," he admits.

Still, the artist did provide a bit of sober second thought in suggesting that rather than waiting three years for whisky, it might be more economically advantageous to concentrate instead on rum, vodka, and gin. And so, when they opened the doors of the distillery store in May of 2017, the product on the shelves was a vodka, which was followed a month or two later by a pair of gins.

View of St. John's from atop Signal Hill. (Photo by Whitney Moran)

Rums came a bit later still, but this time the spirit was not of their own creation. (All other spirits are distilled in-house, the sole exception, Wilkins says, being a bit of NGS purchased on occasion when demand outstrips supply.) Working on the advice that it's wise to source good Caribbean rum while working on perfecting and aging your own, the partners buy from three sources for the fragrant and floral Gunpowder & Rose Rum (flavoured with local rose, kelp, charred birch, and sea salt), and other seasoned rums.

As of early 2019, however, the company's surprise bestseller is its Seaweed Gin, which also delighted the duo with a double gold award at the San Francisco World Spirits Competition in 2018.

"It's all been quite extraordinary," says Wilkins. "We made the spirits that we like and I think that we're a bit surprised that so many other people agree with us."

QUÉBEC

When we prepared for our deep dive into Québec's fascinating craft distillation scene, the first question we knew we needed to answer was: what's up with all the gin?

The province is fast becoming known around the world for its weird and wonderful craft gins, distilled with a range of surprising ingredients, including seaweed, chanterelle mushrooms, and, quite famously, parsnips. Its distillers have established a world-renowned boreal forest category, are leaders when it comes to using foraged botanicals, and produce numerous umami-rich gins. At any given time, there may be roughly forty or fifty local gins on the shelves of the Société des Alcools de Québec (SAQ).

Most distillers agree, though, that this wasn't in answer to a specific demand for gin in the province, but instead grew out of a perfect storm of circumstances—abundant clean water, amazing access to a wide range of unique botanicals, and some of the country's toughest distillation laws—which make it very hard and very expensive to start off by opening a grain-to-bottle distillery. So, instead, a lot of crafty people begin with a small still (400–500 litres), source neutral grain spirit (NGS), and distill that with botanicals to make gin, or, in some cases, absinthe or aquavit. In response to all these new and interesting gins, Québec, traditionally a wine and beer market, is seriously embracing cocktail culture, to the point that Montréal appears to be at "peak gin" these days.

While this isn't a universal story, a lot of the province's craft distillers, having tested the waters and built up a reputation with gin, then set out to expand into grain-to-bottle distilleries. A lot of new-make grain spirit has been laid down at facilities transitioning out of NGS over the past year or two, so in the next few years we can expect a second Québécois craft spirits boom—only this time it will be whisky!

Absintherie des Cantons

800 rue Moeller, Granby, QC, J2J 1K7
(438) 877-0290
absinthequebec.com

When you walk into the still room of the Absintherie des Cantons, the unmistakable scent of anise, lemon balm, and bitter wormwood practically smacks you in the face. Funnily enough, though, when we comment on the aroma to Jean-Philippe Doyon, the twenty-eight-year-old founder of the micro-distillery, he responds that he doesn't even notice it anymore. After untold batches, he's fully acclimatized.

Doyon became interested in absinthe five years ago, when he was drawn to its history, lore, and culture—and frustrated by how hard it was to find a genuine bottle of absinthe in Canada. When he finally managed to special-order a bottle from Switzerland, he knew right away he wanted to be part of the absinthe revival.

"I was charmed by the complexity of the product and I wanted to know everything about what was inside it and how it was made," says Doyon. "So I began to read a lot about absinthe and I went to Europe in 2014 to travel the Route de l'Absinthe from Pontarlier to Val-de-Travers."

Over the next three years, in between applying for permits, buying equipment, and sourcing ingredients that met his standards, Doyon took courses in microbiology and did an apprenticeship with a distiller in Switzerland. The obsession has paid off, since both his white and green spirits show technical proficiency and an excellent palate. Made according to European traditions (one Swiss, the other French), they're easily among the best absinthes we've ever tried.

ABSINTHE JOUAL VERT (68%)

A delicate, fragrant spirit with a lovely fresh anise flavour and the perfect amount of bitterness and herbal complexity. Far from an aggressive taste, it's mellow and would work well on a leisurely spring afternoon spent in a backyard with a book.

ABSINTHE FLEUR BLEUE (53%)

This is a really pretty, slightly floral blue with a strong anise backbone, some herbal notes from the chamomile, and a touch of salinity to balance it all out. As is typical with this type of absinthe, it's best with a touch of sugar and carefully administered water.

Jean-Phillipe Doyon (left), founder of Absintherie des Cantons, with sociologist Simon-Pierre Savard-Tremblay (right), who is lending a hand with the absinthe harvest.

He knows the flavour profile of his absinthe "by heart," and so spends a lot of his time obsessively tracking down different expressions from around the world, given that the spirit, like gin, can be made anywhere. Oh, and speaking of gin, he makes that, too, including one called Panoramix that, thanks to butterfly pea flower, changes from blue to pink with the addition of acids. On top of all that, Cantons has a signature aquavit.

Artist in Residence Distillerie

243 rue Bombardier, Gatineau, QC, J8R 0C6
(844) 735-8800
airdistillerie.com

Artist in Residence founder Pierre Mantha never considered opening a craft distillery until one fateful trip to Colombia, where he visits regularly with his wife (who is originally from Barranquilla).

"Each time I go, there's this one guy that's always talking about liquors," recalls Mantha. "I don't drink...so I said to the guy, 'Why are you always talking to me about liquor?' And he said, 'Because you've got the lifestyle for it.'" Mantha asked him to elaborate. His friend explained: "'For us, Québec is green with lots of water. And liquor is made of water.'"

Mantha, a truck mechanic and dealership owner, says he never considered the importance of water in spirits, since he'd spent most of his working life thinking about the trucking business. But recalling that some land he owned had an underground spring, as soon as he got home, he started investigating.

The next three years were pretty hectic for Mantha, who had no prior experience in the industry. Despite this, he was determined to go all in, consulting multiple experts in the fields of distillation, filtration, and branding, and ultimately spending $5 million on a 15,000-square-foot facility outfitted with a top-notch 3,000-litre still. His goal is to eventually produce a million bottles per year over fifteen separate brands. When we met in late 2018, he had already launched a gin, a "light" vodka, and a ginger liqueur, with plans for a white rye, a coffee liqueur, and an aperitivo.

WAXWING BOHEMIAN GIN (41%)

You can't smell the juniper in this floral, corn-based gin, but once it hits the tongue, it kicks in with a perfectly pleasant amount of heat. Some of the more unusual botanicals include rosehip berries and mountain ash berries, both part of the diet of the Bohemian waxwing, a regional bird.

VODKALIGHT (30%)

No question, this diet-friendly corn vodka is soft and smooth—no burn to speak of. Neither does it have much of a distinctive flavour profile, though, as you'd expect from a vodka that has been watered with the property's spring water to get the calorie count down.

MAYHAVEN GINGER LIQUEUR (30%)

Crisp, clean, natural-tasting, and properly spicy, this ginger liqueur steers clear of syrup territory. Less sweet than many ginger liqueurs, it is an excellent option for cocktail enthusiasts looking for a local product.

Cidrerie Michel Jodoin

1130 rang La Petite Caroline, Rougement, QC, J0L 1M0
(450) 469-2676
micheljodoin.ca

Few people probably realize that one of Canada's first micro-distilleries is situated in the idyllic hills of Montérégie, Québec, about 45 minutes east of Montréal, and is quietly producing some of North America's best apple brandy. It's under the radar, probably, because it's better known for the other half of its operation, the acclaimed Cidrerie Michel Jodoin, up and running for eleven years before the distillery was added in 1999.

Of course, Michel Jodoin had a head start—he grew up making cider on the family orchard, a property in Rougemont that his great-grandfather bought back in 1901. Eager to take things to the next level, Jodoin went to Europe to visit some of the most famous wine- and spirits-producing regions, including Champagne, where he got the idea to make sparkling cider, and Germany, where he was awed by the distillers' *savoir-faire* in making fruit spirits. He picked up an artisan cider licence as soon as the province of Québec started issuing them in 1988, establishing what would become a thriving cider house. He later added an alembic still to turn his cider into apple brandy, as they do in Normandie.

Since then, Jodoin's gone on to make a few other odd ducks that you don't often see in Canada, such as an apple liqueur, a vermouth, and a mistelle—grape juice spiked with brandy. He also had a hand in creating PUR vodka, Canada's "most-awarded" vodka, in collaboration with entrepreneur and marketer Nicolas Duvernois. Still, most people probably visit Jodoin for the cider. Well, that and the lively party atmosphere that spills out of the red-brick cider house to the Muskoka chairs every summer weekend.

BRANDY DE POMME, 3 YEARS (40%)

Buttery-rich, but still perfectly dry, this award-winning apple brandy consistently impresses. Aged in new American oak, the vanilla and caramel appear close to the finish but don't overwhelm the natural deliciousness of this clean-tasting, nicely crafted, pure apple spirit.

BRANDY DE POMME, 8 YEARS (40%)

This rich, super-dry, and elegant spirit has an amazing tannic structure that responds brilliantly to conditioning in oak, where it seems to have picked up a touch of maple candy flavour. Pair with a cheese plate and call it a night.

Distillerie Shefford

1125 chemin Denison Est., Shefford, QC, J2M 1Y6
(450) 531-6672
distillerieshefford.com

Ever heard of acerum? Even among avid craft spirit enthusiasts, the answer is likely "no." But if a clutch of small distillers get their way, acerum—maple syrup spirit—will become a new category unto itself and, long-term, may become just as much of a household name as cognac or Scotch. At least in Québec.

There are already spirits made with maple syrup, but acerum is the only spirit actually distilled from maple sap—just like rum is made from molasses or sugar cane juice. Distillerie Shefford's founders, Gérald Lacroix and Josée Métivier,

have already secured a "regional designation" for the spirit, started the Association for Maple Spirit Distillers, and are working towards establishing it as a distinct spirit from the region—sort of like Demerara rum, rhum agricole, or cachaça. Shefford was the first to distill acerum and has since been joined by St. Laurent (see page 84) and we expect several more releases to follow soon. Adding an interesting layer to this story is the fact that the couple never set out to distill maple sap in the first place. The original plan was (and still is) to make whisky. In fact, they laid some down in 2018, made from barley and rye they grew themselves on the property. They knew, however, that they'd need to sell something while waiting three years for the whisky to age. Having a sugar bush on their land, they decided to give sap fermentation a try.

ACERUM BLANC (40%)

On the first whiff and sip, this would appear to be a clean white rum, with a better-than-average body and sweet, soft finish. A few seconds later, though, a rich maple flavour reveals itself—one so pronounced that it's hard to imagine how you missed it. Drink neat. Ideal for those who love sipping eaux-de-vies and white brandies.

ACERUM BRUN (40%)

Six months in oak has made a big difference to this maple spirit's flavour profile and weight—it's rich, oozing with caramel, and yet still light on its feet at the finish line, leaving only the slightest trail of pepper. Delicious. Drink as you might a good whisky.

THE QUÉBEC GIN BOOM CONTINUES TO BOOM

Québec has a way of continuing to surprise the craft spirits lover. We knew it was a young, dynamic scene, but even we were caught off guard by the number of distilleries (almost all making exclusively gin) that opened after we finished editing this section and just before it went to press. So here are a few, either recently opened or slated to open in 2019. And don't take your eyes off Québec—not even for a second; it might soon merit an entire book of its own.

The biggest boom in new distilleries is in the St. Laurent region, which is home to five new distilleries, including the Distillerie du Quai, which makes Super Sonic London Dry Gin in Bécancour, across the river from Trois-Rivières. In Québec City, there are three new gins in town—red, blue, and "noir" (actually colour-free)—thanks to the launch of Distillerie Stadaconé, a new facility in the central Limoilou neighbourhood. Just up the river, in Lévis, the Distillerie des Appalaches has plans to go beyond gin, with acerum in the works.

Acerum, made with maple syrup sourced from the Gaspésie, also figures into the plans being made at Distillerie Mitis—a new distillery in Mont-Joli, north of Rimouski. And, finally, there's a new gin mill on the north coast—Distillerie Puyjalon in Havre-Saint-Pierre, which makes Betchwan Premium Gin with lingonberries and some locally sourced juniper.

In Salaberry-de-Valleyfield, near Montréal, the Distillerie Trois Lacs launched its first gin in 2019 and nearby Sainte-Hyacinthe saw the newly opened Distillerie Noroi ship out its first cases of Noroi Dry Gin. Due south of that, in Granby, a fairly ambitious facility, Distillerie de la Chaufferie, opened up in a shuttered tobacco factory. Unlike many other of the province's distilleries, it *will* be open to the public—and not just for tours—and boasts a large, stylish area that will eventually be a cocktail lounge. It's starting out with a gin and a vodka, both of which are made in-house and from scratch, with rye grain.

Obviously, it worked, but not without challenges—many of those stemming from the fact that maple sap's flavour profile starts to change mere hours after it's been tapped. And, in the fermentation process, which takes about two weeks, sap has a tendency to acquire fruity and floral notes and lose its maple aroma. Lacroix experimented with several yeasts, finally settling on a fairly neutral strain that helps achieve the desired profile—a completely dry, slightly fruity spirit with a round and buttery texture, smooth finish, and very subtle maple aroma. Shefford currently has two styles: Acerum Blanc and Acerum Brun, the latter of which is aged for about six months.

Although it's early days, everyone who has joined the association has high hopes for the future of acerum, since it's a chance for Québec to invent a unique new spirit that truly represents and expresses both the region's culture and terroir.

Domaine LaFrance

1473 chemin Principal, Saint-Joseph-du-Lac
QC, J0N 1M0
(450) 491-7859
lesvergerslafrance.com

Located about a twenty-minute ride from Au Pied de Cochon's famous Cabane à Sucre, and situated in a charming town stacked with cheese shops and cider houses that overlooks the Lake of Two Mountains, Domaine LaFrance is a must-stop on any food and drink tour of the lower Laurentians.

Domaine LaFrance is spread across two separate buildings: the distillery, with its Stupfler alembic still, installed in 2013 by owner Eric LaFrance, and, about one hundred feet away, a bakery and retail store, packed with meat pies, apple donuts, jams, syrups, and ciders. Most of it is made from the bounty of the land—twenty-five hectares of apple orchards that the LaFrance family has been stewarding for three generations.

At the rear of this store of amazing temptations, there's a small, slightly hidden bar stocked with an amazing range of hyper-local products, such as vermouth, gin, eau-de-vie, an apple spirit, an aperitif, and, of course, Georges-Étienne LaFrance Apple Brandy. All the spirits are made from apples (plus some pears and a grape or two, we hear) and some of them are really quite dandy.

DANDY GIN (42.3%)

A wildly aromatic gin, with a perfumy nose that brings fresh spring elderflowers to mind. Still, there's plenty of juniper here, punching up a distinctly tannic structure and assertive flavour profile that could use a splash of dry vermouth to mellow it out and bring it all together.

GEORGES-ÉTIENNE BRANDY (42%)

Named after the grand patriarch who first bought the orchard, this award-winning apple brandy is dry and mature-tasting, with the perfect amount of vanilla and spice you'd expect from three years in oak.

Domaine Pinnacle/ Ungava Spirits

150 chemin de Richford, Frelighsburg, QC, J0J 1C0
(450) 298-1026
ungavaco.com

It all started in the year 2000, when Charles Crawford and Susan Reid decided their family needed a break from the busy daily grind of the city. Not fond of half-measures, they bought a heritage property and 430-acre orchard in the Eastern Townships south of Montréal and moved the whole family to Frelighsburg to work, full-time, in the cider business.

After ten years, Crawford decided it was time to branch out into spirits—specifically, gin. In the course of his research, he learned that juniper grew wild in Northern Québec's Ungava Bay region and was immediately inspired to use it—plus other wild botanicals native to the tundra—for his unique gin, made with cloudberry, crowberry, and wild rosehips.

Ungava's signature bright yellow colour comes about during maceration—an infusion that takes place before the second distillation. Crawford thought of clarifying it, but discovered people really like the gin's unique golden tone and decided that standing out in a crowd was a virtue. Although some people still aren't fans of the hue, it's worth noting that

QUARTZ VODKA (41%)

The big draw here is a combination of Québec's ESKA water and a filtration through quartz, which combine to create a perfumed alcohol nose and gentle, faintly sweet body with a dry, slightly spicy finish.

UNGAVA CANADIAN PREMIUM GIN (43.1%)

Immediately identifiable by its bright yellow hue, this gin boasts a boldly foresty aroma and an equally expressive flavour of bright peppery-herbal notes layered over piney juniper. For a curiously-hued Martini or mixing with grapefruit juice.

CHIC CHOC SPICED RUM (42.1%)

A spiced rum that is relatively subtle in its expression of ingredients, benefiting from the use of boreal botanicals rather than tropical spices. Cocoa-ish on the nose, it has a soft and enigmatically spicy body that suits it well to creative cocktailing.

CABOT TRAIL MAPLE WHISKY (31.7%)

If the idea of whisky and maple syrup puts you off, look elsewhere. But if you like the notion, this is where to start: maple-y on the nose with whisky notes, and sweet and round but balanced on the palate. For coffees or dessert.

Crawford was one of the first distillers in the world to launch a coloured gin—years before the present day's rainbow of pink, blue, purple, green, and even red gins.

Ungava is no longer made at Domaine Pinnacle, since Corby Spirit and Wine bought the spirits side of the enterprise. But you can still visit its birthplace and enjoy a nice tour of a picturesque cidery.

BOOTLEGGERS IN THE ORCHARDS

Hard cider was actually *illegal* in Quebec until 1971—a strange state of affairs, given that it is generally viewed as a wholesome, low-alcohol product. Some claim the prohibition stemmed from an error in provincial alcohol legislation written back in 1920—somebody literally forgetting to add the word "cider" to the list of legal alcoholic beverages. Others, such as cider-maker Michel Jodoin, say it was deliberate and that the government, aware that cider was easy to make, didn't want to deal with the nightmare of trying to control the stocks and regulate the industry.

As a result, you couldn't find cider on the province's shelves for fifty years, though if you knew an apple producer, you could get contraband cider. The legislation was fixed in 1971, but industrial giants immediately dominated the industry and flooded the market with poor-quality, mass-produced cider, ruining its reputation. In 1988 the province finally started issuing artisanal cider licences to small producers and, in a few short years, the craft cider scene started to boom—so much so that in 1998, Quebec officially established a "Cider Route" in Montérégie. Given that at least two cidreries have begun making apple brandy as well, the "Cider Route" may eventually equally attract spirits and cider enthusiasts.

Maison Sivo

Montérégie (not open to the public)
(514) 773-9460
maisonsivo.ca

Cherry blossoms on the Maison Sivo orchard.

Almost any write-up about Janos Sivo, founder of Maison Sivo, contains an awestruck mention of the impossibly charming host of this idyllic farm distillery. This will be no exception. On a chilly Sunday morning, Sivo generously showed us around his eighty-five-acre orchard and distillery in Montérégie (which, like many of the province's distilleries, is not open to the public)—all the while talking about his background, his process, and a little bit of his philosophy. He's the sort of person you could happily listen to for hours, over a couple of glasses of his delicious aquavit.

This is Sivo's second venture, having sold his software-engineering business nearly a decade ago. Not quite ready to retire, he bought an orchard in 2011 with a view to making fruit spirits inspired by the Hungarian pálinkas of his youth. "That's what I knew from Hungary and that's what my taste buds were for, but I soon saw there was no real market for eaux-de-vie, so I got into whisky, which I realized was at least as complex... probably even more complex," recalls Sivo. "I realized I just wanted to be an excellent whisky maker."

VALKYRIE AQUAVIT (41%)

This gorgeous aquavit is a veritable Nordic salad of rich fennel, anise, and dill, peppered with the perfect level of subtle caraway that shows in the finish. Keep it in the freezer and serve straight, alongside smoked fish, sausages, or a hearty cheese fondue.

SHÁMÁN (36%)

This herbal spirit, made from a German recipe, opens up with caramel, which melts away as the caraway takes over, the latter lasting only briefly, as a lovely light layer of medicine finishes things off. Perfect as a digestif.

RASPBERRY LIQUEUR (22%)

Rich, tart, full-bodied, and natural-tasting, this raspberry liqueur is uncommonly delicious. It's sweet, of course, but not the sort of sugar bomb you might expect. Ideal in a Bramble cocktail, since it delivers a powerful berry flavour and a lovely sour punch.

RHUBARB LIQUEUR (23%)

This light pink liqueur has a near-perfect combination of sugar, alcohol, and rhubarb—not an easy recipe to manage. Dry and refreshing, it makes a lovely afternoon cooler with a little added soda.

Janos Sivo.

With a background in engineering and an understanding of the basics of distillation, Sivo had a good knowledge base. But for his whisky production he turned for help to Frank Dieter, a pioneer in craft distillation in Canada. Dieter was happy to mentor Sivo and, in the process, they became good friends.

In 2017 Sivo became the first micro-distillery in Québec to release whisky—a rye and a single malt, both made and matured in Hungarian oak at his grain-to-bottle distillery. In the future, we're going to see even more interesting flavour profiles, since, like all excellent whisky-makers, he has a lot of different aging experiments on the go. And while we wait, he has plenty of unique aquavits and liqueurs to keep us happy.

WHY AREN'T MORE OF QUÉBEC'S DISTILLERIES OPEN TO THE PUBLIC?

Although Québec's craft spirits trail is slowly emerging, it's had a slow, rocky start, owing mainly to the province's byzantine liquor legislation which, for years, didn't allow on-site sales at craft distilleries. That changed in 2018, an announcement which spurred considerable new construction.

However, not every distillery jumped at the chance to install a retail boutique, since, as Janos Sivo explained to us, you can only sell those products that are already listed at the SAQ—and at the same price as at the SAQ. Because it is then required to send the SAQ its share, a distillery makes the exact same amount of money no matter where its product is sold, except that if it offers a retail experience it must also set up and staff a boutique. Most craft distillers expect eventual changes to this law, so that they will finally have an incentive to open their doors.

Distilleries Cirka

2075 rue Cabot, Montréal, QC, H4E 1E2
(514) 370-2075
cirka.ca

When Paul Cirka was in the planning stages for his new enterprise, he knew that establishing a direction for the project was the most important—and most difficult—part of the process. Since whisky is one of his favourite spirits, Cirka kept coming back to it, but with misgivings. He wondered, given the amount of existing Canadian whisky, if the world really needed another. Then he went to visit Colorado brewer and whisky connoisseur George Stranahan, who offered to show him the ropes at his famous Denver distillery. Stranahan told him to make a truly memorable whisky.

"I said, you're right. If your approach to the market is to make a great whisky, there's always opportunity," Cirka recalls. "So I decided right there that I was going to be a whisky-maker, because, quite frankly, out of all the spirit categories, that's the one that intrigues me the most."

But Cirka knew that the three or four years before the release of your first whisky were truly miserable, so he set about making some memorable gins and a vodka while he waited. And they are, indeed, memorable—as well as delicious—the results of Cirka's phenomenal knowledge of botany and, it appears, perfectionism, the latter shared with Isabelle Rochette, production distiller, and marketing manager Victoria Slodki.

It took the team six "grumpy" months before they came up with the final recipe for their Gin Sauvage, and with that under their belts they looked for an even bigger challenge, namely, creating a gin to commemorate Montréal's 375th anniversary—one made only from indigenous plants that would have been available in the region in the seventeenth century.

VODKA TERROIR (40%)

Somehow this intriguing vodka manages to be both creamy and crisp at the same time—a rare (and tasty) combination of characteristics. It's smooth, well integrated, balanced, and almost umami-ish, best enjoyed all on its own with ice.

GIN SAUVAGE (44%)

Opening with a fragrant complexity that fades as you savour the spirit, this is a delightful, spritely, and fresh mix of citrus and herbal flavours that practically dances on your tongue. It's soft, but not thin, with a tremendously warm and savoury finish.

GIN375 (40%)

Some might argue that this is more a thinker than a drinker, since its esoteric botanicals are unusual, but the subtle honey, bitter cranberry, and pronounced juniper finish grow on you. Distinctly Christmassy, it is best reserved for after-dinner sipping on a cold winter night.

Distillerie Les Subversifs

850 route 132, Sorel-Tracy, QC, J3R 4T9
(514) 926-6576
subversifs.ca

Although the distillery has moved, some players changed, and the labels and branding re-invented, Distillerie Les Subversifs still deserves credit for opening the province's first craft gin micro-distillery in 2011.

You might remember it as the facility that brought us Piger Henricus gin, which got a lot of publicity for its novel use of parsnips in the botanical mix. And it wasn't just the novelty that got the brand so much attention—it was also a first-rate gin.

In 2018, Fernando Balthazard and Pascal Gervais, two of the original partners, moved their operation from a farm in Saint-Alexandre to an abandoned mid-century church in Sorel-Tracy, a community located on the St. Lawrence about seventy-five kilometres northeast of Montréal. In part, the move was motivated by changing alcohol laws that permitted on-site retail. It helps, too, that the new location is gorgeous and destined to become a must-stop on the region's slowly emerging craft spirits trail, with pews removed to make room for barrel-aging and the still sitting just a few feet to the right of the altar.

Also with the move came a thorough re-branding for all the expressions, including the Piger Henricus, and it might be an uphill battle communicating that Le Gin de Marie-Victorin is the same product. That's a shame, say the partners, but they also believe that the gains they make with the new branding—where each expression is named after a different subversive historical figure from Québec's past—will quickly make up for the loss, especially since it's more in line with the name of the company itself.

LE RÉDUIT DE LÉO (23%)

An homage to the old sugar shack drinking traditions, this maple liqueur tastes completely natural—the essence of maple—but with none of the cloying sweetness you might expect. Delicious at room temperature, but highly recommended heated up for a Maple Toddy.

LA CRÈME DE MENTHE DE ISABELLE (24%)

An unmistakeable Peppermint Pattie aroma introduces this liqueur, which tastes *exactly* like what we've always wanted a crème de menthe to be—natural, mellow, and fresh. It will give new life to Grasshoppers and Stingers and might just make you re-think the entire category of mint liqueurs.

LE GIN DE MARIE-VICTORIN (43%)

This wonderfully complex, artfully balanced blend of sharp and earthy notes makes for a unique and, frankly, delicious gin that somehow manages to check boxes on both the London Dry and New World lists. Works splendidly with a good tonic water or in a dry Martini.

IN DEFENSE OF NGS

Although it's quite controversial in some circles (especially outside of Québec), a lot of the province's gin starts off as sourced NGS (see sidebar on page 20), which is then re-distilled to make a wide range of products. This practice isn't considered a shameful secret in Québec but rather a way to achieve quality and consistency. As Andrew Mikus of 1769 Distillerie explains:

"The way I look at it is that, when a baker make[s] cakes…they don't go out and grow their own flour. Instead, he gets the flour that he wants, be it a particular brand, flavour profile, or grade, then he makes his cake with the best one from then on, so it always rises to the same level and tastes the same. We just couldn't make our own base and guarantee that level of consistency with a small still."

Mikus points out, as do many other distillers, that it's also cheaper to buy NGS than to create a base in-house. In fact, a lot of distillers will quietly tell you it's extremely hard to sell a grain-to-bottle gin for under fifty dollars, and using NGS helps a lot of distillers keep costs down so they can compete with the big, foreign brands.

"At the end of the day, we're running a small business and we have to be profitable, since the margins at the SAQ and the LCBO are very, very slim; so the only way you can survive is to use a neutral base," says Mikus. "I think the guys that are doing it grain-to-bottle are great and I think they should promote that as part of their flavour profile and sell it that way. But it's hard to retail a gin at forty-eight dollars a bottle."

le gin from Distillerie Wabasso (see page 87), one
ny Québec distilleries that employs NGS.

1769 Distillerie

Verdun, QC
(514) 507-1243
1769distillery.com

Booze history buffs may already know the significance of the year 1769 referenced in the name of this Verdun distillery, a nod to one of the dates often cited for the birth of distillation in Québec. (See sidebar on the next page about conflicting dates). Back then, they made rum. Now, founders Andrew and Maureen Mikus are busy pumping out a range of gins—London Dry, pink, barrel-aged, and "breakfast" versions—as well a little vodka and whisky.

MADISON PARK GIN (40%)

A smashing example of a classic London Dry, this light cotton candy pink-hued gin has just enough perfectly balanced juniper and citrus to bring together all the other botanicals. Makes a top-notch dry Martini.

MVODKA (40%)

This is a delicious, corn-based vodka with a fresh flavour profile, a super-velvety mouthfeel and a beautiful, round presence. Finishes off clean with a perfect spark of heat on the tail. Serve chilled with caviar.

MADISON PARK BREAKFAST GIN (40%)

Invented by Andrew and Maureen's son, Alexander, who had the bright idea of turning the distillery's signature cocktail into a spirit, this amber-coloured "gin" is uniquely dry and citrussy. Just add ice and soda for a pre-mixed cocktail.

What, exactly, is a "breakfast gin"? It's actually 1769's own concept: basically the distillery's standard gin re-distilled with bergamot and a blend of five teas, which tastes a lot like Earl Grey with a hint of orange marmalade. Since Andrew's mom served him tea and toast with marmalade every day when he was growing up, he decided to call it breakfast gin.

As to the pink gin, Andrew Mikus is pretty candid about his motivation: "Colour sells," he says, adding that they didn't decide on pink until seeing the colour of one of their better maceration experiments. "When it came out pink, that was great since if you Google 'paint,' 'favourite colour,' and 'millennials,' pink comes up at the top."

Mikus has obvious business smarts, but takes great pains to point out that these are serious, dry gins—not gin liqueurs with added sugars—borne out of a love for craft cocktails and spirits that he and Maureen picked up while travelling. He'd been thinking about starting a distillery for a long time, but it was a trip to Nova Scotia's Ironworks (see page 40) that settled it: "When I left Ironworks, I thought, this is what I want to do, so it's kind of like that's where the final inspiration came from."

QUEBEC'S FIRST DISTILLERY: CONFLICTING DATES

It's been argued that some of the very first spirits in North America were crafted in Québec City, under the guidance of Jean Talon, the iconic saviour of New France and, famously, spiritual father of the colony's beer industry. Yet even though Talon appears to have had a still at his brewery (circa 1668), it was always his hope that colonists would drink more beer and less of the hard stuff, which, given the extreme temperatures and vast distances in New France, was somewhat unrealistic. It was just way easier to carry distilled spirits rather than ale on winter trapping expeditions.

It was a full century before a second distillery was established, in the 1760s—that we know of. And although 1769 is a commonly referenced date for the first licensed distillery in Québec, some historians have claimed that a rum distillery was in operation at least two years before that. Still, it's a long gap between the 1660s and the 1760s and, while it's tempting to put that down to Jean Talon's sobering influence, it probably had more to do with the fact that importing rum from the Caribbean was cheaper than making your own.

THE BEST BARS FOR SAMPLING CRAFT SPIRITS IN MONTRÉAL

So many gins, so little time.

That's the problem a lot of craft spirits lovers face in Québec, where there are just so many gins to try. Fortunately, in Montréal, there are a lot of first-rate bars dedicated to showcasing the province's bounty.

One of our favourites is **Le Pourvoyour** (184 Jean-Talon Est), a two-level "gin pub" with a first-rate patio that backs onto the Jean-Talon market and offers over one hundred gins—both local and from around the world. A similar number are on offer at **Pub Bishop & Bagg** (52 rue Saint Viateur) and at least thirty are homegrown Québec spirits.

Similar to the G&T menus you might encounter in Lisbon or Barcelona, **Bartizen** (901 rue du Square-Victoria) has designed custom gin-tonics to show off the flavours of eight specific Québec gins, with several more featured in the bar's signature cocktails.

Finally, there's the **Atwater Cocktail Club** (512 Atwater Avenue), a gorgeous, semi-hidden space with an impressive bar stocked full of Québec spirits, and expert staff who can help you navigate the wild and ever-changing scene of local offerings, including many of the province's spiced rums, moonshine, and acerums.

Montréal skyline at night. (iStock)

Distillerie Blue Pearl

5650 rue Hochelaga, Local 125, Montréal, QC, H1N 3L7
(514) 317-2250
bluepearldistillery.com

Located in an industrial park in the city's north end, Distillerie BluePearl is, at present, devoted to making just one product: BleuRoyal Gin. As you'd guess from the name, it's a bright blue (*bleu*), a nod to both the colour of the Québec flag and the French coat of arms from colonial days. Of course, it only starts off blue—its colour being

BLEUROYAL GIN (45%)

Far more expressive than many of the butterfly pea flower gins we've tried, this has a good hit of spice and quite an attractive finish. Absolutely smashing with a good artisanal tonic and, of course, perfect for Instagram.

derived from butterfly pea flower, the hue changes to a pinky-violet after you add a bit of acid, such as tonic water or lemon juice.

The partners at BluePearl—Francis Bluteau, Karl Fortin, and Jonathan Perlstein—serve as an excellent illustration of the kind of people who choose to get their feet wet with gin distillation. Karl and Jonathan, old friends, used to dabble in home-distillation experiments and at some point realized they were getting pretty good at it, so began to discuss going pro. It would take meeting Francis, with his vision for sales and marketing, before they finally committed.

In 2016 the trio rented a two-room facility, bought a 400-litre still, and got cracking on a recipe they hoped would set them apart. They estimate this approach to starting up a spirits business in the province is about one-tenth the price of opening up a grain-to-bottle distillery—roughly $100,000 to $150,000 versus an investment of at least $1 million or more. Given the limited capital available to the millennials (all three have day jobs and work the distillery at night), this is an attractive option—arguably, the *only* option available to many interested in a start-up distillery.

Distillerie Oshlag

2350 rue Dickson, local 1400, Montréal, QC, H1N 3T1
(438) 387-6500
oshlag.com

When a legend in the Canadian brewing industry starts to dabble in gin, beer and spirits lovers alike tend to sit up and pay close attention.

We're talking about Peter McAuslan here, recipient of the Order of Canada (2017), and the man credited with forever altering Québec's craft beer scene—for the better, that is. In 1988 he founded his namesake Brasserie McAuslan in Montréal's Saint-Henri neighbourhood and, the following year, released his first flagship beer, St-Ambroise Pale Ale. This was followed by an oatmeal stout and, over the next two-plus decades, dozens of other memorable brews.

After twenty-five years in the business, McAuslan sold the brewery in 2013, but retirement was apparently not a good fit, since in 2017 he surprised everybody with an announcement about his new distillery project. Given McAuslan's, and partner Ellen Bounsall's, reputation for brewing beers with integrity, it probably shouldn't surprise us that his distillery is grain-to-bottle. His first two spirits are gins—Oshlag Gin Hibiscus and Holy Smoke! Gin—and we hear a rye is in the works.

Rue Saint Denis in Montréal's Plateau neighbourhood. (iStock)

HOLY SMOKE! GIN (43%)

One of the most esoteric and aromatic gins we've sampled. Made with frankincense and myrrh, the aroma is one of exotic, rich, and smoky sandalwood and the flavour has a delightful candied fennel taste. Phenomenal with a light, low-sugar, high-quality tonic water.

GIN HIBISCUS (40%)

This lightly perfumy and floral gin has a gorgeously spicy flavour profile and a finish that definitely recalls hibiscus in bloom. A fascinating pink gin, with slightly over-the-top botanicals—ideal for fresh rose-coloured cocktails.

Distillerie Tower Hill Road

1 place Ville-Marie, Suite 4000, Montréal, QC, H3B 4M4
(Head office—not open to public)
(514) 312-3125
towerhillroad.com

Distillerie Tower Hill Road uses iStills (small, stainless steel "Smart Stills") to make its award-winning Houpert & Frère vodka. The advantage of stainless steel is that it's a lot more durable than copper, which has to be replaced quite regularly in frequently used stills. Copper, though, is the most effective tool distillers have to remove sulfates, so the iStill manufacturers came up with a copper "waffle," which can be easily removed, cleaned, and re-inserted into the still for the next batch. The owners, brothers Philippe and Laurent Frère, swear by their high-tech, energy-efficient systems, which make good use of computer management to make their spirits. Houpert & Frère is named after their bootlegging great-uncle, Pierre F. Houpert, who used to make moonshine in his barn during Prohibition.

Spirits not available for tasting.

Distillerie Wolfelsberger

5447 rue Chapleau, Montréal, QC, H2G 2E3
(Not open to the public)
(514) 282-2022

Opened in 2014 by Sylvain Lague and Lilian Wolfelsberger, this small Montréal distillery is located in Rosemont, where its owners work on a gin, a vodka, and an outstanding spiced rum. Both had separate spirits projects prior to becoming partners: Lague, with plenty of experience working in the SAQ, launched White Keys vodka and in the process met Wolfelsberger, a political science professor from Alsace who had previously owned a distillery in the Eastern Townships that didn't work out. They seem to have found their muse now, with a brilliant spiced rum, inspired by the history of the nearby Sainte-Marie neighborhood, a formerly working-class area once known as "Faubourg à m'lasse," for its residents' reliance on molasses, at that time considered the "poor man's sugar." The distillery's molasses is sourced from Guatemala, distilled in Montréal, spiced, and then aged in American oak for a year. And it's outstanding.

SAINTE-MARIE MONTREAL SPICED RUM (40%)

Very little can prepare you for how special this rose-coloured rum is. In a category saturated with overly sweet, boring, baking-spice products, this is fresh-tasting, lively, and utterly original, with Szechuan pepper, allspice, cranberry, and cantaloupe. Diverse and delicate, with just a hint of medicine to balance it out, it is best sipped neat, so you can appreciate what just may be the best in its class.

☞ ST. LAWRENCE

Distillerie Fils du Roy

37 rue de l'Église, Saint-Arsène, QC, G0L 2K0
(418) 894-7956
distilleriefilsduroy.com

Fils Du Roy is the only craft distillery we're aware of with operations in two provinces—Québec and New Brunswick. Distinguishing the two from one another can be a little confusing at first, especially since both distilleries offer many of the same products and share all their branding. Its website attempts to clear it up with its tagline: "Two Provinces, A Passion, Two Distilleries, A Family."

It started in New Brunswick in 2012, when Sébastien Roy opened up the first Distillerie Fils du Roy in a northeastern corner of the province. Between international awards, critical acclaim, and because it was in the right place at the right time, New Brunswick's first craft distillery quickly exceeded expectations and began exploring the possibility of expanding into Québec.

"So we went to see the SAQ and it was very expensive to bring a product into Québec," recalls Roy. "Just in marketing costs and fees for each product, it was going to be something like $14,000 every year just to ensure that product would be on the shelf. We did the math on three products and realized it would cost less to start a new distillery in Québec than to try to import product from New Brunswick."

With his brother Jonathan, a Québec resident, Sebastien opened the new outpost in 2015, in Saint-Arsène—about five hundred kilometres away from the original. At first it was a tiny room, but Jonathan has been expanding slowly and, in 2018, began construction on a large facility with space for a boutique. It opened in 2019.

Are the products the same in both provinces? Not exactly. The New Brunswick location offers more expressions, and even those that are essentially duplicates have minor differences. "It's the same recipe, same equipment, but it tastes different," says Sébastien. "It's because the person who makes the cuts from the head, the heart, and the tails has a different nose and no two people cut the spirit run in the same place. And then there's the water, which is probably an even bigger difference."

Spirits not available for tasting.

Distillerie du Fjord

48 chemin de Price, Saint-David-de-Falardeau, QC, G0V 1C0
(418) 815-7915
distilleriedufjord.com

President and head cocktailian Jean-Philippe Bouchard calls the Distillerie du Fjord the "most beautiful distillery in Québec"—a claim that's pretty hard to dispute, even with the dozens of jaw-droppingly gorgeous craft distilleries in the province. It's set in a stunningly beautiful location, surrounded by crisp lakes and boreal forest, a little north of the St. Lawrence in Saguenay–Lac-Saint-Jean.

Of course, "most beautiful" is a subjective term. Other claims about the distillery are more easily quantifiable, such as: first in the region, most gin per square foot, and, certainly, one of the fastest-rising. Distillerie du Fjord only opened in early 2017 and, a little over a year later, broke ground to expand from a tiny garage still into a full-fledged, million-dollar facility across the street with twice the capacity.

"We were really protective with our business model, so we started with a tiny shop with a little alembic still and it didn't take long for us to hit our peak production," says Bouchard. "When the SAQ ran out of our KM12 gin on December 18, we decided we had to increase production."

Some of Bouchard's caution stems from his academic background. In pursuit of a management degree, he actually wrote a thesis on Québec's craft distillery scene. The project convinced him that a gin mill was a viable business. His father, Serge (an engineer), and brother Benoit (who happens to be a chemist) both agreed and worked with him to open the distillery's first incarnation. He says they tried out much of his theory "on the ground," which, he thinks, helped them to achieve a lot quickly.

They started with KM12, a boreal forest-y twist on a traditional London Dry, which he calls "a walk in the forest on a spring morning," and then, once the expansion took place, began work on their second product: a botanical-forward gin made with a blueberry eau-de-vie base. An herbal liqueur made from Labrador tea is also in the works.

Foraging along the fjord.

KM12 GIN (40%)

The promised boreal forest is delivered with an aroma of spruce and pine and a flavour that hovers between medicinal and transformative, ultimately falling on the side of a spa-like experience. First shocking, later entrancing.

Distillerie Mariana

531 avenue Dalcourt, Louiseville, QC, J5V 2Z7
(819) 448-6966 / (819) 668-9000
distilleriemariana.com

We think you're going to be hearing a lot more about Distillerie Mariana, which, at the end of 2018, made a massive upgrade to its equipment in order to speed up and increase its production process. It was already one to watch, since Jonathan Couturier and Jean-Philippe Roussy were distilling some absolutely lovely spirits, both under their own label and for other brands. The pair were childhood friends who grew up together in the Gaspésie but went separate ways, with Couturier focusing on business and Roussy following his love of brewing and distilling to an internship at a cider house/distillery on San Juan Island in the Pacific Northwest. At a reunion, over a glass or two of Roussy's gin, they decided to try going into business together—a bold move for two men who were not yet thirty years old.

The recent upgrade came at the end of a pretty dramatic year for Couturier and Roussy. Three years into the project, they landed a spot on *Dans l'oeil du dragon*, the Québec version of *Dragon's Den*, a show that evaluates start-ups and, for those deemed worthy, provides investment from the venture capitalist "dragons." They bargained for a really great deal—and won. They later refused the deal, however, since the dragons' vision for the company didn't fit their own. Preferring to go it alone, the pair raised money from other sources, including Investissement Québec, to fund their expansion.

In early 2019, the pair was just starting a cautious expansion into Ontario, getting ready to launch an orange aperitivo, and dealing with growing families—Roussy is having his first baby in the fall, a few days away from Couturier's wife's due date. Nobody knows who will make the spirits with two newborns added to the happy families, but they're confident they'll work it out.

CANOPÉE DRY GIN (40.3%)

Bold, fresh, and packed with plenty of black spruce, cedar, and juniper, this pushes the limits on a forest gin—in a good way. Best in a potent and punchy Gin Soda, so you can fully taste the powerful pine balanced with lovely hints of citrus and vanilla.

MORBLEU SPICED RUM (40.3%)

Aged in bourbon barrels, this rum (sourced, for now) has picked up the perfect amount of vanilla and caramel to complement the chocolate and orange. Not overly sweet, and with a little bit of tingly fresh mint to perk it up, the restraint and balance make it a leader in the category—and far superior to the big brands.

VIOLETTE (45%)

This floral, delightfully perfumey, lightly sweet gin manages to offer the best of delicate wildflowers and still steer clear of that over-the-top potpourri sensation of some floral gins. Certainly one of the best floral gins we've had.

AVRIL AMARETTO (26%)

On opening, pure and rich marzipan aromas fill the room, setting you up for a unique amaretto experience—packed with vanilla, icing sugar, maple, and truly indulgent marzipan flavour. A little on the sweet side, save it for guests who want dessert in liquid form—served straight-up.

Menaud Distillerie et Brasserie

1 rue de la Rivière
Clermont
QC, G4A 1B5
menaud.ca

Menaud Distillerie, an ambitious grain-to-bottle distillery, brewery, and event space, joined ranks with a small clutch of interesting Laurentian distillers in late 2018, when it opened the Charlevoix region's first craft distillery. Charles Boissonneau, the youngest of five partners (he was twenty-four years old when we spoke in early 2019), called the relatively remote and northern location for the project a "brilliant and a stupid idea." On the negative side, Boissonneau says the partners had to be pretty resourceful and self-reliant to build up a business in an area lacking in support for entrepreneurs. "On the other hand, though, we believe that in doing this project, people will follow," says Boissonneau. "We're actually seeing other people starting other breweries this year in this area, so we believe we started some kind of movement here in Charlevoix."

It's unlikely any are quite as well-equipped as Menaud, with a capacity potential of about 300,000 bottles per year—thanks to a 5,000-litre stripping still and a 1,500-litre polishing still. It's not all running at full speed yet, since they're planning to grow into it. For its first year, the distillery is projecting about 50,000 bottles, split between a gin and a vodka.

Although they will have to source a few botanicals from outside the province to make their gin, the idea is to work with all Québec products. The vodka is made from rye and wheat grown on l'Île aux Coudres, a tiny island in the St. Lawrence, where most of the population of about one thousand work either in tourism or agriculture. The more the island's farming economy is supported, the less dependent on tourism and the more sustainable life will be.

That's a really nice example of the distillery's mandate—a philosophy that's even reflected in the name, which is taken from the 1937 book *Menaud, maître-draveur* (Menaud, River-Master) by Félix-Antoine Savard. In this classic French-Canadian *roman du terroir* (novel of the land), Menaud, a Charlevoix area farmer/wannabe lumberjack local hero wages a lifelong battle against those who failed to appreciate Québec's precious resource and would sell them to foreigners.

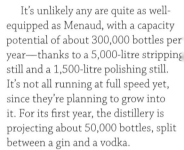

VODKA MENAUD (40%)

Wheat and rye from Île aux Coudres brings a robust character to this fruity vodka that leans towards the eau-de-vie category while retaining a spicy, herbal character to its finish. A vodka with *terroir* to stir into an interesting Martini or sip with ice and a bit of soda.

Distillerie de Québec

6-400 rue du Platine, Québec
QC, G2N 2G6
distilleriedequebec.com

Although Trait-Carré Dry Gin and Vodka Cap Diamant only hit SAQ shelves in 2018, the Distillerie de Québec had been in the planning stages for years before, as Christophe Légasse and David Lévesque slowly turned their dream of making a gin in Québec City into a reality. Some of that planning sounds like it was pretty fun—a massive road trip exploring craft distilleries across North America, for example—and, some of it, a little less so—an exhaustive search for the perfect location that landed them in an industrial area northwest of the city. Production began in 2017.

Since both partners are from Québec City—Légasse from Charlesbourg; Lévesque from Sainte-Foy—the pair wanted to pay tribute to the region's geography and history, especially since the first distillery in New France was located here, eventually finding itself alongside a rich and diverse assortment of small brewing and distilling facilities all over the city. Vodka Cap Diamant is named after the cape on which the city is located and Trait-Carré is a reference to the region's earliest urban planning efforts, which deliberately laid out plots of land around a central common area—the Trait-Carré.

TRAIT-CARRÉ GIN (40.4%)

Made with fourteen botanicals (including blueberries and sea buckthorn), this lightly sweet, refreshing, and subtle gin isn't the kind of spirit that offends people with its aggressive or piney flavour profile. It's mellow and would disappear in a strong tonic, so best stick to serving it with a light splash of soda.

Distillerie du St. Laurent

327-A, rue Rivard Rimouski, QC, G5L 7J6
(418) 800-4694
distilleriedustlaurent.com

In the craft distillery world, there are certain oft-repeated clichés and catchphrases, most of which have to do with unique expressions of the local *terroir*. A lot of distillers do justice to these ideals, but few embody them as perfectly as do Joël Pelletier and Jean-François Cloutier of Distillerie du St. Laurent in remote Rimouski, halfway to Gaspé Bay.

The pair got their licence in 2015—relatively early in the evolution of Québec's craft distillation scene—and were determined to do something that would represent the spirit of the region's fierce Nordet winds, sugar shacks, boreal forest, salty air, barley fields, and fish smokehouses. And the first step in realizing that vision was their flagship gin, one of the first made with seaweed.

"We are located right along the St. Lawrence and we wanted to add a botanical from the river, so we went

ST. LAURENT DRY GIN (43%)

An archetypal New World gin, the aroma sets you up for an esoteric experience with fragrant notes of dried herbs and sarsaparilla, but the body is more conventionally formed, with a sweetish herbal character and spicy finish. A playground for experimentation.

ST. LAURENT GIN VIEUX (47%)

The gin equivalent of reposado tequila, this has a spicy woodiness on the nose and body that sports a caraway note reminiscent of aquavit. It might take a sip or two to understand, but once grasped it is a solid late-evening sipper.

ACERUM (41%)

There is a fair amount of perfumey maple on the nose of this light gold spirit, but don't expect anything liqueur-like. The body is soft, round, only hinting at sweetness, with a bit of spice in the mid-palate and a long and lingering essence of maple finish. A lovely aperitif or digestif.

LAURENTIAN SPIRITS

With at least a half-dozen distilleries populating the shores of the St. Lawrence River, you could almost make a case for a regional denomination of Laurentian spirits, especially since some of the most interesting gins in Canada are coming from there. We suspect part of the reason gins from northeastern Québec are so fascinating has to do with how far afield Rimouski, Percé, and Saguenay are.

With devastatingly high shipping costs, it only makes sense to make the most of what you've got, which has led to a region rich in esoteric gins made with seaweed, wild mushrooms, and a wide range of botanicals foraged from the boreal forest. And if you have the time to take an ambitious road trip from Québec City to Gaspé, well, big bonus: you've just done one of the most beautiful spirits trails in the entire world.

to the university here and asked about seaweeds," recalls Pelletier. "The first one we tried was awful [but] we kept trying until we found this kelp, kombu, that we fell in love with. It's quite distinctive and special and it's okay if some people don't like it, since we'd rather do something polarizing that some people really love."

The seaweed is added at the end, so the gin is tinged with a light green hue, another polarizing factor, and features a hint of salt and umami. Their current main focus, single malt whisky, will be approached similarly, with local barley dried in a fish smoker with maple wood—a nod to the Scottish tradition, but in a distinctly Canadian fashion. In addition, St. Laurent is working on corn and high-rye whiskies and its own acerum maple spirit—see Distillerie Shefford, page 62), which launched in 2019.

The St. Laurent crew celebrates the filling of their one-hundredth barrel of whisky. Left to right: Jean-François (co-founder), Emmanuel, Joel, and Samuel.

Distillerie Vice & Vertu

15 rue de Rotterdam, Local 11
Saint-Augustin-de-Desmaures, QC, G3A 1S8
vicevertu.ca

Established in 2017 by Dr. Franck Sergerie, a spirits-loving radiologist, Vice & Vertu is meant to refer to the duality of shadow and light inside everyone—especially Sergerie, who's happy to discuss the potential tension involved in being both a medical doctor and a spirits distiller.

It all began as a hobby but, happy with recipes he was creating on his small research still, Sergerie impulsively decided to invest in some serious equipment—four fermentation tanks and two stills he calls Ève and Viktor, which together make it possible to distill over 500 litres of pure (95 percent) alcohol per week. His first two spirits fit in nicely with the brand—two gins, a classic London Dry called BeOrigin and the more herbaceous and New World–styled BeDirty. Both won big at the 2019 Canadian Artisan Sprit Competition (a gold and a silver, respectively), so between that and the overall commercial success of his operation, we wouldn't be surprised to hear that Sergerie's cutting back on radiology and devoting himself more to his spirits business. The dark side, it seems, might well take over the light.

BEORIGIN GIN EXCLUSIF (43%)

Bold and savoury, this has an unusually spicy and herbal profile, with a lovely hit of cardamom and possibly sandalwood that ensures it stands out in a crowd. Ideal for spirit-forward gin cocktails, modified with vermouth or sherry.

BEDIRTY DRY GIN (41.7%)

A phenomenally fresh and herbal flavour profile: waves of green peppercorn, spruce, peppermint, and light candied fennel wash over your tongue. Smooth and sweet with just enough heat to keep it interesting. Dry Martini material, for sure, but would also hold its own in a G&T.

Distillerie Wabasso

1024 rue Albert-Durand, Trois-Rivières
QC, G8Z 2M7
distilleriewabasso.com

Opened by Maxime Vincent and Guyaume Parenteau in 2017, Distillerie Wabasso is named after an old textile factory that dominated Trois-Rivières, as well as Canada's cotton industry, for most of the twentieth century. Wabasso had been one of the largest employers in town—Parenteau told us that virtually every family had a member who worked at the Wabasso cotton mill—and the pair one day hope to be just as important a part of the fabric of the community.

The partners started producing Wabasso Dry Gin in early 2018, and, while they have a long way to go before it's a household name in Trois-Rivières, it's done well in a short period—they anticipated making five thousand bottles in the first year and, instead, wound up filling orders for thirteen thousand. The hope is that the gin (as well as two new products being launched in 2019, including a maple-gin liqueur) will eventually pay for the upgrade needed to transform their gin mill into a grain-to-bottle facility.

As such, it's a great example of how Québec entrepreneurs can use NGS-based gin as a stepping stone to grain-to-bottle distillation, although that's not necessarily the end goal for every small distillery. Parenteau

estimated that they would need a pricey 1,500-litre still, at minimum, to distill whatever regional grain or fruit base they might eventually source to a level suitable for making quality gin. So, like many other distillers in Québec (and elsewhere), they opted to build up their business by buying a small still, sourcing NGS, then re-distilling it with their own signature botanicals that include red clover flower and wild wintergreen leaves. It's likely they'll opt to expand the distillery in time, since their gin has been successful—winning bronze and silver international awards and wildly exceeding first-year sales projections almost three-fold.

Spirits not available for tasting.

☞ GASPÉ

O'Dwyer Distillerie Gaspésienne

6 rue des Cerisiers, Gaspé, QC, G4X 2M2
(418) 360-0160
odwyerdistillery.com

Gin Radoune, a spirit distilled with foraged mushrooms, has, as you might expect, a pretty wild origin story.

It had been the brainchild of Michael Briand, an engineer in the Gaspésie with a passion for home-brewing, who became interested in gin after he tried Piger Henricus—the parsnip gin made by Distillateurs Les Subversifs in Sorel-Tracy. The seaweed gin from Distillerie du St. Laurent inspired him to dig deeper.

"I looked at the philosophy of gin and, right from the beginning, it was that you use what's around you," says Briand. "That's what the monks did in Italy when they gathered juniper berries from all around the monastery, so

I decided to take that philosophy and apply it to my own situation where I live in Québec."

We know where this leads, obviously. Briand's backyard, located in the Radoune region of the Gaspésie is covered in wild mushrooms, including chanterelles, yellowfoot chanterelles, honey mushrooms, and matsutake—all of which go into Gin Radoune.

Still, it wasn't a slam dunk for Briand. Initially, he had no idea if mushroom gin would even be palatable and was reluctant to invest six figures into getting a distillation permit to find out. So he started by simply infusing vodka with mushrooms, liked it, and, in 2016, posted his results, along with a prototype of the label on Facebook. It went viral, netting eighty thousand views in the first twent-four hours. The media followed up and, at one point, even Revenue Canada called him up just to make sure he wasn't actually selling mushroom gin under the table.

GIN RADOUNE (43%)

With its rich umami and sweet, earthy flavours, lovely pepper, and coriander, this one-of-a-kind gin is really more a cult classic, likely to attract obsessive fans. Count us in that camp, since we're fully hooked on this iconoclastic gin that should be taken neat, chilled, or in a dry Martini with excellent French vermouth.

Gin Radoune, with the Gaspé's Percé rock in the background.

Briand took that as a sign that a mushroom gin would go over pretty well with the public, so with partner Frédéric Jacques he started working on establishing a distillery and a final recipe. Gin Radoune was launched in 2017, was an immediate hit, and to the partners' delight continues to have a steady demand. Their success led to the distillery becoming grain-to-bottle and it has since released St. Pierre, a "single malt grain spirit"—a preview of things to come, since Briand barrelled off some of that spirit so that it will, one day, grow up and become whisky.

La Société Secrète

1164 route 132 Ouest, Cap-d'Espoir, QC, G0C 1G0
(514) 796-2056
www.societesecrete.ca

When asked about La Société Secrète, people in the province's craft distillation business get really excited—often going on to explain how the founders are artists, elevating craft distillation for the entire province. We tend to agree.

It all started, as many good things do, at a bar—the Microbrasserie Pit Caribou, a microbrewery and pub in Percé, a town perched on the Gulf of St. Lawrence, where three of La Société Secrète's four founding partners were working. As the Pit Caribou started to gain a reputation for making quality beer, they began formulating a plan for a micro-distillery down the road in an old Anglican church. All four founders (Geneviève Blais, Amélie-Kim Boulianne, Michaël Côté, and Mathieu Fleury) worked on the restoration, installation, and distillation—training themselves and apprenticing at friendly distilleries that offered to help out.

To this day, they share the labour, all four working as a team of distillers

Percé on the Gaspé peninsula. (iStock)

LES HERBES FOLLES DRY GIN (42.8%)

A dry, delicate, herb-forward, lightly sweet and citrusy gin with a pleasing melange of mint, caraway, and pepper on the clean finish. Tonic water would drown out the subtle symphony of flavours, which shows best in a Martini.

to turn wheat and barley into grain spirit in their 600-litre, 27-plate column still. The spirit then undergoes a second distillation with wild, local botanicals foraged from an area within walking distance of the distillery. It took two years for the foursome to come up with a final recipe for its gin, Les Herbes Folles, which is then finished for a few weeks in oak.

This makes La Société Secrète one of very few Québec distillers to make the spirit for its gin from scratch, something the collective says they struggle with, since it's not as profitable as working with NGS. But, for them, there was never any question of using sourced bulk alcohol, since their mission statement from the start was to produce 100 percent Québec gin that represents the region.

In addition, they're working on un-aged whisky, craft tonics, and seasonal releases, such as an amaro called La Troisième Vie that sold out quickly, as well as many collaborative projects with Le Pit Caribou that see spirits aged in beer casks and vice versa.

ONTARIO

ong before the rise of Ontario's famous whisky barons—James Gooderham Worts, Henry Corby, Hiram Walker, Joseph Seagram, and J. P. Wiser, who would dominate the whisky business in the late 1800s—the province had a thriving micro-distillery scene. In the 1850s, Ontario was home to about 150 small, independent "distilleries," to use the word loosely, since most of them would have just been tiny pot stills (about 100 litres) located on farms, bought and used, largely, to deal with the problem of surplus grains. In other words, about 175 years back, Ontario was a pioneer in zero-waste craft distillation.

Not every spirit was a gem. These farm distilleries often produced small quantities of oily, pungent, swampy-tasting whisky and sold it, unaged, for a song—the equivalent today of about five dollars per litre. So where did that distillation culture go? The vast majority of operations

were driven out of business by the industrial giants known as the whisky barons, so that by the 1870s, small still operations were an endangered species, with fewer than twenty distilleries—big or small—in existence.

But, 150 years after the big boys started dominating Ontario's spirits industry, things have come full-circle, with dozens of small distilleries turning the region's grain (and, in fact, grapes, apples, potatoes, and even dairy surplus) into tasty spirits. The province still has a lot of work to do if it wants to rebuild its heritage and reach 150 distilleries again, but, since the early 1990s, it has gone from zero to nearly 30 small distilleries, with many more in the works. And, instead of pungent, swampy, pot-still whisky, the province's distillers now make excellent expressions of gin, brandy, aquavit, nocino, vodka, rye, absinthe—nearly every type of spirit you can imagine.

Collective Arts Brewing & Distilling

207 Burlington Street East, Hamilton, ON
(289) 426-2374
collectiveartsbrewing.com

As a rule, we have decided not to include in this book spirits companies that do not operate their own distilleries, but rather have others make their products for them. But Collective Arts is a little different, so it is our lone exception.

Started as a contract brewer, Collective Arts made an almost immediate splash in the Ontario craft beer market when they opened in

ARTISANAL DRY GIN (43.5%)

An immensely approachable London Dry–style gin with a terrific body, this has a floral juniper perfume on the nose and a classic flavour profile with a peppery juniper as the star—and fruity roundness making it all work. A Martini gin, or just sip it neat.

RHUBARB & HIBISCUS GIN (43.5%)

The rhubarb, or at least something aromatic and vegetal, is notable in the aroma of this pale pink gin, while the body offers a balanced note of sweetness with floral acidity from the hibiscus. Chill and enjoy on its own.

2013, with almost equal emphasis on the independent art that adorns their cans as on the beer inside them. The approach worked, and they quickly went from contract brewing, to sharing a production facility in Hamilton with another brewery, to operating that same brewery on their own.

Then came distilling, and with it, unanticipated problems. Although Collective Arts had already purchased a still and was set to install it, city officials had other ideas and refused to issue the necessary permits, forcing the aspiring distillery to assemble its botanicals in-house and take its gin recipes to Dixon's in Guelph (see page 97) for the actual production. As a result, the company is unable to even offer samples of its spirits in Hamilton.

Having watched the evolution of the company's brewing side over the years, however, we believe co-founder Matt Johnston when he says that, one way or another, he is determined to open a distillery at or near his brewery. Until then, we're happy enough with the gins to include them here.

Dillon's Small Batch Distillers

4833 Tufford Road, Beamsville, ON, L0R 1B1
(905) 563-3030
dillons.ca

Long before the craft spirits boom was even a fleeting fantasy for most, Geoff Dillon did what few people realized was even within in the realm of possibility: He bought a still, named it Carl, and, in 2012, started making Dillon's Gin 22—a spirit distilled from grapes and infused with twenty-two botanicals.

Why grapes? Well, that has a lot to do with the distillery's location: Beamsville is a small, lakeside town in the heart of Niagara wine country. Wine growers use a lot of grapes—but not all of them, since they have to thin the vines before harvest. Rather than let those clusters go to waste, Dillon bought them up, since, even though they're not ripe enough for winemaking, they're perfectly suitable for distillation.

The location was also ideal for attracting visitors, who flocked to Dillon's out of curiosity—few had had the chance to visit a working distillery in Ontario before that—and to enjoy a break from wine tasting. Dillon anticipated this and focused on education

UNFILTERED GIN 22 (40%)

Some of the stated twenty-two botanicals are certainly quite floral in nature, as evidenced by the rose and marigold notes in this gin's aroma. On the palate it is sweet-ish and silky, turning spicier and drier towards the finish. A characterful mixing gin.

DRY GIN 7 (44.8%)

The roundness of the aroma here is expressive of this gin's 100% straight rye base, accented by floral notes and a soft spiciness. On the palate, herbal notes precede a vibrant and peppery body that finishes with a solid dose of juniper. Straight or with tonic.

RYE WHISKY (43%)

Aged in three distinct forms of oak barrel, this all-Ontario whisky emerges bright and fresh. Expect citrus and spice on the nose, more spice and a pleasing oakiness in the body, and a generally complex but approachable character.

PEAR BRANDY (40%)

Bottled in 2018, this Niagara Fruit Belt brandy has a candied pear and baking spice nose and a full body that expresses its fruit without being overly fruity, finishing with a stomach-settling warmth. A Niagara after-dinner drink.

(Image by Insite Design)

Geoff Dillon at the Dillon's bar. (Photo by Nataschia Wielink)

through distillery tours from Day One. The distillery has moved on since from gin and vodka to other spirits, including a more traditional London Dry–style gin, rye whisky, vermouth, fruit brandies, peach schnapps, limoncello, a pre-bottled "Professor's Negroni," and a highly acclaimed absinthe.

With all of this on the go, Carl (450-litre capacity) couldn't keep up with demand, so, as of 2018, it now has some support, in the form of a new, 5,000-litre still, Carl, Sr. And there aren't enough thinned grapes anymore, which means that the distillery also employs grain, such as the Ontario rye it uses for its whisky.

Dixon's Distilled Spirits

Located in an industrial park on the outskirts of Guelph, Ontario, Dixon's is about as far as you can get from being a quaint little tourist attraction on a spirits trail. This is a very busy distillery, established in early 2015 after four years of research, business plans, installation, and licensing. The bottle shop is small and, at times, noisy and cramped, especially if it happens to be cluttered with cases waiting to ship.

Production takes place about fifteen feet away in the bustling distillery area, where a 2,800-litre still runs pretty much around the clock. That might be a slight exaggeration, but business is brisk at Dixon's, which supplies to the LCBO, sells spirits on-site, and also does a considerable amount of contract distillation for brands across Canada.

As such, founders Vicki and J. D. Dixon have worked with a diverse range of raw ingredients and expressions, including ready-to-drink products, a.k.a. RTDs, a.k.a. coolers. Dixon's has been an important part of the revitalization of that category, since the distillery was an early pioneer in the introduction of gin RTDs that actually tasted like real gin—not to mention ginger, mint, cucumber, and other mixes.

Aside from their clean-tasting, sweet corn vodka, they've also developed a roster of creative products, including spicy vodka for Bloody Caesars, citrus- and licorice-infused gins, "Oatshine," made with 100

SILVERCREEK VODKA (40%)

Vodka lovers who like that creamy and lightly sweet mouthfeel that is almost always a sign of a corn base will be pleased with this peppery, floral, and super-smooth spirit.

WICKED CITRUS GIN (40%)

Traditional London Dry stalwarts aren't likely to understand this citrus-forward gin that sees almost all of the botanical impact play out in the second half. The strong lemon oil flavour makes it ideal for a tall, citrusy cocktail such as a Ramos Gin Fizz.

FLAMING CAESAR VODKA (40%)

The interesting thing about this award-winning Caesar vodka is the intense garlic nose and flavour, which really overwhelms any of the spiciness you might be looking forward to in a pepper vodka. Definitely for mixing—and only for savoury cocktails.

WICKED LICORICE GIN (40%)

Our favourite spirit in the Dixon's portfolio, this licorice gin has an extremely subtle and round aroma and flavour profile, which demonstrates the perfect amount of restraint during distillation. Truly a little bit of brilliance.

percent Canadian oats, and, at the time of writing, a chocolate gin they were readying for release. Expect to see a whisky soon, too, since laying down some spirit had been pretty much the first order of business for J. D. since the beginning.

Unit 106
355 Elmira Road North
Guelph, ON
N1K 1S5
(519) 362-1850
dixonsdistilled
spirits.com

Junction 56 Distillery

45 Cambria Street, Stratford, ON, N5A 1G8
(519) 305-5535
junction56.ca

I n fall 2018, Junction 56 celebrated its third birthday with the release of its first Canadian whisky. And even though distiller and founder Mike Heisz says he probably likes making his award-winning gin best, since the flavour profile can be so

JUNCTION 56 VODKA (40%)

Perfect for cocktails, this vodka is a great example of a classic standard mixing spirit, with a faint hint of pepper and mint on the nose and a subtle taste of a stone fruit on the tongue before the clean finish.

JUNCTION 56 GIN (41.3%)

A pronounced juniper and aniseed aroma sets you up for the candied black licorice flavour—one of the more assertive botanicals in this gin—but the lightly spicy, herbal finish is a complete surprise. Ideal G&T gin, since the flavour won't get lost in the tonic.

JUNCTION 56 RHUBARB GIN (33%)

A standout flavoured gin, with botanicals balanced perfectly against a delicate and only lightly sweet rhubarb flavour. Pour over ice and add an ounce of soda to while away a summer afternoon in the garden.

JUNCTION 56 CANADIAN WHISKY (40%)

Released in April 2019, the second expression of Junction 56's Canadian whisky is still a touch rustic but the flip side of that is that it's robust, exploding with rich pronounced caramel, chocolate, and cinnamon flavours—a whisky which suggests that Junction 56 will, one day, be responsible for some of the province's most delicious whiskies.

diverse, the first whisky is an important milestone.

"It's almost like we're getting this impression from people that, now that we have whisky on the market, we're a real distillery," he says. "It's kind of weird, because making gin is definitely a real thing, but it's almost like a prestige thing to have whisky."

Of course, it also indicates a distiller has at least three years' experience under their belt. We can expect to see this release (a blend) followed up with a 100 percent rye, and, of course, the continued quest for perfection of his many acclaimed white spirits. When Heisz entered the Canadian Artisan Spirit Competition in 2017, all six of his spirits were awarded medals and he used feedback from the judges to tweak them further.

Distilling is a second career for Heisz, who used to work as an engineer in the tech sector but had a "eureka moment" while listening to Davin de Kergommeaux at a whisky tasting. After considerable research, and with a lot of help from his friends and family, he realized his dream in 2015 and set up a 1,200-litre still. His right-hand man is a former tech colleague and all his corn and wheat comes straight from his cousin's farm.

Murphy's Law Distillery

2-90 Earl Martin Drive, Elmira, ON, N3B 2P5
(519) 669-2500
murphyslawmoonshine.com

We were just about to award the prize for Youngest Founder of a Moonshine Distillery in Canada to Ben Murphy, since he was but twenty-three years old when he opened the doors to his distillery in 2015. When we suggested that to him, though, Murphy pointed to younger brother, Sullivan, who is also a big part of the project. At the time, Sullivan was only eighteen—legally allowed to get his Smart Serve certification and work in the industry, but not yet old enough to drink.

The idea for the distillery, though, was all Ben's, who learned the craft of moonshine distillation in West Virginia while at school on a hockey scholarship. Moonshine was not on the official syllabus, but he made friends who gave him instruction in the local traditions, all the while successfully completing his degree. Like many craft distillers in Canada, Murphy is adept at doing two things at once; even after the distillery opened, he started pursuing his Master's in disability studies, a field in which he still works.

Although Murphy makes it look easy, it didn't start out that way. The name Murphy's Law is a reference to

APPLE PIE MOONSHINE (22%)

You don't have to add much to turn this into an apple pie–laced cocktail. Serve on the rocks or warmed up like a hot apple cider—and enjoy a drink that could not be any closer to a liquid version of classic apple pie if it tried.

ROOT BEER MOONSHINE (22%)

Ben Murphy suggests mixing this with root beer, but, in fact, this seems redundant, given that the moonshine already tastes exactly like a high-quality, old-fashioned root beer, replete with sarsaparilla, earthy bitterness, and a touch of mint.

all the things that went wrong—personal and professional—around the time he was trying to establish his business. Once the product started getting out there, though, things started to turn around, with his Apple Pie Moonshine selling well at the LCBO, probably because it tastes like old-fashioned apple pie with a perfect hit of baking spice—a result of the locally-sourced, high-pectin apple cider he uses in the process. It would seem that the Murphy's Law curse is finally lifted.

Niagara Falls Craft Distillers

6863 Lundy's Lane, Niagara Falls, ON, L2G 1V7
(289) 477-1022
niagarafallscraftdistillers.com

It's hard to know exactly what might be going on behind the curtain at Niagara Falls Craft Distillers, since they weren't terribly open to tours or tastings when we dropped by. (And yes, we emailed before, too.)

Located at the back of a restaurant called the Syndicate, located on Niagara Falls's famous Lundy's Lane, is a tiny retail store with a few gins and vodkas, distilled by owner Chris Jeffries, who has a background in craft brewing. He and partners Andrew Murison and Ian Kowalchuk established this small distillery in 2017 and have launched spirits meant to celebrate the history of the area, including its Lundy's Lane 1814 gin—commemorating the battle of Lundy's Lane—the Lucky Coin Motel Vodka, and Barrelling Annie's Rye Whisky, named for a woman who celebrated her sixty-third birthday by going over the Falls in a barrel.

Spirits not available for tasting.

NIAGARA COLLEGE ARTISAN DISTILLING PROGRAM

To date, Canada's small-batch distillers have learned their trade via a variety of routes, from apprenticeships at other distilleries to privately run courses to degrees from Heriot-Watt in Glasgow, Scotland. In the future, however, another avenue will be available to wannabe distillers: the Artisan Distilling program at Ontario's Niagara College.

Conceived as long as a decade ago, during the launch phase of the college's acclaimed Brewmaster and Brewery Operations Management course, development of the program pretty much coincided with the recent boom in small-scale distilling in the country, and finally launched in the fall of 2018. According to course director David Dickson, formerly the head distiller at Dillon's, the first course

had far more applicants than the college could accept and plans are already in place to increase the class size from sixteen to twenty students and run it twice, rather than once, per year.

The two-semester course covers everything from distilling science to regulation, distillery management, and, of course, practical distilling, culminating in each student creating their own spirit from start to finish. Unlike at the brewing school, however, getting these student projects to market is legally a challenge, albeit one the college is working to overcome. In the meantime, the students'"thesis spirits" will be either stored indefinitely or redistilled into a neutral spirit that can be re-employed by the next class.

Niagara Falls. (iStock)

Polonée Distillery

380 Vansickle Road, Unit 450, St. Catharines, ON, L2S 0B5
(905) 380-1669
polonee.com

At the same time that Polonée moved from Ancaster, Ontario, to its new home in St. Catharines in the summer of 2017, it also launched its signature product—Kannŭk vodka. Its creators, Patricia and Adam Szymków, are proudly Polish-Canadian and

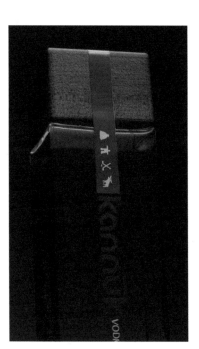

wanted to pay homage to Canadian diversity with their flagship spirit, which is why it's a blend of corn, sweet potato, wheat, and wild rice, representing indigenous and imported staples. The custom bottle is uniquely square and they make its maple-wood tops themselves.

Despite the fact that they hand carve their bottle tops the hard-core, old-fashioned DIY way, the Szymków are also early adopters of smart distillation technology, employing a G-Still—a high-efficiency alternative to a copper plate still that makes it possible to produce the high-alcohol distillate needed for vodka with the assistance of a computer that monitors the entire process. This family-run distillery is a fascinating blend of tradition and high-tech innovation.

Spirits not available for tasting.

Spring Mill Distillery

43-A Arthur Street South, Guelph, ON, N1E 0P9
(226) 780-2215
springmilldistillery.com

It is a reasonable bet that most Canadian beer drinkers will be familiar with John Sleeman, the founder of what is now Canada's third-largest brewing company, Sleeman Breweries. After selling his company to Sapporo of Japan in 2006, and despite remaining under contract with the brewery to this day, Sleeman had been, for at least a decade, nursing an urge to return to company-building.

"I've always enjoyed spirits," he told us in the spring of 2019, "and when I looked at the spirits market about ten years ago, it looked a lot like the beer industry in the 1980s."

And so, just as he had done decades earlier in brewing, Sleeman set about raising money to build a distillery larger than most of the current crop of craft distilleries, yet still much smaller than the massive legacy distillers. The parallels don't stop there: While investigating Ontario distilling history, Sleeman's daughter discovered that her great-great-great-grandfather not only brewed beer, but also had a distillery in St. Catharines. That distillery's name? Spring Mill.

Spring Mill's head distiller is former Sleeman Breweries head brewer Doan Bellman, who took a retirement package from the brewery and studied distilling via correspondence at Edinburgh's Heriot-Watt. The distillery itself is similarly Scotland-connected, having been fabricated by Scottish still-maker Forsyths, which Sleeman believes to be the only one of its kind in Canada.

The goal for Spring Mill is single malt whisky, but as at so many other smaller-scale distilleries in this country, the lights will be kept on while the whisky is aging through sales of a gin and vodka. Both are distilled from soft red winter wheat and are no stop-gap spirits, but rather seriously impressive creations. A retail store and attached cocktail bar complete the tourist-friendly locale on the bank of the Speed River in downtown Guelph.

VODKA (40%)

This has a soft aroma that is faintly floral but mostly fresh cereal grain. The body has a distinct sweetness, particularly at the front, balanced by hints of stewed fruit in the mid-palate and gentle heat on the finish. Straight, mixed, in a cocktail—impressive in any format.

GIN (40%)

Made in the London Dry style, this has a strikingly fragrant aroma, mixing juniper and citrus with a yellow berry fruitiness. On the palate, the sweetness of the base spirit shows first, then round fruit and citrus, and finally the juniper and spiciness. Definite Martini material.

Tawse Winery

3955 Cherry Avenue, Vineland, ON, L0R 2C0
(905) 562-9500
tawsewinery.ca

seasonal

As Paul Pender, the director of viticulture and winemaking for Tawse, recalls, the idea to add a distillery to the award-winning winery came when he and owner Moray Tawse were touring the French wine region of Burgundy.

"We were visiting wineries when we saw this mobile still driving around

DRY VERMOUTH (18.5%)

Pale gold and certified organic, with a base featuring Riesling grapes showing brilliantly in a rich fruity-floral perfume. The body seems sweeter than it actually is thanks to its robust pear-grape-ripe melon personality. Serve over ice for a terrific aperitif.

LA PRESSATURA: GEWÜRZTRAMINER (45%)

The liveliest of the three Pressaturas, this has a gently yeasty, under-ripe grape fruitiness on the nose and a hint of sweetness on the front of the palate leading to a clean, dry, faintly grassy and lightly fruity body. An afternoon pick-me-up.

LA PRESSATURA: PINOT NOIR (45%)

For those who suggest that the character of the grape does not carry on through distillation, we present this spirit with the soul of pinot: notes of dark fruit on the nose and a round, heart-of-the-grape body. A robust after-dinner tipple.

DRY GIN (40%)

This corn-based gin is almost clinical in its use of botanicals, definitely in the London Dry style but with reduced emphasis on juniper and a delightfully perfumey citrus character. Gentle and assertive at the same time, this belongs in a Martini.

making *marc de Bourgogne*," he says. "Since pretty much every wine region in the world except Ontario has a side distilling industry, we thought this made sense."

That was in 2016, with the release of the company's first products occurring in the spring of 2019. Their hybrid still, which Pender says converts from column to pot "with the switching of a couple of valves," was custom-made in Italy, and comes with a basket attachment for the making of gin.

"I'm a big lover of gin," says Pender. "It's also a great way to have fun and be creative, to really put your mark on it as a distiller."

Pender notes that gin makes commercial sense in Ontario where people tend to buy gin more than they do grappa, and their white vermouth made with Riesling wine and fortified with Riesling-derived spirit further ensures that Martini fans keep coming back for supplies.

The gin and vermouth are accompanied by three Pressaturas—their interpretation of grappa—and three cocktail bitters. Pender also reports that large quantities of grain spirit are being barrelled for eventual whisky releases, distilled from various combinations of wheat, barley, rye, and corn.

Vieni Estates Wines & Spirits

4553 Fly Road, Beamsville, ON, L0R 1B2
(905) 563-6521
vieni.ca

Given the number of wineries in the Niagara region, it comes as a bit of a surprise to the casual observer that so few follow the European custom of distilling the pomace left over after wine production. To Vieni manager Steven DiMora, however, it's a question easily answered.

"It's expensive!" he explains simply, adding that the taxation on spirits is very high. So why do it? "We like that we are able to use all of the products of the vineyard," he explains. "And that's why we've been distilling since Day One."

Founded by three partners with a fondness for the Niagara Escarpment, Pasquale Raviele, Alex Spassiani, and Paul White, Vieni opened its doors in 2012, although the property was purchased and planted fourteen years earlier. The decision to add a still to the winery, explains DiMora, was an attempt to introduce the North American palate to a new set of flavours. To ease that introduction, the decision was made to put a Canadian twist on things.

"Maple syrup, well, that's Canada, isn't it?" says DiMora, explaining the descriptively named Brandy Infused with Pure Maple Syrup.

To avoid conflict with the denomination-protected spirits of Italy, Vieni's main line of products are called Graspas rather than grappa. And that Dolce Piccante version? Another attempt to "Canadianize" the style of spirit.

In addition to the winery and distillery, Vieni also operates a three-bedroom B&B on the picturesque piece of land it occupies.

CABERNET GRASPA (40%)

The Old World meets the New in this grappa-style spirit with a bready, grassy aroma and elegantly rustic body that combines the best of farm-distilled Old Country spirits with the sophistication of a modern winery.

PINOT NOIR GRASPA (40%)

The aroma of this lovely spirit is best described as pillowy, with yeasty bread dough, marshmallow, and soft red grape notes. The body is rich and dryly spicy, making this a truly elegant after-dinner tipple.

DOLCE PICCANTE GRASPA (43%)

A deft mix of maple and pepperoncini combine to make this unexpectedly appealing spirit, with mostly maple on the nose, a spicy mid-palate and finish, and a lingering mix of sweet and spice.

BRANDY INFUSED WITH PURE MAPLE SYRUP (52%)

Light cognac coloured, this is pure maple essence on the nose, but sweet without being cloying in the body, with the surprising strength providing peppery pinpricks of alcohol. A lovely digestif spirit.

Wayne Gretzky Estates Winery and Distillery

1219 Niagara Stone Road
Niagara-on-the-Lake, ON, L0S 1J0
(844) 643-7799
gretzkyestateswines.com

Although the "Great One" has been involved in the wine industry for some time, in 2016 he expanded his roster to include No. 99 Canadian whisky, made with more than a little help from Joshua Beach, the estate's master distiller.

Beach got to work making whisky even before the team opened the doors to the Wayne Gretzky Estates Winery and Distillery in Niagara-on-the-Lake in the spring of 2017—an impressive facility with a number of experiences available to visitors interested in wine, whisky, and, most recently, beer. In addition to the sprawling gift shops, there are tours, tasting rooms, a cocktail bar, and the Whisky Bar Patio, a hot spot with a full menu and a great view of the vineyards or, in the winter, the skating rink. (Of course.) Owned in partnership with Andrew Peller, Gretzky Estates represents a next-level whisky trail/wine country attraction, modelled after the more expansive facilities found in Kentucky or California and, likely, a harbinger of things to come for the region.

Most interesting, perhaps, is the range of products being made in the impressive, state-of-the-art 3,000-litre still. In addition to Canadian whisky, Beach works with the winemaker, Craig McDonald, to make grape-based spirits, such as the Muscat and Vidal "Spirited Wines." Other crossover projects include wine barrel–finished whisky and whisky barrel–finished wine.

VIDAL ARTISANAL SPIRITED WINE (40%)

A blend of grain distillate and grape distillate, this marks a new category unto itself, rather than a traditional grappa as you might expect. Highly aromatic, with a round body and a flavour that speaks to the light sweetness of the Vidal grape.

CANADIAN CREAM WHISKY (17%)

This is a delicious, rich, and almost walnut-y whisky cream liqueur, with a wholesome and natural taste, built on a base of Red Cask Whisky. Suitably destined to be quietly snuck into thousands of coffee cups at hockey rinks across the country.

RED CASK WHISKY (40%)

A blended whisky that has been aged in red wine casks from the winery side of the operation, this is slightly biscuity, with a light and smooth body holding some weight, and a hint of vanilla from the wood. Perfect highball fodder.

WAYNE GRETZKY NINETY NINE PROOF CANADIAN WHISKY (49.5%)

Best-in-show from the Wayne Gretzky whisky lineup, this has good character, with deep toffee and coffee notes that make for a very pleasant finish. Despite its being high-proof, it is perfectly lovely when served neat.

PROOF POSITIVE

We can recall a time when nearly everything on the shelf in Canada was bottled 40 percent ABV. Of late, though, when it comes to gin and whisky especially, it almost seems as if we're more likely to see odd levels, such as 43.7 or 46.2 percent. What's up with that?

Most distillers will tell you that after days of blind tasting at various different proofs, they determine the perfect level of dilution to express the spirit. Besides finding that sweet spot where the spirit shines, though, sometimes there's a little more to the story. Hiram Walker's Dr. Don Livermore, for example, chose to bottle his special release "The Dissertation" at 46.1 percent so that he could make a nerdy little science joke: 46.1 is the molecular weight of ethanol.

At Reid's Distillery in Toronto, they had a similar opportunity they couldn't resist. "We were tasting [the spirit] at different strengths to see what we wanted to proof it down to, and there was one we really liked at 42.2 percent," recalls Jacqueline Reid, one of the owners. "My older brother, Calvin, said, 'We should definitely do 42.2, because it's fate.'" It took the rest of the family a moment to realize a marathon is 42.2 kilometres and that, between the four owners, they had, combined, run over fifty marathons. Needless to say, every bottle of Reid's gin is proofed down to 42.2 percent. Fate, indeed.

Willibald Farm Distillery

1271 Reidsville Road, Ayr, ON, N0B 1E0
(226) 556-9941
drinkwillibald.com

It's almost impossible not to make a cheeky *Field of Dreams* reference when writing about the Willibald distillery in Ayr, Ontario—a tiny hamlet truly in the heart of bona fide farm country. There, three young men, Cam Formica and brothers Jordan and Nolan van der Heyden, had a vision to turn the van der Heyden family farm into a craft spirits distillery, despite the fact that there isn't exactly a lot of foot traffic nearby. Or even traffic traffic.

Well, they built it. And in the summer of 2018, when they opened to the public, the people came. Over six hundred visitors descended on the farm distillery, anxious to finally get a taste of Willibald gin. They ran out of nearly everything that day—including parking spaces. Since then, things have only become more exciting, as they've rolled out their farm-to-glass cocktail bar, a wood-fired pizza oven, and, on select Saturdays in the summer, live music festivals, which have been a hit with the locals.

It helps that Willibald is a lovely facility, set back from a rural road, with Marilynn, a striking, German-made, 18-foot, 1,000-litre Kothe still, visible through the glass wall of a gorgeously renovated and retrofitted old barn. That still is used to crank out Willibald Farm Distillery Gin, their flagship spirit—barrel-aged with a fairly unique botanical mix and flavour profile. In addition to this, they've laid down whisky, and are patiently waiting for it to mature. And that's pretty much it. Willibald, unlike many other distilleries that have a wide range of products, is concentrating on building up its brand by making the best aged gin and Canadian whisky possible, which for them includes working towards getting an organic certification so it can become the province's first certified organic grain-to-glass distillery.

WILLIBALD FARM DISTILLERY GIN (43%)

This is one of the few aged gins we've tasted that really seems to work. Unlike others, it is rich, sweet, and tastes like minty vanilla balanced perfectly with spicy caraway; a bridge between gin and whisky, which is probably the point, since the Willibald founders can't wait to get going on their whisky!

PINK GIN (38.3%)

Aged in wine casks, this is less pink than it is pinkish-gold, with a gently fruity nose sporting light berry and more prominent juniper notes. The wildflower honey in the recipe adds a fair amount of sweetness but doesn't obscure the spice-accented finish.

Wolfhead Distillery

7781 Howard Avenue, Amherstburg, ON, N0R 1J0
(519) 726-1111
drinkwolfhead.com

The Windsor region has been dominated by one single distillery, Hiram Walker & Sons, for, well, quite possibly, ever. That changed in 2016, when Tom and Sue Manherz opened Wolfhead distillery, attracting something like one hundred job applications right off the bat—a reflection of how much the people in that region have counted on jobs in the liquor sector for the better part of 150 years.

Manherz had been working on his concept for a couple of years before opening, inspired by the fact that he knew Canada was far, far behind the United States when it came to numbers of craft distillers, and because he knew he could build on the legend of rum-running and bootlegging for which the Detroit–Windsor corridor is famous. So far, his lineup of unusual flavoured spirits—banana-caramel vodka, grapefruit vodka, and coffee whisky liqueur—has done quite well on the awards circuit.

The distillery also has a restaurant on site, offering a locally focused menu.

KAVI RESERVE COFFEE BLENDED CANADIAN WHISKY (36.2%)

Made with cold-brew coffee and Canadian whisky, Kavi is one of Wolfhead's "sister brands." It's well-balanced, relatively dry, finishes up with a nice, sweet burn, and shows well the quality spirit underneath the coffee the whole way through. Sip neat, pour over ice cream, or make a boozy dessert coffee with it.

Last Straw Distillery

9-40 Pippin Road, Vaughan, ON, L4K 4M6
(416) 564-5971
madebyhand.laststrawdistillery.com

Although they can't say for sure, Don DiMonte and partner Mike Hook believe they have the distillery with the smallest footprint in Ontario, and considering their tightly packed eight hundred square feet, they may be right. In addition to the fermenters

VAUGHAN VODKA (40%)

Made in small batches, Last Straw's vodka is generally only available at the shop. A perfect base for a Bloody Caesar, this is a soft-bodied spirit with a quick finish.

GIN TWENTY-ONE (46%)

This award-winning gin is potent and light-tasting, a diplomatic gin that's perfect for those who object to the piney, oily punch of a juniper-forward spirit. Serve straight-up, well-chilled and extra-dry.

LAST STRAW DARKER SIDE (45.5%)

Although it could easily pass for whisky with its rich, burnt caramel and buttery corn notes, this delicious spirit aged in charred American oak is more a whisky pretender. Purists will care. Moonshine fans who like easy-drinking spirits won't.

BLACKSTRAP RUM (46.5%)

Slightly hot, but in the most pleasant manner, this very Caribbean-tasting rum has a slight touch of funk and a body miles ahead of many big-brand rums. Aged one year in oak, it's suitable for straight sipping and next-level Dark 'N' Stormy cocktails.

and two stills with a combined 1,000-litre capacity, the pair also do all their aging in that space. The first Last Straw whisky, which they laid down as soon as they started distilling in the summer of 2016, should be ready by the time this book's out on the shelves.

This is a second career for DiMonte, who used to work in sewer and watermain construction, all the while planning to one day open a brewery. One night as he was doing research and enjoying a glass of The Balvenie, however, he checked out how many people were making whisky in Ontario and discovered nearby Still Waters (see page 117). DiMonte dropped by the shop and Barry Stein welcomed him in.

"He showed me the equipment, showed me the units, and he said, 'We'll answer any questions you have,'" recalls DiMonte. "And I said, 'Okay, every time I ask a stupid question, I'll buy a bottle.' And so, at one point, I was their best customer."

Now, Last Straw and Still Waters are neighbours, and DiMonte pays it forward by offering classes to interested wannabe distillers, although never as frequently as he'd like. The rest of his time is spent stacking barrels as high as they'll go and making the most of his small footprint.

Mill Street Brewery and Distillery

21 Tank House Lane, Toronto, ON M5A 3C4
(416) 681-0338
millstreetbrewery.com

In the brewpub

Despite the slowly changing gender norms in the spirits industry, there still aren't all that many women distillers in Canada, which distinguishes Mill Street: it has not one, but *two* women distillers. It all began with Kaitlin Vandenbosch, an Ontario native who was snapped up by Mill Street before she handed in her thesis for her Master's in Science, Brewing and Distilling at Heriot-Watt in Edinburgh. Although hired as a production brewer, Vandenbosch's duties expanded in 2013 when the company acquired a 4,000-litre beer still and a 1,000-litre spirit still.

Mill Street's first available distilled product was bierschnaps, a spirit distilled from beer that's commonly found in Bavaria. At the same time, Vandenbosch was also distilling rye malt and barley malt, laying it down to age in ex-bourbon barrels and bringing whisky production back to the Distillery District for the first time since Gooderham & Worts shuttered its facility in the 1990s. In 2016, Mill Street released its first single-barrel Canadian whisky.

More recently, Vandenbosch moved up to become Mill Street's brewmaster, while distillation duties have been passed on to Martha Lowry, who previously worked at Dillon's. Lowry's signature spirit is a gin with an unusual botanical—hops—but she also intends to expand Mill Street's whisky business.

SMALL BATCH BOTANICAL GIN (45%)

The El Dorado hops used are abundantly evident on the nose, but may be a bit too profound in the body to appeal to non-beer drinkers. If you're an IPA fan seeking to make the switch to gin, however, this is a good place to start.

SMALL BATCH CITRUS CRAFT GIN (40%)

A slightly better integration of the Citra hop notes and the rest of the gin botanicals makes this a less hop-forward gin, with a commensurate effect on the palate, which is perfumey and lemony. A Gin & Tonic spirit, hold the lime.

SINGLE BARREL WHISKY, BARREL NO. 2 (43%)

This early whisky release, sampled in late 2018, shows a considerable amount of oak, both on the nose and in the body. Perhaps bottled a bit early, hopefully future iterations will be somewhat less woody.

TANKHOUSE BIERSCHNAPS (45%)

Distilled with Cascade hops then aged on oak, this has a fragrant hop perfume, grassy and citrusy, and a lightly sweet palate entry that grows drier and more herbal as it progresses to a spicy, warming finish. Best enjoyed alongside a pint of IPA.

Nickel 9 Distillery

100-90 Cawthra Avenue, Toronto, ON, M6N 3C7
(647) 341-5959
nickel9distillery.com

When we dropped by one Saturday afternoon, Nickel 9 founders Chris Jacks and Harris Hadjicostis, along with their head distiller, Greg Morrison, were distilling an unusual ingredient—their Christmas tree.

Not quite as strange as it sounds, when you consider that spruce tips are often used in gin; the point is, these guys are having fun and are game for trying nearly anything, which is how they hit upon apples as the foundation for their spirits in the first place. Jacks and Hadjicostis had been hobbyists, playing around with distilling everything and anything, and after trying a range of things including kiwis, raspberries, and strawberries, realized apples were best. The next spirit they're working on is one made from wild mushrooms—a collaborative project with Forbes Wild Foods, one of the country's first food foragers. Nickel 9 also sources its botanicals from Forbes—and six out of its nine gin botanicals are actually wild Ontario ingredients, including the juniper.

"The way we came up with the final recipe is that we did all individual distillates, starting with the juniper, the coriander, orris root, angelica, and the anise," says Jacks, "Then we just started having fun with it and we'd distill things like Szechuan peppercorns, different fruits, spruce, and cedar, and we wound up with about forty different distillates. Then we started blending."

One of the more interesting ingredients that made the cut is chaga, a wild mushroom—the one that grows out of a tree like a shell. Though you can't actually taste it in the spirit, Jacks says it plays a crucial role as a binder, bringing all the disparate botanicals together. Sounds like a strange discovery but, hey—it's a great gin. So maybe there's hope for the Christmas tree, too.

NORTHERN TEMPLE (40%)

A whiff of sweet apple indicates this isn't your standard vodka, although neither does it resemble an eau-de-vie. It's lightly sweet, clean, and clear, owing to the fact that it comes off the still at about 93 or 94 percent.

HIDDEN TEMPLE GIN (40%)

Also made from apples, this is a nice oily spirit with a good, clean, and lightly peppery finish, and, worth noting, far less of the evergreen forest flavour than you might expect, given the presence of spruce tips, cedar, *and* juniper. An expertly balanced Martini gin.

TORONTO'S CANADIAN SPIRITS BAR TRAIL

At the end of a long day touring craft distilleries, you'll be needing to unwind with a smart cocktail at one of the many bars in Toronto that like to show off their Canadian spirit.

EAST
The Rye & Ginger Highball, on tap at the Canadiana-themed **Maple Leaf Tavern** (955 Gerrard St. E.), pays tribute to our original national cocktail—the Rye and Ginger that was *the* staple call drink at taverns across the country until the Bloody Caesar started to inch it out. This elevated version of a lowbrow classic is made with spicy, dry craft ginger beer and good Canadian rye, like many of the cocktails at this whisky-centric bar.

DOWNTOWN
In anticipation of the Canada 150 celebrations in 2017, the CN Tower decided to up its local craft spirits game by partnering with more regional producers, including Dillon's and Still Waters, the makers of Stalk & Barrel whiskies. It starts with a little shrine to Canadian spirits at the **360 Restaurant** and extends to its cocktail menu and spirits list. Sadly, the revolving restaurant has no cocktail bar, *but* the main observation level features does—and they recommend ordering a cocktail and walking the entire circumference—drink in hand!

The second-best view in Toronto is at **Canoe**, a financial district restaurant on the 54th floor of the Toronto Dominion Tower (66 Wellington St. W.), where Canadian food and drink have always been a priority. About half of its signature cocktails feature Canadian whisky, including rare birds like Glen Breton and local heroes like Dillon's Rye.

Char No. 5 (75 Lower Simcoe St.) is a veritable shrine to Canadian whisky, offering flights and both signature and classic cocktails with a Canadian twist—subbing in our nation's blends and single grain expressions at every opportunity, including in the food.

Since "Unapologetically Canadian" is **Bannock**'s tag line, it should come as no surprise that the restaurant's cocktails are made with a good range of Canadian ingredients—many of them craft, such as Kinsip's Woodland's Whisper Pine Vodka and Dillon's Unfiltered Gin. Located in the Hudson's Bay building (401 Bay Street), Bannock is also a good place to duck into for a quick break on an exhausting shopping trip.

WEST
It's hard to find a bar with a section devoted to Canadian single malts, but that bar does exist and it's called **The Emmet Ray** (924 College St). In addition to the single malts, this casual and relaxed bar also boasts an awesome selection of Canadian blends and pure rye expressions.

kyline, showing the CN Tower. (iStock)

Reid's Distillery

32 Logan Avenue, Toronto, ON, M4M 2M8
(416) 465-4444
reidsdistillery.com

Toronto's fifth urban distillery is unique in a couple of ways, beginning with the fact that it launched with one product to sell—and it's a gin. Reid's Distillery may not be the only one to have ever done so, but, given that one month after opening they still had no plans to extend the line, it's unusual. Especially given that since they make their own neutral grain spirit (from local wheat and barley), it would have been practically effortless to launch with a gin and a vodka.

"We might do a vodka at some point," explains Martin Reid, a co-owner, with his three adult children, of the distillery. "But we don't want to focus on that, since we're first and foremost a gin distillery, which is a little unusual because most people only do gin because they're waiting for the whisky to age and need something for cash flow. For us, it's all about the gin."

If that sounds risky, well, it might just be. This is a family that's pretty comfortable with taking risks, though. When the children, Calvin, Jacqueline, and Graham, were on the cusp of becoming teens, their parents pulled them out of school and packed up to spend two years sailing around the Caribbean and Latin America. As adults, the younger Reids still embrace adventure and it was Jacqueline's decision to study and work in the United Kingdom for a decade that nudged the family towards craft gin distillation—since the family fell in love with British gin culture when they visited her in London, after brainstorming ideas for a family business.

Graham, the youngest, is finishing up his Master's in Brewing and Distilling at Heriot-Watt in Edinburgh, and has loose plans to eventually stray from gin, perhaps into rum. For now, though, expect to see specialty gins, such as a rhubarb gin, a spicy gin, a citrus-forward gin, and, eventually, a barrel-aged version of their flagship "modern-style" London Dry gin.

REID'S GIN (42.2%)

A bold, juniper-forward aroma lets you know before you ever taste it that this gin is made by and for serious gin people. Still, possibly as a result of the use of wild, foraged juniper from Canada in addition to imported Italian berries, rather than being piney it offers a lovely balance of sweet, citrus, and spice with a perfectly oily body and a dry finish.

Spirit of York Distillery Co.

12 Trinity Street, Toronto, ON, M5A 3C4
(416) 777-0001
spiritofyork.com

Located in the old malting room of the former Gooderham & Worts distillery, the Spirit of York has a pretty daunting legacy to live up to. Of course, Gooderham & Worts, a monster industrial facility, wasn't nearly as stylish as the Spirit of York, where visitors first encounter a circular cocktail bar covered in plant life—the herbs used in the fresh drinks. From the bar, almost all of the distillery's operation is visible as a backdrop through glass—a beautiful copper hybrid still amongst fermentation tanks. The real showstopper, though, is out back: a 44-foot copper rectifying column housed in a glass tower in a courtyard outside.

The staple spirits are vodka and gin, which are always available, but they've also been quietly laying down whisky to age. While they wait, they offer special, limited-edition releases, such as an aquavit in 2017 and a Red Fife Wheat Vodka in the fall of 2018. Although they're rolling out the one-offs relatively cautiously in comparison with a lot of distilleries today, they have big plans for eventually making spirits that reflect the city's diversity.

VODKA (40%)

Lightly sweet and creamy, with a touch of fresh honeydew melon on the nose, this vodka is great on the rocks or in an equal-parts Vodka Tonic. It's an elegant and classic vodka with a clean taste and a perfectly spicy finish.

AQUAVIT (44%)

This is a delightfully bright, round, and rich spirit, imbued with a distinct roasted caraway flavour that melds perfectly with a little honey and black pepper on the finish. Store in the freezer and serve straight-up for a taste of one of the better aquavits we've had in Canada.

GIN (40%)

With a little hint of perfume and juniper on the nose, this light-bodied crowd-pleaser of a gin is perfect tonic-fodder. Fifteen botanicals go into its making, including some odd ducks, such as cubeb pepper, cinnamon, and fennel, giving it a lightly spicy and fruity finish.

HAWTHORN BERRY GIN (35%)

Inspired by sloe gin, this is made with a rye distillate and Ontario hawthorn berries harvested from Manitoulin Island. The result is an intensely chocolate and ripe berry spirit with a lot of Christmas cake flavours and a dry, tannic finish.

Toronto's Distillery District, in the shadows of the Gooderham & Worts distillery. (iStock)

"When we called it the Spirit of York, one thing we were trying to communicate is how we want to work with all the Toronto communities," says Gerry Guitor, one of several founders. "We believe that the sum of all the different social, cultural, and ethnic groups is greater than its parts, so we're going to try to develop products for Little Italy and Greektown and all the other communities. Ideally, we want this to be their distillery."

Still Waters Distillery

26-150 Bradwick Drive, Concord, ON, L4K 4M7
(905) 482-2080
stillwatersdistillery.com

Established in 2009, Still Waters Distillery is, by about three years, Ontario's first craft distillery. The pioneering duo behind this remarkable accomplishment is a pair of old friends, Barry Bernstein and Barry Stein, who bonded over their love of whisky and who, after many tastings, distillery tours, and much consideration, decided to make a go of it. Having toured far too many distilleries with overly romanticized and over-the-top stories, they decided not to invest a whole lot of time developing the lore of their operation and, instead, concentrate on making the best Canadian whisky possible.

That's why they were also perfectly happy to set up shop in what is, objectively speaking, a wildly un-romantic industrial park just north of Toronto. The small bottle shop doubles as a reception area; through the open door, you can see the 600-litre still and, behind that, the fermenters and small barrel storage area.

The distillery is anomalous in at least one other way, too, in that it pretty much only sells whisky. Sure, they had a vodka once and they make a batch once in a while, and they make spirits for other Canadian brands, too, including a bottled Toasted Old Fashioned cocktail they worked on with cocktail legend Frankie Solarik of Toronto's cocktail oasis, Barchef. But, unlike the many distilleries that throw a lot of experimental products at the walls and see what sticks, Still Waters is determined to stick with what they know, and only sells Stalk and Barrel whisky—rye, two blends, and a single malt. The last represents the province's first single malt.

STALK & BARREL SINGLE MALT (46%)

The nose of this pale gold whisky speaks solidly to its oak cask aging, although an exact age is left undeclared. The slight lemony note of the aroma translates into a dryly fruity, lightly citrusy palate and soft, vanilla-accented finish. An aperitif whisky.

STALK & BARREL 100% RYE (46%)

Lovers of bold rye whiskies will enthusiastically embrace this emphatically rye-forward spirit, with its peppery, vanilla-tinged aroma and richly expressive palate of spicy grain, melon rind, and black pepper finish. For sipping over ice or in a Manhattan.

STALK & BARREL RED BLEND (43%)

Caramel-coloured and forcefully vanilla-ish on the nose, this blend seems designed to bridge the gap between traditionally light Canadian whiskies and artisanal ones, a task it does brilliantly with its round, sweet-ish, and yet still spicy palate.

STALK & BARREL BLUE BLEND (40%)

Paler than the Red Blend, the Blue is less expressive of its cask with a drier, more floral nose and a palate that follows suit with a correspondingly drier—but not completely dry—body with spicy notes and hints of pear and red apple. A solid spirit for any cocktail.

The White Distillery

22–400 Matheson Boulevard, East, Mississauga, ON, L4Z 1N8
(647) 546-4291
whitedistillery.ca

When Kevin Dahi opened The White Distillery in 2016, there were only a couple of brands of Levantine arak available in Ontario, neither of which, he felt, were as good as the ones he was used to drinking at home in Hafar, Syria. There were only two solutions available to him: become an importer and bring in some better brands, or make his own. The latter appealed to him as a newcomer, since he was able to tell the story of the traditions he grew up with in Syria with Canadian ingredients, including maple syrup—the only sweetener used for his spirits. In a way, it's the Canadian "mosaic" dream of immigration and multiculturalism.

At first, Dahi wasn't sure people in Canada would buy arak, so he did something very unusual—he made "house calls," offering tastings at people's homes, weddings, parties... anything. At those events he introduced people to arak, and then he started adding new spirits to his portfolio, including a pastis and "berrycello"—a strawberry-maple liqueur with berries right in it.

Now he doesn't have time for personal tastings, since his arak is doing quite well at the LCBO and at the many Mediterranean restaurants in Ontario that want to offer up a taste of Syrian spirits tradition.

BERRYCELLO (24%)

The berry sediment might be a little off-putting, filling as it does a good inch at the bottom of the bottle, but the fresh and fragrant strawberry nose and mildly sweet and fruity body does much to dispel such aesthetic concerns. Keep in the fridge and serve chilled.

DAYAA ARAK (50%)

The label reads "Ultra Smooth" and, despite its potency, there is considerable truth to the claim. Complex anise notes define the aroma while an oily body supports the strong and slightly fruity, anise-dominated spirit. A must for aficionados of the style.

PASTIS DU HAMEAU (40%)

Dark for a pastis, this nonetheless has all the appeal of a southern French version, with a very fresh, herbal aroma reflective of the twenty-four herbs and spices employed, and a body that tends a bit towards sharpness but settles down nicely with a drop of water.

Yongehurst Distillery

346 Westmoreland Avenue,
Toronto, ON, M6H 3A7
yongehurst.com

   Pending

Most craft distilleries start off by producing one or two flagship spirits—usually gin and vodka—then build up a portfolio of limited and experimental releases after that. That's not the exactly the case at Yongehurst Distillery, where founders Rocco Panacci and John-Paul Sacco occasionally run out of the basics, but always have something interesting from the Libation Lab—from a Japanese-style Katsutori shōchu and whey vodka to limoncello and apple brandy.

"One of the things we thought about when we started this was how we'd have a lot more foot traffic in the city than the farm distilleries," says Panacci, already distilling in North York when he moved Yongehurst to its new, more central, location in 2016. "So we could talk to people one-on-one, explain what we're doing, explain things like, for this apple brandy, these are local apples [that we] picked ourselves and processed ourselves."

Despite this, Yongehurst is slowly becoming associated with one specific product—rum. And that's largely because of Panacci's philosophy of total transparency, something that's maddeningly hard to find when it comes to rum, which is sometimes sourced and often contains added sugar and/or colour. Yongehurst distills *everything* from scratch and they are proud to say that their rum is additive-free.

"To us...if it's something you can get at any other distillery, there's really no point in doing it," he says. "I always hang my hat on the fact that, when I look at other distilleries, I think what we're doing is really different and really innovative and that's important to me."

NOCINO (30%)

If you can get your hands on this seasonal walnut liqueur, by all means, do. It's not just that it's a rarity, it's also delicious—not overly sweet, but rich and nutty, with a touch of the bitterness that a proper Nocino should have.

APPLE BRANDY (42%)

There's a lovely hint of natural sweetness and vanilla in this apple brandy, which balances and softens the tannic structure for a spirit that tastes a little like a buttery apple tart, but with a perfectly clean finish. A seasonal product that we think, but can't guarantee, will return.

HARBOUR RUM (44%)

What makes this spirit truly special is the subtle esters on the nose that suggest a Caribbean-style spirit, round and slightly grassy. It's a beauty of a rum, achieving some of its unique character from a longer-than-usual (weeks, not days) open fermentation.

☞ NORTH

Beattie's Distillers

6673 Line 13, Alliston, ON, L9R 1V4
(705) 435-2444
beattiesdistillers.com

The craft spirits business can be a pretty small world. In 2013, Harrison Torr was working at the Prince Edward Island Distillery, giving tours and learning how to make potato vodka and gin, when he met Liz and Ken Beattie, on vacation from their potato farm in Ontario's Simcoe County. Nobody realized at the time that this would turn out to be a fateful moment for both Torr and the Beatties, the latter of whom were inspired by the PEI distillery to do something similar at home.

Fast-forward a few years and Torr, now fully versed in distillation, moves back to his hometown of Innisfil, Ontario, and hears about a distillery being built over in nearby Alliston. He decides to drop by to see if they need help, only to discover they'd all met before. The rest is history, since Torr is now the head distiller at Beattie's, Ontario's first potato distillery. You hear about jobs that are "meant to be" all the time, but this is really one for the books.

Better yet for Torr is the fact that the Beatties weren't messing around, a fact obvious from the 55- and 40-foot double-column still. It has a capacity of 5,000 litres, making it one of the biggest stills of its kind in Canada.

"Ninety percent of vodka today is made with grain or grape and the reason for that is you need about four times the product to make potato vodka," explains Torr. "Right now, I'm averaging, per bottle, between ten to seventeen pounds, which is huge."

The first batches of their vodka went out in 2016 and, since then, the line has been extended to include a gin, a sweet potato vodka, and a *poitín*-style spirit—a pot-distilled Irish potato moonshine that uses the whole potato, peels and all, and is briefly aged in wood—pronounced "put-cheen." Another great Canadian first.

Distiller Harrison Torr.

POTATO VODKA (40%)

You expect a certain amount of earthy rusticity with a potato vodka, but none of that is present in this clean-tasting, sweet, rich, and buttery spirit that finishes with a hint of caramel corn and pepper. Not to be wasted in a Caesar—enjoy on the rocks.

SWEET POTATO SPIRIT (30%)

Easily one of the most original—and successful— spirits we've tried, with a completely natural-tasting and intriguing candied yam flavour that's just subtle enough that it keeps you coming back for more.

POITÍN (40%)

Some of the earthy rusticity that's missing in the vodka can be found in the poitín, distilled according to tradition. This spirit has an edge that's slightly mellowed out by oak and vanilla notes and finishes off with a touch of damp vegetal flavour.

POTATO GIN (40%)

From the aroma, you know pretty quickly that this isn't a London Dry but, rather, a diplomatic gin, with a light aroma and a lot of crisp, refreshing citrus and mint notes. Perfect in a Tom Collins or any tall, fruity gin cocktail.

Crosscut Distillery

1347 Kelly Lake Road, Sudbury, ON, P3E 5P5
(705) 470-5323
crosscutdistillery.ca

Before it even opened in April 2018, one product at Sudbury's Crosscut Distillery was already generating a fair bit of excitement—bacon vodka. Owner Shane Prodan, though, had mixed feelings about what was only ever meant to be a fun experiment, and despite its success, he still considers putting an end to it.

"People sometimes expect synthetic bacon flavours as if we were Frito-Lay, but it is more smoke, brine, pepper bite with subtle caraway," he says, "which some people complain about, so we fought between shutting it down and doing our third batch."

Prodan eventually decided to give the people what they wanted, releasing a third batch of bacon vodka for the holidays. And despite releasing more than half a dozen spirits in his first eight months, he still fields requests for new flavours.

As long as it lets him shine a light on Northern Ontario raw ingredients, he'll probably be happy to keep coming up with new things; because he thinks his region's produce is often overlooked, his core mission statement involves staying as local as possible. He's got a source for foraged wild juniper, as well as other botanicals, and uses regional rye, wheat, and oats as a base for his white spirits.

"I used to work as a toxicologist for the Canadian Food Inspection Agency, on the alcohol side of things," he says. "And maybe it's not the most romantic way to look at it, but a distillery is basically running a chemistry lab. There's still an art to distillation, but the science part came pretty easily."

TRIPLE GRAIN VODKA (40%)

Made from Ontario wheat, oats, and rye, this sweetish vodka has a soft and creamy countenance, with a slightly spicy mid-palate and a finish that calls to mind oatmeal with a sprinkle of brown sugar on top. Sip straight, chilled, or at room temperature.

LOCAL HARVEST GIN (43%)

A layered gin if ever there was one, this segues wonderfully from sumac on the nose to a fruity front, more peppery and piney mid-palate, and a lovely fennel-ish finish. The stuff of an extremely dry Martini or straight sipping.

HASKAP RHUBARB GIN (40%)

Though it might suggest sweetness, this fragrant, berry-ish gin is actually quite dry, slightly spicy and floral, and layered in its complexity. A fruit-flavoured gin for people who think they wouldn't like a fruit-flavoured gin.

SEASON FOR TREES-IN (40%)

A vodka flavoured with northern spruce tips, this, not surprisingly, has an aroma reminiscent of a walk in the autumn woods. The flavour is subtler and slightly sweet, with spruce notes that again evoke the forest floor. Serve over ice or mix with tonic.

Grand Spirits Distillery

27 Main Street N, Grand Valley, ON, L9W 5S6
(647) 928-9934
grandspirits.com

Think truly great speakeasy cocktail bars only exist in big cities? Even though that's probably a pretty good rule of thumb, Grand Spirits in Grand Valley, population 2,956, is the exception. Located in a circa 1892 schoolhouse that was abandoned for over thirty years after being damaged by a tornado, Grand Spirits is a micro-distillery with a twist—it's a front for a little cocktail bar, hidden off to the side of the still room. What's more, it's a *seriously* first-rate speakeasy with absinthe fountains, smoked cocktails, house-made syrups, a full food menu, and a *really* well-stocked bar that includes spirits other than those made on the property. Unlike other craft distillery bars that, by law, may only use their own spirits, Grand Valley has a "tied house" licence, which allows it to operate like a normal cocktail bar.

That's integral to founders Jamie and Sheila Stam's master plan, namely, to build up Grand Spirits as a destination and community centre for the town, while the distillery slowly finds its legs. Their still is tiny, at only a 400-litre capacity, but that's also intentional, since it affords the pair the flexibility to make small batches as they learn the ropes from the consulting distiller they hired, who commutes from the United States. Currently, they convert locally sourced malted barley into vodka, gin, and a single malt that will one day grow up to become whisky.

Before that happens, though, Jamie Stam has further renovations in mind, including a newly completed event space and a pair of guest rooms upstairs. Long-term, the Stams hope to be a part of bringing back more of the building's and region's Prohibition history, with plans to help establish a full "bootlegger's trail" in the region.

SCHOOL SPIRIT REAL BARLEY VODKA (40%)

A bit of a chill tempers the inherent earthy rusticity you might expect of a malted barley spirit, leaving an exceptionally smooth vodka with a very gentle finish. Eventually to be joined by a gin and a single malt, the latter resting in oak barrels.

Muskoka Brewery

1964 Muskoka Beach Road, Bracebridge, ON, P1P 1R1
(705) 646-1266
muskokabrewery.com

Already well known in Ontario for its line of craft brews, Muskoka Brewery and Distillery (est. 1996) added a still to its operation in 2015 and, a year later, after a lot of paperwork and a lot of recipe development, launched its Legendary Oddity Gin. It raises the question, after a decade of building up a successful beer business, why take on the hassle of adding a new sideline?

Well, a lot of the inspiration for that came from a trip Muskoka president Todd Lewin made in 2014 to a brewery-distillery in San Francisco called Seven Stills, where whisky is made from craft beer. "That's where the genesis really came from," says Lewin, "since all their products were tied back to beer, [including] a stout whisky distilled out from the beer mash. It was such an interesting play that made a lot of sense."

We just felt for the Muskoka brand that it was a real good natural extension, and started thinking of making a gin 'born from beer,' since we had this Legendary Oddity Belgian beer that we'd done every spring for a few years. (It) had juniper berries, orris root, orange peel, and heather tips, which we decided would make a great base for a gin," says Lewin. "We just felt it was a natural link back to the beer."

LEGENDARY ODDITY GIN (40%)

The nose is soft but pleasantly foresty, with the delicately sweet spruce tip notes most obvious, while the body is similarly gentle and soothing, with notes of spruce evident mostly on the finish. A good base for creative mixology.

LEGENDARY ODDITY OAK RESTED GIN (45%)

Vanilla notes accent the nose of this aged gin, while the rest of the aroma remains fairly true to the unaged version. The wood becomes even more obvious on the palate, which might make this more appealing to whisky rather than gin drinkers.

MUSKOKA PINK PEPPERCORN GIN (40%)

A Christmas 2018 release, this is flavoured with Brazilian peppercorns, hibiscus, and Sorachi Ace hops in addition to the usual botanicals, for a soft and fruity flavour with the peppercorn spice reserved for the dry, zingy finish. Serve chilled.

Rheault Distillery

6 Highway 583 Nord, Hearst, ON, P0L 1N0
(705) 362-8263
rheaultdistillery.ca

Located north of Timmins in Hearst, the "Moose Capital of Canada," Rheault is the province's northernmost distillery—at least it was at the time of writing—but even if someone were to set up shop farther north, this fascinating distillery has other distinguishing claims to fame. First, it's Ontario's only licensed still located in the living room of a residential house, and the only North American producer of an "alpha vodka"—considered the spirit's highest grade.

What, precisely, is an alpha vodka? It's a classification for a vodka distilled according to a specific method, using only high-grade wheat and distilled to a higher level of purity. Alpha vodkas cannot contain more than .002 percent methanol, which is well below what most regulatory bodies call for—usually in the 0.3 or 0.4 percent level. That's not a typo—regular vodka can contain more than ten times the amount of methanol as an alpha.

Marcel Rheault and Mireille Morin.

LOON VODKA (40%)

The lightly sweet aroma on this vodka in no way prepares you for this spectacular, bright-tasting, fresh, and sparkly spirit that practically jumps off the palate. The mouthfeel is creamy, yet not in the least bit filmy; the taste puts you in mind of a lemony wheat field and it ends with a perfectly clean finish. We can't say it's the best vodka in the world—we haven't tried them all—but in our estimation, it's pretty darn close.

SINFUL CHERRY (24%)

This completely natural-tasting cherry liqueur is a delightfully dry after-dinner sipper with a cherry compote aroma and a pronounced sour cherry flavour. We can't help but think this would be an amazing topper on vanilla ice cream or simply served *as* dessert.

SINGLE MALT BARLEY IRISH STYLE SPIRIT (50%)

There are two expressions of this, one aged in American whiskey oak, the other in port barrels. Both are smooth enough, but have a slightly thin and rustic character that might well change by the time they've hit the three-year mark.

Rheault's residential still—housed in the distiller's living room.

Rheault's Loon vodka is only .018 per cent methanol, a level achieved through five distillations and a not-so-secret ingredient—cow's milk, which is added on the second distillation. The theory is that the milk "polishes" the alcohol molecules, picking up impurities that are then trapped in a sediment. There are three other ingredients that distiller Marcel Rheault says are factors in the quality of his vodka—silver ions, glacier water, and high-starch, high-grade northern wheat.

If that seems like an awful lot of effort, well, it is. But it was Rheault's goal to make the best vodka in the world, in part to shine a light on the pristine natural ingredients of the region. The whole family—his wife, Mireille Morin, and the kids (at least the ones of legal drinking age)—are keen on the project and pitch in to help distill, bottle, and sell it, along with Rheault's other spirits, which include liqueurs and a "not-for-the-faint-of-heart" whisky that they'll custom blend for customers who buy it by the barrel.

Spy Cider House and Distillery

808108 Side Road 24
Clarksburg, ON, N0H 1J0
spydistillery.com

When this book was being written, Spy Cider House and Distillery was just getting up and running. Partners David Butterfield and Piers Roberts were all set up, but still working on getting local permission to invite the public into their retail shop. So, having seen little and tasted nothing, it's hard to justify our opinion that this is going to be one of the most exciting distillation projects and destinations in Ontario.

Most of our enthusiasm comes from having spent some time speaking with Butterfield, a Toronto kid who studied history in Montreal and then, in an unexpected turn, moved to France and started learning how to make world-class Burgundian Grand Cru wines. Partner Roberts is an experienced Ontario cider-maker, and one day the pair began wondering about the untapped potential for Calvados-type spirits in Ontario— a province rich in apple orchards.

Their first plans didn't involve a cider house, since they were keen on the potential of apple spirits, but since both had more expertise in fermentation than distillation, they decided it would be foolish not to also work on building up a cider business. And what really has our mouths watering is this: they've planted two thousand cider apple trees—the kind of small, bitter, highly tannic varietal used in Normandy and Spain to make the less-sweet versions of *cidre* and *sidra* common in Europe.

That's a good sign for the eventual apple brandy they'll be releasing, not so much because it will matter that much for the distillation, but rather because it's an indication of the lengths the pair is willing go to produce high-quality products in keeping with exacting traditional standards.

Spirits not yet available for tasting.

ONTARIO COMING ATTRACTIONS

Aside from the hotly anticipated Spy Cider House, two more distilleries will be opening soon in Collingwood—Heretic Spirits and Georgian Bay Spirit Co., both of which already have brands on the market.

Just before this book went to print, Heretic had opened up a small retail space with a tasting room and cocktail bar to showcase its gin and vodka at 395 Raglan Street and a much larger, more ambitious space is expected to follow.

Possibly as early as the end of 2019, Heretic will be joined by Collingwood's second craft distillery, Georgian Bay Spirit Co.—the company's first bricks-and-mortar location. Since the brand has become a household name in Ontario with its ready-to-drink Gin Smash, it's hardly surprising that it will open with its gin, then wade into the whisky business, which will obviously take a little time.

In addition, a little south of the Georgian Bay region, we can expect two new distilleries—a gin mill in Mapleton called Pepprell and, down the road in Arthur, an ambitious new project called Silver Fox.

At the time we went to press, Viritus Organics, a gluten-free, organic vodka distiller opened in Etobicoke.

☞ EAST

Black's Distillery

99 Hunter Street East
Peterborough, ON, K9H 1G4
(705) 745-1500
blacksdistillery.com

It's easy to come up with adjectives to describe Robert Black, founder and distiller at Black's Distillery. He's a purist, a man with deep roots in the community, delightfully opinionated, and, above all else, down to earth. In fact, it was his love of *terroir* in spirits that convinced him in 2018 to embark on the ambitious project of opening up a grain-to-glass distillery in Peterborough. Several trips to Scotland, from where his family hails, helped him along.

"When I was out in Islay visiting Laphroaig and Lagavulin, I got to see the way they harvest the peat from the fields there, cutting it up into squares," Black recalls. "Then, when you see them heating the barley to stop the malting process, you understand how the peat smoke gets infused right into the barley. That was it for me, 'cause that's mother earth right in the grain."

As you might expect, Black plays around with a little peat when he's working on producing new flavours but, to him, respecting the taste of the Kawarthas region is far more important than Scottish whisky traditions. That is why he uses Red Fife wheat, a frost-resistant strain of wheat developed in Canada, for most of his spirits. Black thinks the developed-in-Peterborough grain is an important piece of Canadian history;

HERITAGE VODKA (40%)

One of Canada's most distinctive vodkas, this Red Fife wheat spirit has a touch of thyme on the nose, a buttery body with a little vegetal complexity, and, somehow, a distinct freshwater character that brings it all together.

GIN (40%)

A savoury combination of cubeb, sage, and apple helps push this towards an intoxicating fruity-juniper aroma, with more pepper in the body, a robust symphony of herbals, and a finish to write home about. Enjoy as close to straight-up as possible.

WHITE RYE (43%)

Leading the pack in terms of white rye spirits that are actually worth sipping, this offers a gorgeous, rich, slightly oily, and layered experience of light sweetness and spice, with a lingering finish that seems to last for ages. Sip neat; enjoy fully.

he honours it by using it as the base for his gin and vodka and by featuring the history of Red Fife wheat on his labels.

Dairy Distillery

34 Industrial Drive, Almonte, ON, K0A 1A0
(613) 256-6136
dairydistillery.com

Until recently, Almonte's biggest claim to fame was that it's the birthplace of basketball—the game invented by James Naismith in 1891. Nearly 130 years later, it's able to boast a second world-first, namely having devised a solution for turning "milk permeate" (a lactose-rich by-product of dairy processing) into a tasty little spirit.

That may not sound like as earth-shattering an invention as, say, nailing a pair of peach baskets to two posts and writing up the original rules for one of the world's best-loved team sports, but the advent of milk permeate spirit might just have a huge impact on both the viability of dairy farms around the world, and the environment. Why? Well, thanks to a perfect storm of changing consumer tastes, technologies, and trade regulations, dairy farmers have a lot more milk permeate than they used to, and it's very expensive to treat.

Omid McDonald, who was far more interested in craft spirits than milk, learned about this problem from his wife's cousin, Neal McCarten, who spent a lot of time at his uncle Jimmy's dairy farm. They agreed there had to be some smart solution for the waste and, of course, McDonald's first thought was to distill it.

The problem with permeate, though, is that wine and beer yeasts aren't able to ferment lactose and bring it up to an alcohol content suitable for distillation. This didn't deter McDonald, who went to the University of Ottawa for help and, after a year with a specific yeast working at high temperatures, came up with something that produced a "low wine" that McDonald recalls thinking was a little odd-tasting.

VODKOW (40%)

A delicate, soft spirit that's naturally sweet and makes you think of a really light vanilla cake icing with a hint of cinnamon or baking spice. It actually tastes—a lot—like the distilled version of *horchata*, a rice "milk" drink common in some parts of Mexico.

LEGAL DEFINITIONS OF SPIRITS IN CANADA

No book on alcohol would be complete without a section on wacky liquor laws, of which Canada has its fair share. For example, when Almonte's Dairy Distillery started work on its project to distill from milk permeate, it discovered that Canadian Food and Drug regulations, last altered in 1959, didn't permit calling a liquor "vodka" if it was made from anything other than grain or potatoes. That's why they came up with the name "Vodkow."

As we went to print, however, the regulations had changed to allow vodka made with other agricultural products, including fruit, honey, and dairy—a change that Dairy's Omid McDonald may have had a hand in, since he started lobbying the federal government to revise it in January 2019. McDonald wasn't alone, of course, since there are a lot of craft distillers in Canada making a vodka-ish spirit from grapes, apples, sugar beets, and honey who would prefer to label their spirit "vodka" as opposed to, say, "apple spirit," which might confuse the consumer.

And it wasn't only vodka that had an outmoded definition, either. When it comes to rum, there are a few distillers who object to the fact that they're confined to sugar cane and molasses derived from sugar cane, since we don't even grow that in Canada. Beet sugar rum producers have to call their spirit "Brum" or "Rhumb," which, again, might be confusing to consumers looking for something local with which to make Daiquiris. In addition, regulations require proper "rum" to be aged in wood for a full year, which many object to on the grounds that it makes it much harder to make a white rum. Unlike the vodka overhaul, however, we know of no plans to change this regulation at the moment.

Would it taste better as a spirit? The only way to find out was to bet the farm: drive to West Virginia, buy a second-hand CARL still, then build a gorgeous home for it in the north end of Almonte. The design is inspired by the idea of "modern barn"—nearly everything a crisp white, except the striking copper 23-foot column still that you see through the glass front when you pull into the parking lot.

When the first spirit came off the still, everyone got to breathe a long sigh of relief. It was a fine product. In fact, the first blind Vodkow tasting saw a majority pick it above other imported brands. The first batch of one thousand bottles sold out in ten days and the new goal is to produce a quarter of a million bottles per year.

King's Lock Craft Distillery

5 Newport Drive
Johnstown, ON
K0E 1T1
(613) 704-2529
klcraftdistillery.ca

There's a lot of talk about sustainability in the spirits industry these days, but few operators have lived their philosophy as completely as Laura Bradley, Rob Heuvel, and Joey Kelly, owners of King's Lock Craft Distillery, a small, super-green operation located near Prescott on the St. Lawrence River. Right from the start, when this locavore, fully organic, and kosher distillery opened in 2016, it was using *only* renewable energy sources and energy-efficient LED lights, as well as recycling all its grain mash and water.

Bradley and Heuvel, an electrical engineer and an organic farmer, were pretty well-equipped to set up a sustainable distillery, but they've still faced challenges, mostly in the form of negotiating the tricky ground between conforming to people's expectations and staying sustainable. Their prices are ever-so-slightly higher than some other premium local spirits'—but still less than many of the splashier imports—and some of their other choices, such as their barrel-free process for aging spirits, can lead to consumer confusion.

Oak barrels are common in whisky production, and mandated in bourbon making, but Heuvel and Bradley weren't interested in felling whole trees for their spirits and opted for wood chips, a move that's still controversial with traditionalists. But given the show-stopping nature of Prescott White Rye, made with 100 percent organic, un-malted rye grain, maybe the wood-aging won't matter. The grain is unmalted because the distillers wanted to respect its full flavour, in keeping with their field-to-glass philosophy. It paid off, showing that sometimes doing the right thing isn't a tough choice at all.

1000 ISLANDS MOONSHINE (40%)

The term "moonshine" doesn't really set you up for this elegant and light sugar cane spirit. Although it's got plenty of light honey and subtle vanilla from oak contact, it's not old enough to be legally called "rum" yet, which is why King's Lock chose to call it "moonshine."

VON SCHOULTZ VODKA (40%)

A classic vodka, with a touch of sweetness, a creamy mouthfeel, and a little more complexity than you get in your average corn vodka. Finishes off with a touch of corn and the perfect hit of pepper on the tail. Just keep this one in the freezer.

PRESCOTT WHITE RYE (40%)

This award-winning rye spirit is double-distilled from un-malted rye, a gamble that pays off in a spicy yet rounded white rye that represents one of the better un-aged and grain-based spirits we've ever had the pleasure of trying.

Kinsip House of Fine Spirits

66 Gilead Road, Bloomfield, ON, K0K 1G0
(613) 393-1890
kinsip.ca

It's all in the family at Kinsip House of Fine Spirits, a Prince Edward County farm distillery owned and run by four kindred spirits: Jeremiah Soucie, the first to catch the craft distillation bug; Sarah Waterston, his wife, who works with the Ontario Craft Distillers Association; Michael Waterston, his brother-in-law; and Michael's wife, Maria Hristova.

Soucie, a New Brunswick native, had been looking to open up his own facility in Ottawa when the clan discovered that 66 Gilead—the second craft distillery ever established in Ontario—was for sale. So in 2016, the foursome bought the farm and now work on the enterprise together, doing everything from marketing and promotion to cleaning out the chicken coop. The chickens can often be seen casually clucking and wandering around the patio cocktail bar, which is situated between the old oast house—once used for drying hops, but currently used as a barrel room—and the gorgeously restored Cooper-Norton farmhouse.

COOPER'S REVIVAL CANADIAN RYE WHISKY (42%)

Coopers are those who make barrels for whisky (and other uses), so it is an apt name for this barrel-defined spirit, which speaks to its oak in both its lightly charred aroma and earthy, almost rustic palate. More for mixing than sipping neat.

JUNIPER'S WIT GIN (40%)

A somewhat barnyard, herbal-citrus nose introduces this soft and retro-olfactory perfumey gin. On the palate, it is strongly citrusy with orange coming to the fore and a slight juniper pepperiness on the finish. Try with tonic.

BRANDY (40%)

A youthful brandy that declares its age in a profoundly fruity nose, this has a soft and fruity palate with minimal to moderate sweetness and a hint of oak. The finish is warming and slightly herbal. An after-dinner digestif.

DUCK ISLAND RUM (45%)

The charred American oak in which this is aged comes through on the caramelly, vanilla-accented aroma of this coppery-gold spirit. The body is similarly sweet and toffee-ish, with a gentle fruitiness and warming finish. Enjoy with cheese after dinner.

Kinsip's fully restored Cooper-Norton farmhouse.

Kinsip's owners are seeking to revive the region's grain farming heritage by growing barley on their eighty-acre farm, so they can become next-level grain-to-glass producers. At present, while they still have to source some ingredients, some, like the vodka, are estate-grown. They've also distilled several delicious single malts from the farm's barley which are currently being aged in unusual ways, including a tasty one that was finished in an old brandy cask.

With a lot of creative minds at play, Kinsip makes a wide range of products, from a sweet-tasting vodka to a pair of whiskies and shōchū to a lovely, dry cassis made from local blackcurrants. You can also expect occasional liqueurs inspired by what the neighbours are currently growing, since the idea of local collaboration is one of the things the owners are most excited about, especially now that the region's reputation as a food and drink hub is starting to truly take root.

North of 7 Distillery

North of 7, which opened in 2013, isn't just Ottawa's first micro-distillery, it's also one of Ontario's oldest—established during the first wave of the province's distilleries and well before the explosion of upstarts between 2015 and 2017. Yet, at least outside of Ottawa, North of 7 is under the radar as compared with some of the others, possibly because Greg Lipin and partner Jody Miall don't really spend that much time building the brand and working on a "brand story." They're too busy making really good whisky—not to mention gin, vodka, rum, and even absinthe.

That makes North of 7 something of a hidden gem, with a line of well-made products from experienced distillers with a genuine love of the spirit. "I love to climb. So I used to go down to Kentucky and Tennessee all the time on climbing trips," says Lipin. "I've also always been a big bourbon lover, so I'd go to the distillers down there and see what was going on. And it was around the same time that I saw Toronto Distillery Co. was opening up and basically thought, 'Hey, you can do this?'"

Lipin is a firm believer in long-aging, which he says is the single most important thing you can do to influence the flavour of whisky and rum, which is why North of 7 uses only new oak imported from Kentucky. Not only is he happy to invest in

the right wood, he's also fine with having money tied up in inventory, pointing out that if you sell everything the moment it turns three (and becomes legal age), you'll never have anything aged any longer than that. By contrast, Lipin still has whisky he laid down in 2013, which is certainly something to look forward to.

1733 St. Laurent Boulevard, Ottawa, ON, K1G 3V4
(613) 627 4257
northof7distillery.ca

ILLUMINATI VODKA (40%)

You really couldn't ask for much more out of a vodka than what you get with this by-the-book, perfectly well-made spirit. It's solid, clean-tasting, and an ideal choice for a spirit-forward vodka cocktail, such as a Cosmo, where you really need the spirit to perform.

TRIPLE BEAM GIN (40%)

A classic gin that achieves a perfect balance of juniper, citrus, and florals on the nose, this has a juniper-led and lightly piney palate and just enough fire on the finish. A gin for all cocktails and any occasion.

LEATHERBACK RUM (40%)

Distinctly estery in its aroma, with sweet honey and tropical fruit notes in the rich body, this is a true Canadian sipping rum, which is a rare beast, indeed. Would also make a world-class Dark 'N' Stormy.

NORTH OF 7 CANADIAN WHISKY (45%)

This four-grain whisky is an exercise in balance, depth, and complexity. The rich, buttery, sweet and spicy flavours run deep, the body is full, and the finish stays with you. Drink neat, since anything else would be a waste.

Top Shelf Distillers

14 Warren Crescent, Perth, ON, K7H 3P4
(613) 201-3333
topshelfdistillers.com

Prior to Prohibition, Ontario was a micro-distillers' paradise. Perth, then a town with a population of about 350, had three stills in operation—one of which, McLaren's, was famous for producing the province's first pure malt whisky. The Ontario Temperance Act of 1916 shuttered these enterprises, though, and for nearly a century, the rich distillation traditions of the town of Perth were only a distant memory. Co-founders Hanna Murphy and John Criswick changed all that when they opened Top Shelf Distillers to the public in 2015, in a space just south of downtown Perth. As of this writing, it offers gin, vodka, a delicious mint liqueur, and a plethora of moonshines. The first barrel of Perth Canadian Whisky was bottled in January 2019, with a single malt following it up later in the year.

The company's ethos is one of cheeky fun, which is evident in their line of Reunion Moonshines, including flavours like Butter Tart and Gingerbread. The former, incidentally, tastes exactly like a butter tart and is, so far as we know, the only of its kind.

Despite all the fun, Top Shelf is very serious about its relationship to the community and the environment, with a hyper-local ingredient-sourcing mandate and a tree-planting program that sees one new tree planted for every bottle sold at the LCBO or directly from the distillery. And never mind a one-hundred-mile diet, all Top Shelf's corn is grown within thirty kilometres. That corn is used in every spirit made in the facility's 1,000-litre Kothe still—the gin and vodka are pure corn; the whiskies (single malt and rye) are a blend of corn and malted barley and rye, respectively; the moonshine is a blend of all three grains.

VODKA (40%)

For a corn vodka, this has a surprisingly delicate body, with an aromatic nose and taste profile—floral, with flecks of lavender balanced with the natural light sweetness you'd expect from corn. We see a lot of Vodka Tonics in this spirit's future.

GIN (40%)

An extremely round and smooth spirit with an unusually minty aroma and a botanical blend that balances out floral notes with citrus and anise with a bit of spicy juniper at the end. Probably best stirred up into a Negroni.

REGIONAL REVIVAL

In the nineteenth century, Perth was the whisky hub of Lanark county, a region that was awash in whisky with something like two-dozen operating stills. The two most prominent distillers were Spalding & Stewart, famous for its "Mountain Dew" whisky, and McLaren's, which made a malt whisky occasionally marketed as "Canadian Scotch"—something you could never get away with today. (Just ask the folks at the Glenora Distillery about that.) The Top Shelf release marks one hundred years since a whisky was made in this once highly spirited region.

Glenora Distillery.

THE *Prairies*

he craft distillery scene in the Prairies is a study in contrasts, thanks to wildly different provincial regulations, population bases, and drinking traditions. Manitoba's craft distillers are just finding their sea legs and struggling to compete with big distilleries; Saskatchewan started relatively early, but has yet to find its "breakout" distillery; and last but not least, Alberta is booming with new start-ups making a combination of grain spirits and "sugarshine"—moonshine made from sugar beets. What they all have in common, though, is access to tremendous resources, being situated as they are in the water-rich bread basket of the country.

Up until five years ago, Manitoba was known for making one thing and one thing only: Crown Royal. That is beginning to change, but the going is slowed considerably by sluggishly evolving regulations and frustrating provincial trade barriers. Still, with its central location—key to Sam Bronfman's years-ago decision to establish his giant distillery in Gimli— and being home to both the Canadian Malting Barley Technical Centre and an important research station for the breeding of triticale, there is ample reason to hope for sunnier, or at least more distillery-dense, days ahead.

Smack in the middle of Canada, Saskatchewan was home to the first small-scale distilling on the Prairies and, in some ways, it continues to lead the way. While the size of the province's distilleries remains generally quite modest, the innovative character of its distillers, whether seen in the invention of dill pickle vodka or the employment of a silver-impregnated carbon filter, bodes well for a future filled with interesting, oddball, and tasty Saskatchewan spirits.

When we started putting this book together in the summer of 2018, our list of Alberta distilleries came in at under twenty; when last we spoke to the Alberta Craft Distillers Association, we were told there would be thirty-seven up and running by the end of 2019. Despite the slow Alberta economy, the distillery business is apparently booming.

While we are concerned about the number of distillers frustrated with provincial legislation, interprovincial trade barriers, and, more recently and acutely, a glut of new local spirits that some say is causing consumer fatigue, we tend to think that Alberta is a market worth watching, perhaps even more than Saskatchewan. In a decade's time, one (or both) may well be a world-class spirits-producing region.

Capital K Distillery

3–1680 Dublin Avenue, Winnipeg, MB, R3H 1A8
(204) 697-2901
capitalkdistillery.com

Located in Winnipeg's St. James Industrial district, Capital K became Manitoba's first craft distillery when Jason Kang opened its doors in the summer of 2016. It remained alone in the field, as well, until Patent 5 surfaced to provide a little company in early 2019.

Kang, who grew up in China and arrived in Canada in 2003, came to the business with a background in engineering and a passion for homebrewing. With general manager Jesse Hildebrand, a Winnipegger with

TALL GRASS OAKED RHUMB (42%)

Brilliant wild and funky aroma, with plenty of molasses and subtle tropical fruit—not exactly the taste of Winnipeg. The round flavour lingers, showing off little specks of pepper, honey, banana, and baking spice. Nothing short of brilliant. Drink neat.

TALL GRASS VODKA (40%)

You can't argue with this sweet, light, and perfectly approachable vodka. Finishes perhaps a bit too quickly for our tastes, but on a super-clean note. Keep in the freezer and serve chilled.

TALL GRASS DILL PICKLE VODKA (40%)

Dill pickle vodkas are polarizing, since at least a few spirits aficionados believe this is a thing that shouldn't exist. This one might change naysayers' minds—it's lightly sweet, the pickle isn't aggressive, and it finishes with the perfect amount of heat. It's got finesse.

TALL GRASS ESPRESSO VODKA (40%)

Every distiller who makes coffee liqueur in Canada should order a bottle of this espresso vodka to see how it should be done. Almost no residual sugar and a potent but perfectly judicious hit of delicious espresso, as opposed to the mocha icing flavour we're often subjected to.

Winnipeg skyline. (iStock)

experience in the restaurant industry, he has created a two-man operation and a rather labour-intensive and grain-to-bottle one, at that. Kang hand-mills his grain on site and distills the spirit for his vodka straight from the mash rather than from a low wine, as most distillers do. He believes this results in a much richer-tasting final product and, from what we've tasted, he seems to be correct.

Capital K started, as many distilleries do, with a vodka made from wheat and rye, but has since added ten more products, including an award-winning gin, a rye, several flavoured spirits, and a product that federal aging regulations require him to call a "rhumb." This is the sort of rule that Kang and Hildebrand hope will slowly change, since between federal and provincial regulations, it's been difficult to make a go of the business. As a way to supplement the sales of spirits, though, they also make a ridiculously popular line of craft canned cocktails.

Patent 5 Distillery

108 Alexander Avenue, Winnipeg, MB, R3B 0L2
(204) 995-4999
patent5.ca

N amed after the first patent filed for a column still in Canada, Patent 5 was opened in February 2019 by Brock Coutts, a former accountant and trained chemist who finally decided to turn a life-long homebrewing hobby and passion for distillation into a business. And he's going for it in a big and beautiful way—converting an old warehouse in the East Exchange neighbourhood of Winnipeg into a 1,700-square-foot distillery with a small-ish still that he hopes he'll have to replace in a few years. He's anticipating not being able to keep up with demand.

While he builds up the spirits side of things, the plan is to make the most of the space as a destination in and of itself, which is why Coutts sourced original chandeliers, stained glass, and wood panelling from a historic 1908 hotel bar (the Oak Room at the St. Regis, which was slated for demolition) to partially recreate that swank, antique cocktail bar in the new building.

"In our original business plan, the tasting room was just going to be a place to sample our product and maybe sell a T-shirt and a bottle, but we got a hold of Heritage Winnipeg and worked with the director long enough that she got us permission to do this," says Coutts. "We're allowed to actually make a cocktail in there, so long as our spirits are the primary ingredient."

He's starting with a vodka and a juniper-forward gin, and is currently working on several whiskies, including a wheat whisky that's another historical re-enactment—this time, of the last whisky distilled in Winnipeg, back in 1880. The most interesting spirit he's working on, though, has to be his Oude Genever, a gin made the Dutch way, with malt wine, minimal sugar, and all of the traditional botanicals.

Spirits not available for tasting.

THE CROWN ROYAL STORY

The blend was initially created by Canadian entrepreneur Samuel Bronfman to celebrate the 1939 royal visit, when King George VI became the first British monarch to visit Canada. It was a historic visit for another reason, too: geopolitical tensions were rising and the Second World War was looming, so the visit doubled as an attempt to boost trans-Atlantic alliances in the face of Nazi aggression. Bronfman, commissioned by the Canadian government to make a blend to commemorate the occasion, apparently understood the weight of the task and even consulted a rabbi for spiritual guidance as he played with hundreds of different blends until he found the perfect one. That "royal blend" is now one of Manitoba's most famous exports, perhaps *the* most famous.

The cocktail bar at Patent 5 Distillery.

Bandits Distilling

3A-22nd Avenue SE, Weyburn, SK, S4H 3J9
(306) 559-4753
banditsdistilling.ca

M ichael Guest was born and raised on the farm, as was his long-time friend and now distillery general manager, Marnie Gruber. So when he says he knows all about grain, and is proud of his "sown, grown, and

RED COAT GIN (45%)

Initially London Dry–like in the aroma, showing plenty of juniper, this shifts markedly towards a more aromatic profile once the nose opens up as well as in the body, with sarsaparilla notes in the former and a floral nature in the latter. Chill and enjoy, with or without vermouth.

TRADITIONAL MOONSHINE (50%)

The nose announces the strength of this 'shine quite effectively, with emphatic notes of grain alcohol. On the palate, however, it becomes a gentle giant, with soft flavours of pear and vanilla and a finish that warms rather than burns. Use in cocktails or sip on its own.

SASKATOON BERRY MOONSHINE (30%)

Sure, this is sweet, but sweet with a depth of berry flavour as much as it is with sugar. Although we have yet to encounter a Saskatoon berry pie filling, this is what we imagine it would smell like, while the body attractively balances berry with sugar and alcohol. Serve over ice.

OATMEAL COOKIE MOONSHINE (30%)

Moonshine is the source of many guilty pleasures, and this is sure to take its place among them. It does smell like a tray of oatmeal cookies fresh out of the oven and actually tastes sweetly oat-y. Enjoy as is—no ice, no mixer, no guilt.

bottled in Saskatchewan" spirits, you can be sure he's speaking the truth.

A self-described "mid-sized grain farmer," Guest's first farm expansion was in 2004, when he opened a meat-packing plant. (Earlier the farm had expanded from grain into cattle.) A decade later, he got the idea to follow the same sort of "value-added" path with a distillery designed to make Saskatchewan spirits out of his grain.

Bandits Distillery, named after Guest's two sons, whom he calls "the bandits," opened officially in December of 2017 with a vodka, a gin, and four moonshines. Guest says the big seller remains the gin, crafted from a mere four botanicals. "I wanted to make a true Saskatchewan gin," he says, "so the mix is 51 percent juniper, plus Saskatchewan birch bud, lilac [from his mother's garden], and citrus zest." The name of the gin is derived from the farm's position on the Red Coat Trail, the path of the North West Mounted Police's 1874 "March West."

The moonshine aspect of Guest's portfolio—twelve flavours and counting!—presumably comes from where he did his distiller's training, which was mainly in Virginia, Tennessee, Kentucky, and South Carolina. It's an area he still visits regularly to keep on top of craft distilling developments, and to hang with his distiller friends.

Black Fox Farm & Distillery

245 Valley Road, Saskatoon, SK, S7K 3J6
(306) 955-4645
blackfoxfarmanddistillery.com

Despite having both studied agriculture at the University of Saskatchewan, husband and wife John Cote and Barb Stefanyshyn-Cote weren't certain what they wanted to do with John's family farm once they took it over. So they rented out their land and went on a two-year sabbatical in South America.

Returning from their trip, the couple discovered they were no closer to reaching a decision on the direction for the farm; at the time the trends were either to buy land and grow or stay small and add value to what was produced. Social animals both, they missed the interaction of dealing directly with their farm customers.

After an early foray into vegetable growing proved rather disastrous, the two thought to get into the business of fruit wine, alongside their highly successful U-pick flower business, the largest on the Prairies. But when they realized that neither of them really liked wine, they turned their attention to spirits and, after taking a couple of courses, opened their distillery.

Black Fox is a "seed to sip" distillery in that 90 percent of the ingredients used in their products, save for such exotics as lemons, limes, and ginger, are grown on the farm. It is also

unusual in that the principle grain for their gins is neither barley nor rye nor wheat, but triticale, a hybrid of wheat and rye developed in the late nineteenth century. The distillers favour it for the combination of sweet (wheat) and peppery spice (rye) that it brings to the spirits, particularly notable in the Oaked Gin.

GIN #3 (42%)

For drinkers fearful of juniper, this presents a fragrant and perfumy juniper berry nose and a spicy body with round fruit punctuated by black pepper and anise, and nary a pine cone in sight. A soft and alluring Martini gin.

OAKED GIN (42%)

With a nose of clove, nutmeg, and juniper, this seems at the outset almost more spiced spirit than gin. On the palate, it's slightly more gin-like with peppery juniper and herbals, but accented by a vanilla-honey character. A digestif gin for the gin-curious.

Last Mountain Distillery

70 Highway 20, Lumsden, SK, S0G 3C0
(306) 731-3930
lastmountaindistillery.com

Although the distillery website says that husband and wife Colin and Meredith Schmidt started on their journey to building Saskatchewan's first craft distillery in 2010, Colin admits the true genesis actually took place about three years earlier. That was

DILL PICKLE VODKA (40%)

The pickle-and-vodka tradition in a single bottle, with an unquestionably dill pickle-ish aroma and a flavour that evokes alcohol-saturated dill and pickle brine in a way that thoroughly lives up to its billing.

VODKA (40%)

Vodka in its most archetypal form, light to faint on both aroma and flavour, with a slight rubbing alcohol aspect to the nose and a lip-tingling alcohol presence on the palate that begs this to be served very cold in small glasses.

CANADIAN WHISKY (40%)

This very pale, wheat-based whisky has a soft, vanilla-y and oak-influenced nose and a surprisingly robust body with gentle spice and rounded grain notes leading to a slightly hot, drying finish. Mix with soda or ginger ale.

LMD SPICED (35%)

A young spiced spirit—hence its billing as a "rum-flavoured beverage" rather than a "rum"—there's a profound spiciness to the nose and an almost equivalent zing in the body, with less sweetness than a typical spiced rum. Use in cocktails or mix with fruit juices.

when he heard from an old friend who reported he was living in Hawaii and making vodka out of pineapples.

Intrigued, after the Schmidts moved back to Saskatchewan from living in Colorado, they investigated what it would take to start a distilling business of their own. What they found was that the idea was so new the province had no regulations to cover the emerging industry, so the couple sat down with legislators to try to figure it all out.

It all came together when Last Mountain opened in August of 2011 in the couple's refitted garage, a space of only about 550 square feet. That served their purpose as a start-up, but lacked the room for expansion, which they very much hoped would become quickly necessary. Fortunately, a golf game in 2012 solved that problem when Colin met a local entrepreneur who had just sold one of his businesses. By the fifteenth tee, Colin says, said entrepreneur had invested in one-third of the business and the distillery moved into its new and much larger premises in 2013.

While Colin is justly proud of all of his spirits, he admits to being a bit blown away by the popularity of the Dill Pickle Vodka, which he believes was the first such spirit in Canada.

DILL PICKLE VODKA

Canadians love our dill pickle potato chips and putting pickle brine or spears into our Bloody Caesars, so we suppose it was really only a matter of time before someone made a dill pickle–flavoured vodka. And that someone was the Last Mountain Distillery.

Or, at least, that's the claim made by distillery owners Colin and Meredith Schmidt. We have been unable to confirm that Last Mountain's was, indeed, the first commercial dill pickle vodka in Canada or elsewhere, although what timelines we have been able to construct suggest it was.

Vodka infusions being such relatively easy things to do, however, and the Prairies being both hotbeds of hobby distilling and enormous consumers of Bloody Caesars, we do think it rather unlikely that dill pickle vodka was a wholly original idea. And as it has spread across Canada and into the United States (where there is even a company, Chilled Dills, that is entirely dedicated to its production), we admire the creativity that people have applied to the category. We just very much hope that we never again need to do a blind comparative tasting of them!

Meredith Schmidt
st Mountain Distillery.

Lucky Bastard Distillers

814 47th Street East, Saskatoon, SK, S7K 0X4
(306) 979-7280
luckybastard.ca

For Cary Bowman, the road to Lucky Bastard Distilling began south of the border, via a story he read about the proliferation of small distilleries in the United States in 2010, and wound through a month he spent touring Italy, Greece, France, and other European countries.

"At one point in Italy," he recalls, "I was in a place where there were about four or five distilleries located within a couple of blocks of where I was staying. I was intrigued by all these small distilleries that covered Europe."

Returning home to Saskatchewan, he began to research the potential for small-scale distilling on the Prairies. Finding it feasible, he went drinking one night with the couple who would

VODKA (40%)

It takes a "lucky" seven distillations to make this all-Saskatchewan wheat vodka, and each of them is done in a copper pot still. The result is a spirit with the faintest note of new-make whisky on the nose and a clean, vaguely grainy body. Sip chilled or mix.

BIRMINGHAM'S DILL PICKLE VODKA (40%)

Using a recipe developed at Birmingham's Vodka & Ale House in Regina, this has a dill pickle nose you can smell from two feet away, courtesy of real kosher dills and brine, and a salty, savoury, dill pickle-y flavour. Reserve for Caesars.

SASKATOON LIQUEUR (24%)

That this pours halfway between a syrup and a liquid suggests it contains a fair amount of Saskatoon berries, and the nose quickly confirms that fruity notion. Balanced sweetness and acidity from the fruit makes this the base of a fine Kir Royale or an excellent ice cream topping.

SINGLE MALT (46%)

Although young—at least three years old, though obviously far south of ten—this has an encouraging character in its grainy-floral nose and dry, spicy-fruity body holding notes of caraway and dried pear. Good now, with a fine future ahead.

Downtown Saskatoon. (iStock)

ultimately become his partners, the husband and wife team of Michael Goldney and Lacey Crocker. The next day, they all went searching for possible distillery sites.

Eventually, after a solid eight months of consulting (alongside the also soon-to-open Last Mountain Distillery) with the provincial authorities on industry regulations, the trio opened their distillery in a 3,000-square-foot space in May of 2012, with ownership split 50–50 between Bowman and the couple.

While their goal was always to produce single malt whisky, that takes time, and so the distillery opened with

gin and vodka—then, as now, made from rectified NGS—as well as some fruit liqueurs. Other spirits, including a rum and some flavoured vodkas, plus a whisky, arrived later.

As for that name, a source of contention that has the Canadian Intellectual Property Office challenging it because, says Bowman, the trademark examiner deems it "immoral, scandalous, and obscene," the distillery came by it honestly. It's the nickname of Goldney, who, years earlier as a newly minted physician, had a lottery win in excess of $14 million. One lucky bastard, indeed.

Outlaw Trail Spirits

1360 Scarth Street, Regina, SK, S4R 2E7
(306) 527-6533
outlawtrailspirits.com

While visiting her brother Chuck in Butte, Montana, Charmaine Styles and husband John were dispatched to pay a visit to what Chuck thought was a new brewery in town. Headframe turned out to be a distillery, though, and in touring, tasting, and buying spirits there, the couple found the "quasi-retirement project" they had been looking for.

A petroleum engineer with thirty-five years of experience in the trade, John felt he could make the leap from industry to consumer beverages, so the couple began investigating the viability of setting up a distillery in Regina. Determining that it made sense, they started the process in early 2016, enlisting the aid of long-time friends Stella Dechaine and Ken Balius.

While John and Chuck worked on product development, Stella and Charmaine put their heads together on branding and marketing. Looking to the history of the area, they came upon the Outlaw Trail, an 1890s route that ran from Saskatchewan's Big Muddy Badlands into Montana and all the way to Mexico, and which was favoured by such notorious Americans as Butch Cassidy and Sam Kelly. Tying their distillery to the Trail, the pair thought, would allow them to add a little fun and history to their eventual tours and tastings.

Not that those tastings would be at all dull, with Balius and John Sykes busy developing spirits like the "limoncello-like" Lemon Vodka and Calamity Jane Ginger Vodka, both made with redistilled NGS, and their pride and joy, Old Foggy Bottom, a new-make single malt aged six months on charred oak staves.

CLIMAX SK COOL CUCUMBER VODKA (38.6%)

This does not immediately announce its flavouring, with a nose that is as much richly herbal as it is cucumber-y. No such confusion on the palate, however, as cucumber dominates over soft grassy notes. Mix with soda for a summer refresher.

LADY LUCK LEMON VODKA (34.8%)

Certainly limoncello-esque, this offers fresh lemon juice and zest on the nose and combines sweet lemon with a slight mid-palate tanginess and a warming lemon peel finish. Serve chilled after dinner or use in a Vodka Collins.

CALAMITY JANE GINGER VODKA (34.8%)

Appealing more to those who prefer the confectionary side of ginger over the root's more peppery character, this is almost a gingerbread man in a glass, with a sweet and fragrant ginger nose and a flavour that is all ginger baked goods with notes of booze and a hint of spice.

OLD FOGGY BOTTOM SINGLE MALT (44.8%)

A whiff of phenolic on the nose of this spirit speaks to its youth, but open-minded whisky drinkers will still find much to like. The body is a bit oaky, but nonetheless spritely, caramelly, and spicy-dry. Pleasant now, with real potential for the future.

Smooth 42 Craft Distillery

400 Cathcart Street, Brownlee, SK, S0H 0M0
(306) 630-7468
smooth42.ca

    planned

Carpenter Adam Dombowsky was more than a little concerned when he noticed a downturn in Saskatchewan's construction industry. So, looking around for less market-sensitive industries, he and brother Daniel concluded that alcohol seemed to be a business that stayed up even when the economy was down and plans to build a distillery in Moose Jaw were born.

When finding the right place in Moose Jaw proved tricky, they started looking elsewhere and eventually settled on Brownlee. After partnering up with a friend of a friend, Sacha Elez, they found local councillors wanted to do whatever they could to speed the project along, including selling the trio the town's derelict hockey arena for—one dollar! The partners jumped at the chance and set about renovating and reopening the building, doing most of the work themselves.

In order to get around an ordinance that would have required sprinklers to be installed throughout the arena, they built a firewall 6,000 square feet into the building and opened on the small side of it, with a vision of eventually turning the rest into an event space. In the meantime, they still use only a fraction of their square footage, and will continue to do so even after they triple their useable space in the spring

of 2019. A proper bar addition to their tasting room is also on tap.

Smooth 42 distills or heavily redistills all they produce, including the NGS used as the base for their liqueurs. Red spring wheat provides the fermentable material and organic, locally grown garlic is used to flavour their Caesar Ready Vodka, while the Apple Pie Moonshine is based on a recipe the partners bought from an amateur distiller Adam met while working on a construction site.

SEXY PEACH LIQUEUR (21.6%)

Forget the peach liqueurs of your youth; this has the aroma of fresh and canned peaches, while the flavour is evocative of someone's mother's peach preserves, with a light peach pie spice and a slightly drying finish. Serve over ice and enjoy without guilt.

APPLE PIE MOONSHINE (34%)

Stronger than most Canadian "apple pie" spirits, the cinnamon and alcohol clash a bit when this is served at room temperature. When chilled, however, the cinnamon brightens, hints of vanilla emerge, and the experience becomes far more apple pie-ish.

HABAÑERO AND GARLIC CAESAR READY VODKA (42%)

Massively garlicky on the nose, there is a hint of pepper in support, but this is apparently not a spirit for anything other than mixing, with some complexity and a lot of pepper in the body. Use in a Bloody Mary or Caesar and forget the spices.

Sperling Silver Distillery

2124 Albert Street, Regina, SK, S4P 2T9
(306) 751-0000
sperlingsilver.com

Adam Sperling is fairly certain that his great-grandfather, Peter Paul Sperling, who opened a hotel in Saskatchewan after emigrating from Russia via Germany and Poland, was supplementing his hotelier income by bootlegging booze to the United States during Prohibition. But, as he says, "We can't be certain because no one was ever arrested."

Not that the head of Sperling Silver has led any less interesting a life, counting as he does stints learning Chinese imperial cuisine in China, studying at Le Cordon Bleu in France, cooking on Russian icebreakers in Antarctica, and finally resettling in Regina to open not one, but two nationally acclaimed restaurants, the Mediterranean Bistro and La Bodega.

Having developed a culinary name for himself, he was faced with the decision to either act on that fame and open a chain of restaurants or retrench to his roots. He chose the latter, opening the Slow Food Brewpub in Regina, which he eventually converted to the current Sperling Silver Distillery.

A pub and in-house brewery remain, with made-in-house cider, mead, and even wine fermented from purchased grapes and juice, but the heart of the business is now the distillery. The leftovers of the brewery's fermentation, known as trub, still forms the base for Ole Jed's moonshine, and a steep learning curve has pared the gin down from twenty-four botanicals to just four.

FRENCH LAUNDRY VODKA (40%)

Sperling boasts that his combination of a silver-impregnated carbon filter and freezing the spirits for forty-eight hours prior to their third and final filtration produces a pure spirit, and by the evidence of this vodka it's hard to argue. Bright, dry, clean, and, frankly, delicious.

EARL GREY TEA GIN (40%)

The colour of very weak tea, the Earl Grey aromatics balance nicely with the juniper on the nose, but are a bit more forward in the round and perfumey body. The appealing result is a gin that speaks to both its pedigree and its namesake ingredient. Serve chilled.

OLE JED'S HOMEMADE SHINE (45%)

This moonshine's brewery origins are immediately evident in the grassy, herbal aroma—think fresh hops—and the grassier still body, with even a vague suggestion of bitterness along the way. An interesting base for a characterful cocktail.

KILLYA (40%)

Made from imported blue agave, this lacks the *terroir*-ishness of a proper tequila, but appeals on a more fundamental level with vague spiciness on the nose and a flavour that trends more to vodka, albeit quite a lively one. Use to positive effect in a spicy Caesar.

Back 40 Distillery

4701 36 Street, Camrose, AB, T4V 0J3
(780) 271 2826
back40distillery.com

Back 40 isn't Lorne Haugen and Rick Lazaruik's first foray into food and drink—in fact, it all started with the duo's sausage and bacon business, a side hustle to their full-time jobs. At one meaty event on Haugen's farm, he and Lazaruik were serving up some special cocktails to pair with their smoked meats and one of their guests commented that they had a natural talent for making great-tasting drinks. They started to research, took a distillation course, and, after a little debate, decided to go for it. Back 40 became a legal entity in 2016 and the spirits followed a year later.

Although neither partner was a moonshiner before starting up, the name "Back 40" is a nod to the Ukrainian moonshine community (largely around Vegreville, Alberta) that shaped the region's distillation and spirits culture. "All the old-timers around here and, I guess even beyond that—to anywhere it was against the law and people made their own liquor—it was literally done in the back forty acres of everybody's property," says Haugen.

Although Haugen and Lazaruik do all the distillation from scratch, "grain-to-bottle" isn't really the right term for what they do, since their spirits are distilled from beet sugar, an increasingly common base in a province that produces over three-quarters of a million tonnes of sugar beets per year. All of it, incidentally, is processed at a single plant—the Rogers plant in Southern Alberta. At present, Back 40 makes four spirits: Wintertime Frost, Farmer's Blend (coffee liqueur), Vanilla Frost, and Ol' Apple Betty. A gin and a rum are next on the docket.

Spirits not available for tasting.

COULD ALBERTA WHISKY BE THE NEXT BIG THING?

Several distillers hope that "Alberta whisky" will become a household name, with a signature style and flavour profile, much like Kentucky bourbon or Tennessee whiskey.

Why? First, Alberta has a long, rich history of unique and characteristic whisky, thanks to Highwood's long-aged expressions and Alberta Distillers's pure rye whisky, which sets the region apart from other whisky traditions in Canada. In addition, Alberta has an exceptionally high number of grain-to-bottle producers working with local grain sources in w every distiller will tell you is the "breadbasket" of Canada. (This is thanks in part to regulations that require "craft" spirits to be made from at least 80 percent Alberta agricultural materials.) Many are looking to showcase the province's natural resources in unique ways, often opting hold back their whisky long after the mandato three-year mark.

Whisky barrels at Eau Claire Distillery.

Black Diamond Distillery

200 16 Renault Crescent, St. Albert, AB, T8N 4B8
(587) 598-2820
blackdiamonddistillery.com

When David and Andrea Scade took home *seven* medals for their spirits from the 2019 Canadian Artisan Spirit Competition—less than a year after Black Diamond Distillery opened in 2018—they couldn't have been more surprised. Or happy, of course. This after taking a leap of faith when they first signed the lease on their 1,400-square-foot space in St. Albert.

"We had no experience in the actual liquor industry," says Andrea Scade. "Both of us were just making it at home and everybody really loved what we were doing. My friends would try it and they would always say, 'You guys really need to do this.'"

It was after their wedding in 2016 that the couple finally decided to go for it, since friends and family raved about the custom flavours they came up with for their reception. The following year was devoted to licensing and in February 2018, they opened their doors, now with newborn Axel

EARL GREY VODKA (40%)

Since we generally expect tea-infused spirits to be dry and astringent, this sweet, perfumy vodka that could actually pass for a light mocha liqueur took us by surprise. Add soda or serve over the rocks with lemon and turn it into a boozy, sweet iced tea.

TART CHERRY LIQUEUR (40%)

Remember those Cherry Blossom chocolates that came in the little yellow boxes? That's almost exactly what this cherry spirit tastes like—rich, relatively dry, and slightly chocolatey.

HOT CHILI VODKA (40%)

With its intense habañero-esque flavours, this hot chili vodka certainly means business. It tastes natural and hasn't been drowned in sugar—as are some others—making it a standout in the spiced vodka category.

CUCUMBER VODKA (40%)

There's a fine line between a pickle vodka and a cucumber one and this one walks it quite nicely by staying on the fresh, crisp side. It's like spiked spa water. Destined for bloody delicious Bloody Caesars.

Black Diamond co-owners, and husband and wife, David and Andrea Scade.

in tow. It's been a learning curve and a lot of hard work with their "itty-bitty" 200-litre still that makes such small batches they've run out of product a couple of times—always, of course, at the worst possible moments. Like Christmas.

The Scades explained their capacity problem to West of the Fifth, another start-up distillery they got to know on the farmers' market circuit, and their new friends lent them a section of their column still—a work-around that was exactly what they needed to keep up with demand. Little wonder the Scades can't say enough about the community in Alberta—distillers and consumers alike.

ALBERTA'S MINIMUM PRODUCTION LAWS

Alberta craft distillers are playing catch-up with counterparts in other provinces, since for decades it was not just hard, but outright impossible to run a craft distillery—thanks to a law which imposed a *minimum* production volume of 600,000 litres of distillate per year.

To put that number into context, British Columbia *caps* craft distillers at 100,000 litres. Anything more than that and they cease to qualify as "craft distillers." What minimum volume regulation

meant was that big players, such as Highwood and Alberta Distillers, were essentially the only game in town until 2013, when the requirement was finally eliminated.

Since then, the craft distillation scene has been making up for lost time, with new distilleries popping up every time you turn around and, at the time of this writing, at least a dozen more in the works.

Broken Oak Distilling Co.

10518 100 Street, Grande Prairie, AB, T8V 0V9
(780) 513-6811
brokenoak.ca

I n the first several months of 2019, Grande Prairie went from being a town with no craft distilleries to the proud home of two brand new facilities—Latitude 55 and Broken Oak Distilling Co., which opened within weeks and a ten-minute drive of one another.

"Great minds think alike," says Shawn Herbert, who opened up Broken Oak with partner Patrick Chute. "We didn't know about Latitude 55 at the time. I guess we all just thought it was good timing to try something like this here."

Neither Herbert nor Chute had any professional spirits industry experience when they decided to open a distillery. The pair worked as truck drivers in the oil patch and, when business was slow, they spent their time homebrewing, which led them into distilling. Encouraged by friends who loved what they were making, they decided to try to take it to the next level. At the time we spoke, they were working on a traditional gin and a wheat vodka, which they cooked up in an 800-litre still with a 20-plate copper column.

"That was one thing we did—we oversized our equipment," says Chute. "When we were building, we visited a lot of distilleries and asked what mistakes they made when they started.

Everybody said they undersized their equipment, then outgrew it in the first year. So we actually went a little overboard on the size of our equipment just so we don't have those growing pains in year one, two, or three."

For now, the goal is just to make enough gin and vodka to not run out of stock. In late 2019, though, the pair hope to start working on new expressions and, of course, barrelling off a little whisky.

VODKA (40%)

A clean, clear, and light wheat-based vodka, this has a gentle, almost vanilla-ish perfume on the nose, with a sweet body that evokes thoughts of butter frosting without straying into confectionary territory. A natural partner for fruit juices.

BLOOD ORANGE VODKA (40%)

Fresh blood orange juice veritably leaps from the glass in high-intensity aromatics, while the natural sweetness of the vodka base makes this something not entirely dissimilar to a dry triple sec. Sip neat as a digestif or mix into a Sea Breeze.

GIN (40%)

By our figuring one of the gentlest gins in Canada, this has a lightly spicy, sandalwood-esque nose and a soft, fruity, Asian spice–accented body, ending with a touch of candied fennel and juniper. A friendly introduction to gin.

Burwood Distillery

4127 6 Street NE, Calgary, AB, T2E 6V5
(403) 276-8410
burwooddistillery.ca

It's not uncommon for a real estate agent to leave a lasting impact on a client. After all, if all goes well, the transaction should lead to you finding the house of your dreams, where you'll hopefully make the memories of a lifetime. With Jordan Ramey, though, not only did his agent, Ivan Cilic, find him a house in 2013, their meeting would also have a

VODKA (40%)

In no way does the whiff of sweetness on the nose set you up for this spicy little number. It has a rich and full-bodied mouthfeel and just a hint of damp barley at the end, which makes it perfect for a dry vodka Martini with a little character.

GIN (44%)

Maybe it's the Szechuan pepper that makes this gin so special. Or maybe it's the perfect balance between fresh flavours and spice in the rich, delightfully playful body. Use in everything and anything, but don't mask its flavour, since it's already a cocktail in its own right.

lasting impact on his work life.

"We became friends because we were driving around the city all day in his car looking at houses," recalls Ramey. "And it turned out we were into a lot of the same things." Beer, for starters, the industry in which Ramey was consulting and training as he transitioned away from life in the university lab.

Ivan's brother, Marko, saw the potential for a business relationship, given that he had helped with rakia distillation back in Croatia before the family emigrated to Canada. He pitched the idea of the three starting up a craft distillery in Calgary, they incorporated in 2016, and the first spirits went out the door in May of the following year.

Gin and vodka were first, of course, and, like most distillers, they got busy laying down whisky right away. Some of the most interesting stuff, however, involves honey, a traditional Croatian spirit base. Conveniently enough, the Cilic family has a hobby farm with several hundred hives, so one of the first products was a honey eau-de-vie. And what doesn't make it into the spirits will likely find its way into the food in their adjacent restaurant and cocktail bar—both of which are heavily influenced by farm-to-table and hive-to-glass philosophies.

Confluence Distilling

507 36 Avenue SE, Calgary, AB, T2G 1W5
(587) 771-1286
confluencedistilling.ca

A red light over a slightly hidden entrance is the universal sign that a swank bar with high-quality craft cocktails is waiting for us on the other side of the door. The one at Confluence Distilling is no exception, although the uninitiated might be surprised to find a great hidden bar in the middle of an industrial park. Arguably, the unlikely location just makes it even cooler, as does the fact that there's a full distillery right next door—one that specializes in craft gin, aquavit, and amaro, as opposed to the usual emphasis on whisky found at a lot of distilleries in the province.

"Part of my love of spirits is the cocktail culture that surrounds it, and so our cocktail bar is a little bit of an old school speakeasy-style bar," says Ross Alger of the cute tasting room, replete with antique bar tools and decor. "It kind of reminds me of my grandpa's basement."

Alger's grandfather, Ross Patterson Alger, was mayor of Calgary from 1977 to 1980—a fact that his grandson feels is partly responsible for his strong feeling of connection to the city and which informs a lot of his ideas about his distillery. The name, for example, refers to the confluence of the Bow and Elbow Rivers. As well, several special products are made in collaboration with local brewers and artists and the raw materials (wheat) and botanicals are almost entirely sourced from a farm about one hundred kilometres from the distillery or foraged locally.

And while Alger reserves the right to work on a whisky one day, right now he's really loving the creative freedom he has with gin. "Creating a whisky is like trying to create a new *Mona Lisa* with the exact same paint colours as the original," he says. "With gin, it's like you can paint any picture in the entire world."

HEADWATER VODKA (40%)

Warm, sweet, with a touch of graininess and a mild herbal finish, this is definitely not a character-free, neutral grain vodka. From our point of view, that's a good thing. You'll want to reserve this one for straight sipping—serve slightly chilled.

MANCHESTER DRY GIN (42.6%)

The chartreuse-y herbal aroma of this gin sets you up for a more esoteric experience than you wind up getting in the end. The sharp notes mellow and meld with pepper, citrus, and earthy notes for a well-balanced spirit. Dry Martini fodder.

Eau Claire Distillery

113 Sunset Boulevard SW, Turner Valley, AB, T0L 2A0
(403) 933-5408
eauclairedistillery.ca

When David Farran, co-founder of Eau Claire Distillery, ordered a spirits still from Germany in 2013 for his new venture, provincial laws still essentially made craft distillation an illegal activity, given the *minimum* production standards (see sidebar on p. 156). Farran boldly forged ahead with his plans regardless, convinced that Alberta was swimming against the current and would eventually have to change the law. Whether or not his lobbying was a factor, the province removed the requirement in December 2013, and Eau Claire launched its first product, a vodka made from malted barley, the following year.

Farran has been building his portfolio ever since, adding a gin, an herbal prickly pear spirit, non-alcoholic sodas and tonics, and, in 2017, one thousand bottles of Alberta's first single malt whisky.

"David's ultimate goal was always to be a whisky-maker, so the plan from the get-go was to make white spirits to pay the bills," explains master distiller Caitlin Quinn. "And then the white spirits took off, so now we're in a balancing act." Quinn, a Canadian-born, Scottish-raised graduate from Heriot-Watt University's renowned program, began working at Eau Claire in 2015 and notes that part of the solution to this balancing act is to increase production. Indeed, they were adding equipment when we spoke in early 2019.

"The funny part is that we're often using the same grains because a lot of Alberta grain is shipped to Scotland," says Quinn. "So essentially we're doing the same thing except getting closer to the source. And we're the first craft distillery here to do that."

Eau Claire Distillery, showing the front patio. (Photo by Colin Way.)

THREE POINT VODKA (40%)

An outstanding spirit, with a distinctly sweet aroma that pulls you in and preps you perfectly for a soft, delicately floral sipping vodka. The slightest tingle of not-quite-heat, but actual spice, keeps you interested and coming back for more.

PARLOUR GIN (40%)

The aptly named Parlour Gin is, indeed, a polite spirit with a subdued and relaxed flavour profile that balances exotic spice notes with perfume. It definitely pulls its punches on the juniper and citrus, making it less of a Gin & Tonic gin and more of a cocktail spirit.

PRICKLY PEAR EQUINEOX (40%)

At risk of turning off readers, this unique spirit tastes an awful lot like watermelon Jolly Rancher candy—but in a good way. It's not overly sweet and has a lovely hit of subtle candy, which makes for an intriguing flavour profile. Enjoy on the rocks.

SINGLE MALT WHISKY (43%)

Alberta's first single malt is going to be a tough act to follow—it's an elegant and balanced melange of treacle, fruitcake, vanilla icing, and light heat. Delightful for straight sipping.

Elk Island Spirits Co.

120 Pembina Road, Sherwood Park, AB, T8H 0M2
(780) 913-1215
elkislandspirits.com

By appointment

For John Stubbington, making spirits is definitely a labour of love. Everything is handmade in small batches by Stubbington, the "head elk," who has been distilling at his farm since 2016. The shop in Sherwood Park is off-site and, since he's pretty much a one-man show, is open by appointment only, although most of his products can be found through Liquor Connect (the distribution system offered through the Alberta Liquor Control Board that helps to organize the privatized retail system in the province).

At the time of this writing, he had five spirits in regular rotation: three young grain spirits, a vodka (Aurora Rare), and a whisky cream liqueur (MooseMilk). The distillery sources rye and as many other ingredients as possible locally and prides itself on aiming for sustainability.

Consistency? Not so much. Stubbington doesn't think that's a high priority for a craft distiller, so he leaves that to the big distilleries, taking pride, instead, in the wandering flavour profile that he gets from making spirits in seriously small quantities.

Before too long, though, Stubbington is likely to start taking the sales and promotion of his spirits a little more seriously, since his goal is, was, and always has been to make high-quality Alberta whisky. Currently, he's busy laying down straight rye and other grains in the barrel room and expects, in time, to have a whisky program that includes three-, five-, and ten-year expressions. For now, you can try the Wandering Elk Albino Foundation Spirit, the foundation for their future whisky.

Spirits not available for tasting.

THE CAESAR TURNS FIFTY

We swear we didn't plan this, but the Bloody Caesar, arguably Canada's most famous spirited concoction, is celebrating its fiftieth birthday the very same year this book is being published.

The story goes that it was invented in 1969 by restaurant manager Walter Chell, who was inspired to create a liquid version of Spaghetti alle Vongole in Rosso for the launch of an Italian restaurant at the Calgary Inn. The Bloody Caesar quickly evolved into the entire country's signature drink and is to many a source of national pride, since it distinguishes us from our neighbours, who tend to brunch with a Bloody Mary instead.

About a decade ago, though, Canadian drinks writer Adam McDowell rained on everyone's parade by digging up precursors to the Caesar in the United States. McDowell concluded, though, that we should still honour Chell's contribution, since his version was more palatable than the American clam/tomato/vodka prototypes that predated the Caesar.

The most important thing about the clam cocktail, though, may well be the boost it gave to vodka, a spirit that North Americans rarely drank before 1950—at which point drinks like the Moscow Mule, Screwdriver, and, of course, the Bloody Caesar promoted the spirit from an obscure import into a bar rail essential. And since Alberta is home to some very fine vodkas made at distilleries both large and small, it makes perfect sense to think of the drink as a bit of a regional treasure—one that inspired distillers to work on making some of the best vodkas in the world. And consumers to drink them.

The Fort Distillery

128–8818 111 Street, Fort Saskatchewan, AB, T8L 3T4
(587) 588-9237
thefortdistillery.com

The pursuit of a degree in chemistry at Edmonton's King's University might have been what stimulated an interest in distilling in Nathan Flim, but it was a visit to Blindman Brewing in Lacombe that cemented in his mind the notion that it could be a viable business. Or to be more precise, it was the visit to the Old Prairie Sentinel Distillery next door—only noticed as he and his wife, Kayla, were exiting the brewery—that did the trick.

PRAIRIE GOLD VODKA (40%)

Distilled from prairie wheat and malted barley, this is a vodka with weight, but not harshness. The nose is fragrant and lightly herbal, while the body begins slightly sweet before growing more floral and soothing, almost toothsome. Best neat with a slight chill.

PREMIUM DRY GIN (40%)

It is hard to miss the grapefruit and lemon peel in the aroma of this zesty gin. Combined with the juniper that lurks more on the palate and a hint of peppery coriander, it makes this a refreshing gin suited to drinking with light tonic or lemon soda.

ESPRESSO VODKA (40%)

Brazilian coffee beans roasted at the local Café Bench and then steeped for two weeks in the vodka bring a forceful coffee nose and full coffee flavour to this spirit, although without any added sugar sweetness. The result is an after-dinner vodka for serving neat.

For although the idea of distilling for a living had intrigued the self-described entrepreneurial spirit, Old Prairie Sentinel was the first place he discovered that distilling could be pursued on a smaller scale. This in mind, he and Kayla embarked upon several other Alberta distillery visits before deciding to set up The Fort Distillery in their hometown of Fort Saskatchewan.

The project came to fruition when the distillery doors opened on September 8, 2018. With a community focus, it took months before The Fort was serving any market outside of Fort Saskatchewan's twenty-six-thousand residents, with sales occurring mainly at the distillery and local farmers' markets. At the beginning of 2019, the couple finally began to serve a small number of liquor stores in the surrounding area, including a dozen or more in nearby Edmonton.

Still, the community-first approach will probably continue, at least until business picks up enough for Nathan to leave his "day job," which he expects to take place sometime later in 2019. In the meantime, local residents are more than happy to enjoy Fort spirits in the distillery's quaint and cozy cocktail bar, with food available from an adjacent restaurant, literally walked across to the lounge when ordered.

Hansen Distillery

17412 111 Avenue NW, Edmonton, AB, T5S 0A2
(780) 341-0682
hansendistillery.com

Many in Alberta's craft distillation industry have some connection to moonshiners, but none that we know of have quite as direct a link to the old outlaw traditions as Shayna Hansen, who, along with husband Kris Sustrik, founded Hansen Distillery. "My great-grandparents were moonshiners, my grandparents were moonshiners, my dad, too—and when I was growing up, everybody around me was moonshining," says Hansen. "But still, it definitely wasn't ever my dream to open a distillery."

It wasn't until Hansen and Sustrik had to sell off a welding company during the economic slowdown of 2014 that they started thinking about new ventures. They were taking it easy, upgrading skills and touring distilleries and breweries in their spare time and, crucially, initiating Sustrik, who was fascinated with the family's moonshine traditions.

BARN OWL GOLD VODKA (40%)

This spirit's sweet, slightly floral aroma is an awesome introduction to a tingly little vodka with a stunning balance between soft flavours and sharp heat. Drink chilled or on the rocks, since it'd be a shame to see all the flavours disappear into a tonic.

BARRELED TROUBLE GIN (42%)

This barrel-aged gin absolutely nails it—a tough thing to do in this category. On the nose, it's fresh and piney, while the body is full and creamy with a caramel–baking spice flavour and a slight bite on the finish. Not for the gin traditionalist, but a real crowd-pleaser.

MORNING GLORY CHOCOLATE HAZELNUT CREAM LIQUEUR (17.4%)

Every other cream liqueur should feel ashamed next to this almost surreally good, rich, and natural-tasting spirit. It tastes like an opulent but not too sweet Nutella crème brûlée with a perfectly caramelized sugar. Serve as dessert.

RED CASK BARREL-AGED RYE SPIRIT (40%)

This release isn't a "whisky" yet, but it gave us a little insight into the distillery's future as a whisky producer. This clean spirit is lightly spicy and we imagine that, by the time it's released, it will be rounded out with a little caramel and vanilla.

Hansen's West Edmonton tasting lounge.

The couple opened Hansen's in December 2016, with Sustrik handling the distillation side, since his wife had less interest in the actual making of the liquid. Flavouring it, however, was another matter, and the self-proclaimed sweet tooth was happy to try her hand at an Irish Cream–style liqueur, probably one of the best we've tried.

These, of course, are in addition to the regular lineup of grain-to-bottle offerings that include a vodka, a gin, a wheat-based moonshine, and an unaged rye. Expect a small offering of pure rye whisky to be released in 2020—Edmonton's first-ever (legal) unblended rye whisky.

Krang Spirits

315–1 Street East, Cochrane, AB, T4C 1Z2
(406) 630-2431
krang.com

lthough the distillery only actually opened in 2016, Krang Spirits was really born four years earlier, when Cochrane business owners Susan Ransom and Michael Guenzel toured the Ironworks Distillery in Lunenburg, Nova Scotia (see page 40). They'd been in the market for a winery, but after checking out the craft spirits scene in the Maritimes, they decided to switch gears.

Of course, at that point, the laws in Alberta still hadn't changed to allow for small craft distilleries, which is part of the reason it took a while for Krang to get up and running. Even after the provincial laws changed, it took a long time for fire departments and municipal governments to figure out logistics and Ransom recalls that it was eighteen months before they got their zoning changed. All the while, the couple ran their other business, a software company, which they still operate in addition to Krang. It makes for busy days and nights, but Ransom says it has its rewards, namely, having fun with the customers who pop in to buy their spirits and learn about their operation.

"If they're not happy when they come in, they're happy when they leave," says Ransom, noting that isn't always the case with their other business. "If somebody calls you at the software company, they're not calling you to tell you how wonderful you are. They're calling to tell you that your software has broken. So we were looking for something a little more fun."

They found it, using a 400-litre Müller still and a 250-litre digital still, to make nine liqueurs, vodka, apple brandy, whisky, and a cloudy gin— unfiltered to maintain more flavour— cleverly named Nimbulus Gin.

Spirits not available for tasting.

Last Best Brewing and Distilling

607 11 Avenue SW, Calgary, AB, T2R 0E1
(587) 353-7387
lastbestbrewing.com

Although there are other brewpubs owned by the Bearhill Brewing Co., only Last Best has spirit stills in addition to its brewery operations. (So, too, did the Wood Buffalo Brewing Company of Fort McMurray, Alberta, which closed its doors in June 2019 after seven years in business.) Last Best opened in 2015, building its 500-litre dual column combination still right into the initial design. Its primary focus is on interesting whisky experiments, such as its current "single farm" batches now aging, although somewhere along the way gin started getting all the attention.

You can blame that on Bryce Parsons, since his New Year's

GIN(S) (46%)

Because distiller Bryce Parsons is dedicated to demonstrating the diversity to be found in gin, the spirits we tasted are not the ones that you will be able to buy by the time you read this. What we can say, however, is that the gins he produces are wildly expressive, beverages to be sipped and considered rather than gulped and forgotten. You may like or love or loathe what he produces, but you won't soon forget it.

resolution for 2018 was to make a new gin every week in order to help people gain a better understanding of both the distillery and the diversity of the spirit. In fact, gin was the subject of his thesis when he got his MS in Brewing and Distilling at Scotland's Heriot-Watt in 2011.

"I really think gin is similar to what we see in the IPA movement," says Parsons. "You know, fifteen years ago, Alexander Keith's *was* your IPA. Now there are mango IPAs, milkshake IPAs, New England–style IPAs, and I think something similar could happen with gin."

One of the gins he liked best was a hopped style, which may well become his flagship gin; it fits in nicely with his overall philosophy of "building bridges" between brewing and distilling. Along the same lines, some of Parsons's whiskies will be made with deep-roasted specialty malts. "It's true that a lot of the flavour comes from the barrel, but you can actually drive a lot of the flavour from the malt, too," he explains. "The science is the same because charring a barrel to create a Maillard reaction is the exact same thing as the malt house's roasting procedures."

Latitude 55 Distillery

12523 101 Street, Grande Prairie, AB, T8V 5S1
(780) 532-9591
latitude55.ca

Coming Soon

In a province full of small start-ups established by moonshiners and distillers who turned to spirits after years of homebrewing, Latitude 55's master distiller Nick Kebalo's resumé sticks out like a sore thumb. Not only does he have a degree in distillation, he hails from Gimli, Manitoba, where his previous job was distillery operations manager for Crown Royal.

Kebalo moved to Grande Prairie in 2015 to work in water management and one day, talking to his new friend Dennis Warren, he mentioned his previous occupation. It didn't take long for the wheels in Warren's head to start turning, since at the time there were no distilleries in Grande Prairie.

"I asked him if he'd ever consider doing it again," recalls Warren. "And he said, 'Well, yeah, but if we did it, we'd have to do it right.'"

That was all Warren needed to get moving on putting together a business plan and finding three other investors. It took a lightning-fast ten months to get the doors open and start selling the first bottles of Latitude 55 gin and vodka in January 2019. Not long after opening day, they had already barrelled off four casks of rye for the future.

Within weeks, the partners decided to invest in more fermenters—they now have twelve—since they've already decided to alter their business plan and try to at least double their capacity from 20,000 to 40,000 litres per year. We've been told that Kebalo is looking at developing five new product lines, most of which are still under wraps. One that's not, however, is an authentic Alberta Rum (not a "brum" or a "rhumb"), possibly the first to be made from sugar cane molasses and aged for a year, which ticks all the boxes under Canadian regulations to qualify as a "rum."

VODKA (40%)

The nose of this clear, crisp spirit is mellow and faintly fruity, with perhaps a note or two of citrus oils, while the flavour has a gentle creaminess and more of that light citrus taste joined by a whisper of melon. A vodka for sipping or mixing, but probably a bit more the latter.

MOONSHINE (43%)

In many ways, this is a classic moonshine: not grain-forward enough to approach new-make whisky; not clean enough to come close to vodka. The appealing roughness runs through the nose to the palate, making this a candidate for shots or the punch bowl.

GIN (40%)

The pale yellowish colour and mildly woody nose makes us suspect this has had some oak contact, although none is stated, while the body has a gentle juniper, malty sweetness, and some spice on the finish. Mix with an assertive tonic.

Old Prairie Sentinel Distillery

3413 Unit C, 53 Avenue, Lacombe, AB, T4L 0C6
(403) 877-7872
opsd.ca

Sometimes also referred to as "Prairie skyscrapers," "Prairie sentinels" are what people call the many distinctive grain elevators that popped up next to railroads in western Canada

PREMIUM SINGLE MALT VODKA (42%)

Even before tasting it, you know there's nothing neutral about it, with its pungent aroma of damp heat and grain. The flavour profile is rich, oily, bracing, hearty, rustic, with a splash of stone fruit—characteristics that not everybody wants in a vodka. We do, though.

BARREL SPICED DISTILLED GIN (47%)

The faint pink hue on this sweet-and-spicy gin is evidence of the barrel aging that gives it so much character. Refreshingly, though, it's not just a vanilla-caramel bomb, as so many aged gins turn out to be. Would hold its own nicely in a G&T.

PICKLED PEPPER VODKA (47%)

This vodka starts off on the esoteric side, with salt and a hint of sweet pickle. You can't argue with the finish, though, which is a perfect lingering heat. Use in a Caesar and skip the seasoning.

BUTTER TART LIQUEUR (20%)

This rich, buttery, brown sugar bomb is certainly tasty. Although it would sweeten up a boozy coffee nicely, its real calling is as a syrup, to be poured liberally over ice cream.

throughout the twentieth century—designed to make shipping grain across the country more efficient. Even though few are left standing in Alberta, it struck head distiller Rob Gugin as a good aspirational name for his new venture when he incorporated in 2016, since he wants his distillery to one day become a beacon of pride for his community.

As you might expect, Old Prairie Sentinel Distillery is serious about grain-to-glass and a commitment to pre-industrial practices. Gugin himself forages for as many botanicals as he can, uses local maltsters, and refuses to use commercial enzymes. He also works closely with farmers—in one case even making a whisky entirely from barley grown and harvested locally with horse-drawn equipment.

"It was a really neat experience for me and then I got to help in various parts of that process," says Gugin. "The barley itself is very different, really green, and it made an absolutely phenomenal distillate that we put into some bourbon barrels and started aging. I can't wait for it to come out."

An old wooden grain elevator, or "Prairie sentinel." (iStock.)

In the meantime, he's playing around with an aged rum (the first batch was released in spring 2019), two vodkas, and a range of interesting gins. The flagship gins include a fresh London Dry style made with saskatoon berries and other local botanicals, and a briefly aged gin with a little "oak and smoke" flavour, thanks to the aging, as well as baking spice and coffee botanicals that Gugin specifically designed to make a great Negroni, his favourite cocktail. On top of these, he does two "Alberta Wild" seasonal gins per year, made exclusively from botanicals he forages in the spring and fall.

Park Distillery

219 Banff Avenue, Banff, AB, T1L 1A7
(403) 762-5114
parkdistillery.com

A s you might guess from its name, Park Distillery is uniquely located in a national park (Banff), and to make it even more unusual, it's also one of Canada's first full grain-to-bottle distilleries located in a full-service restaurant. There are actually a few others in Alberta, which has an unusual concentration of them, although at least two are brewery/distilleries. Uniquely, Park doesn't make beer.

"We were definitely excited to be introducing this model of distillery," explains master distiller Matt Hendriks. "There are a lot of brewpubs out there with a similar idea—you go in and try the beer they make. We're very similar except we're a spirits house, so cocktails are our game."

No surprise then, that Park has a pretty tight cocktail program, developed by operating partner Yannis Karlos, for both on-premises

CLASSIC VODKA (40%)

A clean and clear, high-quality vodka made in the classic style, albeit with a touch of residual sweetness and a mildly spicy finish. For use in spirit-forward vodka cocktails or mixing with a small splash of tonic.

ALPINE DRY GIN (40%)

The aroma of this "Alpine Dry" gin is gorgeously foresty, presumably from the spruce tips that are its signature botanical. But even those who dislike pronounced pine are likely to enjoy this oily and complex herbal blend with a slightly exotic flavour profile. Drink with soda.

BARREL-AGED GIN (42.7%)

Aged 180 days in ex-bourbon barrels, this is a lovely example of what an aged gin can be. It has picked up the perfect amount of sweetness from the cask's former occupant and yet still essentially retains the spruce flavours that are so appealing in the base gin.

MAPLE RYE (30%)

This spirit is more maple than rye, which means it's best drunk after dinner in lieu of dessert or in a boozy maple coffee. Thanks to its high-quality Québec maple syrup, this sweet smooth spirit has a natural-tasting maple flavour profile.

Fifi's Mule, a cocktail featuring Park Classic Vodka, ginger beer, and lime. See the Park Distillery website for the recipe.

Autumn sunrise on Mount Rundle, Banff National Park. (iStock.)

and take-away sales. Park sells a barrel-aged Negròni that gets our vote for one of the best bottled cocktails in the country, and in addition sells kegged cocktails to other restaurants. At the base of all these side projects are the gin, vodka, and unaged rye they distill on site, using hand-milled Alberta grain and glacier water. Somewhere in the offing is a proper, pot-distilled Canadian whisky, but nobody's interested in rushing it.

$\mathcal{RAW}$ Distillery

810 Bow Valley Trail, Canmore, AB, T1W 1N6
(587) 899-7574
rawspirits.ca

The year 2019 was a busy one for Brad and Lindsay Smylie, who actually moved their distillery to the other side of the railway tracks in Canmore, where they joined forces with Blake, a renowned and highly creative restaurant in this adventure tourist hot spot. Now, instead of just visiting the tasting room in the old space, customers can sit at the cocktail bar, enjoy a signature concoction made from RAW spirits, and watch the magic happen in the glass column still on the other side of the divide. The next step will be to add a brewery, which is how Brad Smylie got involved in the industry in the first place—as a homebrewer.

"The untold story of Alberta is really the story of homebrewing," says Smylie, who belongs to the Cowtown Yeast Wranglers homebrew club. "We all really challenged each other to be better. Now, when I look at Alberta and some of the distillers that have really come up in this industry, a lot of them came from that kind of background. It was really grassroots, because it was illegal to have a craft distillery, so it's not like anybody had a lot of professional experience."

Smylie, formerly a firefighter, did take a distillation course in Kelowna, BC, to hone his skills, and he and wife Lindsay (who, helpfully, has a science background) have been running the distillery together since December 2016. They've laid down whisky and are concentrating on their core range while they wait. After that, possibly in 2020, they're going to be ready to take on the world with new special and experimental releases.

BOTANICAL GIN (40%)

This highly but gently aromatic gin is well-named, with juniper and lavender making the most impact on the nose and a strong retro-olfactory effect bringing forward the coriander and spruce on the palate. A definite aperitif spirit.

CITRUS GIN (40%)

The secret ingredient here seems to be grapefruit pu'er tea, the toast of tea addicts everywhere. Here, it combines with lemon verbena to give this gin an earthy, citrusy character with a fuller sweetness and body than most gins. Surprisingly food-friendly!

PEPPERCORN GIN (40%)

The aroma of this emphatic gin is defined as much by its cardamom content as it is by its peppercorn spicing, with a boisterously spicy nose and appealingly peppery-fragrant palate. Try over ice with Indian dishes for a terrific spirits-food partnership.

VODKA (40%)

A bit sharp in its boozy aroma, this vodka mellows out on the palate with a creamy sweetness, a hint of black pepper in the middle, and a soothing finish. A vodka for people who like to drink theirs neat, but also highly mixable.

Red Cup Distillery

3675 44 Avenue East, Edmonton, AB, T9E 0V4
(780) 603-3040
redcupdistillery.ca

In 2018 Rob de Groot moved Red Cup Distillery one-hundred-plus kilometres west, from Vegreville to the Edmonton International Airport, in the hopes of increasing his export business, which he hopes will quickly become the most important market for his "Authentic Albertan Moonshine." What makes it authentic? Most of the moonshine in the province is made from sugar beets, whereas de Groot has revived Prairie moonshine traditions by building his own copper pot still and making his spirit from wheat, a combination he says makes for a smoother product—one that tastes lighter than 30 percent alcohol, despite clocking in at 100 proof.

Well, to be precise, it was really his wife, Barb, who revived it. She worked eighteen hours a day for two and a half years learning how to make high-quality, grain-to-bottle wheat shine—the result of over sixty experimental batches leading up to the launch in 2015. Her efforts were, apparently, in accordance with another venerable regional tradition—one that saw women do all the distillation.

"Women always made liquor better than the men," says Rob de Groot. "Women made all the liquor in the Prairies, 'cause if Mom made the moonshine the police would often look the other way because it was deemed a necessity for the farm. Nobody made tons of money, this was just basic necessities for survival."

Rob de Groot is frustrated, however, with the lack of a domestic market for his product, despite the fact that he considers his spirit to be an homage to the legacy of Prairie moonshine, which he says is no less rich than the more celebrated legacy in the American south.

Nevertheless, the history angle isn't getting him anywhere with other provinces' liquor boards, which typically favour regional producers, and as such he's trying to peddle his wheat shine in the United States and China, two markets he hopes will appreciate this sip of Canadian heritage.

Spirits not available for tasting.

Rig Hand Craft Distillery

2104 8 Street, Bay B, Nisku, AB, T9E 7Y9
(780) 955-2414
righanddistillery.com

You may recall Rig Hand from back in 2014 when it used to be called "Big Rig" and was the province's second craft distillery. Nobody wants to change their name, of course, so, as you can imagine, it was a bit of bad luck that forced the distillery to rebrand.

"Right after the first year of being in business, there was a gentleman in Ottawa, an ex-NHL hockey player, actually, who trademarked his junior hockey nickname and bought into a brewpub in Ottawa with the same name," says Mike Beile, Rig Hand's distiller and general manager. "So his legal team asked us to stop using the name. We thought of fighting, but decided it wasn't worth it."

Especially since they could simply change one word to "Rig Hand," which meant they didn't have to change the logo or bottle design. They just got on with it, which is the way founders Geoff and Karen Stewart have dealt with most everything in their build, the result of which is that they have become the largest craft distiller in the province, not to mention the only one with its own television show, *Still Shots*—Canada's answer to *Moonshiners*. (Some of the first season can be viewed online and Alberta's Global Television has recently committed to another thirty-nine episodes, in production when we spoke to Beile. And while it's arguably just an advertisement for the distillery, it manages to be educational, which was Stewart's goal, since he felt very few people in Canada really understood how spirits were actually made.)

And there's a lot of raw material to work with, given that Rig Hand makes forty different products, including some outliers, a "Brum" made from sugar beet molasses, ZAMA Buca (a dry sambuca), and Habañero Lime Vodka. Plus, Rig Hand's top three sellers, in order: Double Double Coffee Cream, Garlic Vodka, and Wild Rose Gin.

Spirits not available for tasting.

Stone Heart Distillery

Bay 3, 5021 44 Avenue, Innisfail, AB, T4G 1P7
(403) 348-7318
stoneheartdistillery.com

Although Stone Heart had launched a vodka at the time of this writing and has plans for a gin and a berry-infused vodka, this family farm distillery is still a bit of a work-in-progress.

Ian and Marnie Scott had dreamed of being able to use the fruits of their labour and 480-acre central Alberta family farm to make spirits but, of course, were dissuaded for a long time by provincial liquor legislation. After the minimum production levels were lowered, they started slowly working towards making their dreams a reality.

At present, the target launch for a consumer-friendly site, including tours, tastings, a retail space, and a cocktail bar, is 2020.

VODKA (40%)

A perfectly pleasant, well-made, medium-bodied vodka with a bright, citrussy flavour profile that finishes up with a nice touch of heat. Not quite a sipping vodka, but superb in a tonic.

SUGARSHINE

About a half-dozen of the distillers we spoke to in Alberta use sugar beets as a base for their spirits instead of grain or potatoes. Since we haven't seen this in other parts of Canada, we asked what was up with all the sugar beet spirits.

Mike Beile of Rig Hand said they use it to make "brum," which is a rum-like product made from sugar beet molasses rather than sugar cane. "Because we make all our liquor from ingredients grown here in Alberta, that makes it tough to make rum here, since we don't grow a lot of sugar cane in the province," says Beile. "But we do grow a ton of sugar beets."

And the province also *processes* a lot of sugar beets, thanks to a massive Lantic-owned sugar plant established in Taber, Alberta, about a decade ago. Some distillers, such as Rig Hand, buy the molasses from the facility to make spirits; others distill from the sugar itself to make "sugarshine," a new category of spirit unique to Alberta.

Strathcona Spirits Distillery

10122 81 Avenue NW, Edmonton, AB, T6E 1X1
(780) 887-9393
strathconaspirits.ca

Edmonton's first licensed distillery—first *ever*, not just the first since Prohibition—may also just be Canada's smallest operating grain-to-bottle facility. Strathcona Spirits mills, mashes, ferments, and distills three different spirits in less than 800 square feet in an artsy space located in an eclectic neighbourhood on the city's south side. Admittedly, some of the aging is going to start to take place off-site, since owners Adam Smith and Andrea Shubert have recently bought forty acres of land southwest of the city, where they plan to *move* an old abandoned church so they can age whisky there. Long-term, they have thoughts of building up the land, possibly into an outdoor music venue.

This hearkens back to the Edmonton space's past, which Smith used to run as an underground music club—the Baby Seal—a favourite venue for local and touring punk, metal, and indie pop bands. For years, Smith thought he would turn it into a legit licensed live music bar, but when he saw that the regulations around craft distillation were likely to change in 2013, he started drawing up new plans. Still, it took until 2016 before Strathcona launched with two products: a wild juniper–forward gin and a wheat vodka.

SINGLE GRAIN WHEAT VODKA (40%)

Clean, clear, and classic, this award-winning creamy and soft vodka has just the right amount of grainy sweetness, balanced with lingering spice. Ideal for dry vodka Martinis—hold the olive.

BADLAND SEABERRY GIN (40.4%)

From this gin's fresh, minty opening aroma to its lightly fruity and peppery finish, this is easily one of the most successful experimental gins we've had the pleasure of sampling. The flavours are diverse, ranging from wild juniper to wintergreen and anise, but perfectly integrated. Chill and drink neat.

Co-owner Adam Smith at the Strathcona Spirits tasting bar.

"We use 100 percent hard red wheat, which we buy from a farmer who is twenty-three kilometres away from the distillery, just outside the city limits," says Smith. "We think it makes for a softer, creamier spirit, which we then use as a base for our gins. We're also barrelling wheat whisky, which I think will grow significantly in a few years because it's kind of got nice soft notes."

Given how phenomenal their existing products are, we're very much looking forward to Strathcona's whisky, whenever it happens to be ready.

Tippa Inc.

393 Avenue E, Okotoks, AB, T1S 0L1
(403) 399-4589
tippa.ca

As you can tell from the lack of information above, Calgary's Paul Poutanen plays hard-to-get. You can't tour his distillery, he doesn't have a tasting room, and you can't buy directly from him at his facility in Okotoks. But if you drop him a line, he's liable to get back to you lightning fast. It's just that, as a one-man show, he can't keep up a retail operation on top of everything else.

Tippa, which means a "drop" in Finnish, is a reference to the distillery's two tiny stills—one is 100 litres and the other twice as big. Even the largest is less than half the size of the smallest commercial stills we've seen used regularly, and thus they produce his gin one drop at a time. If that sounds labour-intensive, well, it is. And to make matters even harder, he distills his beet-sugar spirit, drop by drop, five times over.

In the short time since he started Tippa in the summer of 2018, though, Poutanen has developed an impressive little cult following among bartenders and consumers in Calgary, who appreciate the smooth and unique character of both of his gins, as well as the absolutely gorgeous packaging. Each bottle sports a bright label depicting birds—lovebirds and a wood duck—designed by local woodcut artist Lisa Brawn. Poutanen has no plans to add new products anytime soon, since two gins are enough to keep him busy for the time being.

TIPPA'S LOVEBIRD GIN (44%)

A delightful, fresh, anise-forward aroma announces that this clean, clear spirit will be unusually lively, but what you can't anticipate is the smooth, almost silky body and the delicious balance of spice, fenugreek, and robust citrus flavours. Poutanen drinks his chilled, straight-up, and we tend to agree that's a good way to go.

WOOD DUCK OAKED GIN (41%)

This is a delicate creature, with a hint of vanilla and caramel mellowing out the fresh citrus notes and bringing out the limonene terpenes and oils instead. A unique spirit that would do really well in a Gin Sour.

Troubled Monk Spirits

5551–45th Street, Red Deer, AB, T4N 1L2
(403) 348-2378
troubledmonk.com

t was a bold move when the Bredo brothers, Charlie and Graeme, decided to open Troubled Monk Brewing in Red Deer, since the central Alberta city had not, in the past, been especially kind to its breweries. Despite a seemingly advantageous location midway between the big markets of Calgary and Edmonton, the only modern Red Deer brewery of note prior to Troubled Monk's opening in 2015 was Drummond Brewing, which changed hands numerous times before ultimately failing in the 1990s.

Adding distilling to their mix in 2017, then, was an even bolder move, particularly since they launched their spirits line with a gin—and a blue gin, at that!

That gin, made from redistilled NGS with butterfly pea powder for colour, has proved pivotal, though, since it was the early product that found the most traction, according to Charlie Bredo, and it inspired a new naming convention for the company once it was rebranded Epitaph Gin. "Troubled Monk makes sense with beer, but less so with spirits," says Bredo. "So we've decided that future products will be launched under different sub-labels."

However, Bredo adds that no plans are currently in place to rebrand the company's other two products, which include an in-house distilled vodka made from a 50–50 mix of wheat and rye and a saskatoon berry liqueur that gets a little extra oomph from blackcurrants. At the time of our visit in early 2019, whiskies had been barrelled for just under a year, including some made from beer recipes, some single malts, and some distilled from 100 percent rye.

VODKA (40%)

The notes of spicy biscuit on the nose speaks to its rye content, while the body begins lightly sweet, grows a bit herbal on the mid-palate, and finishes with a roar of spiciness. Best served chilled, but could also be favourably combined with equal parts soda.

EPITAPH GIN (40%)

Not at all shy of juniper on the nose, this pale blue gin adds some piney herbs to its aroma, and offers a rich, slightly piney, citrus-and-spice body that finishes with resinous herbal notes. Lovely with tonic or in classic gin cocktails.

SASKATOON LIQUEUR (27%)

Deep purple in colour, this has a mildly sweet nose with a mix of dried berry aromas, while the body is round and sweet-but-not-too-sweet, with a combination of berry-skin tartness and fruit juice. Finishes off dry and appetizing.

Shady Lane Estate Winery & West of the 5th Distillery

58029 Range Rd 44, Barrhead, AB, T7N 1N4
(780) 283-1809
westofthe5th.com

As far as we know, West of the 5th is the only distillery in Canada with alpacas. Not that the South American ruminants are an important feature of the facility or anything, it's just that there's a lot going on at the Zdrodowski farm in Barrhead, Alberta. In addition to a distillery and the aforementioned alpacas, the Zdrodowski estate also has a fruit

ESPRESSO SHINE (30%)

This coffee liqueur is more diplomatic than its name suggests, since it tastes more like a mochaccino with a shot of vanilla than a doppio. Refreshingly light on sugar, this would do well in a Brown Cow or an after-dinner Mexican coffee.

SASKATOON SHINE (30%)

With its bright and compelling orange/red colour and intriguing aroma, the saskatoon berry moonshine could easily pass for an Italian aperitivo. And although it's a little fruitier on the palate and far less bitter, it should probably be served that way—with a splash of soda and a twist of lemon.

SPICED SHINE (45%)

If candy cinnamon hearts came in liquid form, this is pretty much exactly what they would taste like. Good spice and the exact right amount of sugar, this is one of the better cinnamon spirits out there.

winery, a U-pick, a working farm, and a destination event space.

The distillery, which, like so many other start-ups in Alberta, makes sugarshine spirits, is the most recent addition to the multi-faceted enterprise, and it's been so successful that the family is considering spending less time on the fruit wines and more on the spirits, especially since three of its products won medals at the 2019 Canadian Artisan Spirit Competition.

"Me and my brother Caleb actually wanted to start up a distillery since we were in high school," says Nathan Zdrodowski. "But the old licensing made it hard to have both a winery and a distillery in the same place, so we couldn't. When the system changed, though, we applied pretty much that very day and started producing spirits as soon as we could—in February 2018."

Since then, they have added a café, tasting room, and cocktail bar, where the family offers signature cocktail creations (recipes for "Inappropriate Auntie Deb" and "The Spiced Grinch" can be found online) made from their beet sugar moonshine, which comes in espresso, cinnamon, and saskatoon berry flavours.

Wild Life Distillery

160–105 Bow Meadows Crescent
Canmore, AB, T1W 2W8
(403) 678-2800
wildlifedistillery.ca

While many Albertan craft spirits producers look to the export market to make ends meet in this tough business, Matthew Widmer and Keith Robinson have taken the exact opposite approach and applied a hyper-local focus to their distillery. Aside from using as much local raw material as possible, including foraged botanicals, they bootstrapped their own business, did all their own recipe development in-house, and worked hard to win the hearts and minds of local residents and businesses.

"The Bow Valley makes up 56 percent of our business and, well, the population is twenty thousand," says Widmer, who grew up in nearby Banff, where his dad runs a restaurant. "Calgary and Edmonton are massive markets that are right behind that, but because we're from here and con-nected here we just keep our focus on winning the home court advantage."

Robinson is a Canmore native who, after working in the energy sector, decided to join forces with his surfing and travel buddy to try distilling pro-fessionally in 2017. Other than hospi-tality and tourism, Widmer says, there weren't many career options in the region, so this was a way to work with that industry, but still have a chance to be entrepreneurial and creative.

Wild Life started with a gin and a vodka, but unlike distilleries aiming to get a lot of different experimental releases on the market right away, the pair are going their own way with a slow, steady buildup that includes a barrel-aged gin and a tonic syrup. They've also laid down three different types of whisky—single malt, rye, and wheat—destined for single grain expressions. No promises on when these spirits will be ready, since they're likely to hold off until they're happy with the results.

VODKA (40%)

Grain-based and very floral/fruity in its aroma, this has a sweetness that suggests a character almost more eau-de-vie than vodka, albeit with a thinner body and a fairly fast finish. A solid spirit for fruit-based cocktails.

GIN (43.3%)

This London Dry–style gin is anything but reserved, with full juniper berry and pine notes on the nose and an oily, almost viscous body that offers bold flavours of peppery coriander and woody spice. Perfect for a cold and dry Martini.

ALBERTA BOTANICAL GIN (42.5%)

Delicate and highly perfumy in its aroma, this boasts floral notes on both the nose and palate, with a spring grassiness in the flavour and an herbal finish. A soft and subtle spirit that should only be enjoyed neat.

British Columbia & THE YUKON

There is something about British Columbia that seems to inspire alcohol-related entrepreneurship. Craft brewing got its start in the province, the first brewpub on the continent was opened there, and while these days they're sprouting like weeds everywhere apples are grown, cideries have been a fact of life in BC for decades. And of course, we needn't even mention the province's remarkable number of wineries!

So it's not altogether surprising that craft distilling caught hold in BC before almost anywhere else. And that was even before the laws changed in 2013 and everything went...well, a little crazy.

The establishment of the "BC Craft" designation in that year (see page 199) with all its associated tax breaks, made distilling in BC more potentially profitable than anywhere else in Canada, and led to the province becoming home to, at one point, a full one-third of the country's small-scale distilleries. And while the laws in other provinces are now beginning to catch up to BC's, a massive appetite for the "drink local" ethos guarantees that the growth of distilling culture in the province won't be slowing anytime soon.

Of course, it helps that BC is not only rich in all manner of fruits, but also home to Canada's only independent maltster of any significant size, Gambrinus Malting in Armstrong. These twin facts help ensure that distillers seeking to employ only local ingredients—and so qualify as "BC Craft"—have adequate supplies regardless of whether they elect to distill fruit or malted grains.

And this raises one other interesting point: Perhaps more so than in any other province, the BC distillers we spoke with consistently expressed a desire to, one day, make whisky the heart and soul of their business, even if they were already faring well with white spirits and/or fruit brandies. Assuming most of them follow through with this, it should make for a very interesting local whisky market in two or three years' time.

Ampersand Distilling Company

4077 Lanchaster Road, Duncan, BC, V9L 6G2
(250) 737-1880
ampersanddistilling.com

When Jeremy Schacht graduated with a degree in chemical engineering from UBC, he took a look around at the jobs on offer and, according to his father, Stephen, decided none were very appealing. So he went to his father with an idea of distilling with a Russian technology, as yet unproven, that would produce a spirit of extremely high purity.

Stephen Schacht, a retired entrepreneur and inventor, was intrigued. So the duo started work on designing a "packed still" that uses small, densely packed coils instead of plates to produce as pure a spirit as scientifically possible in nature. One year later, they realized they'd achieved their goal and transformed from metal workers into distillers.

Stephen credits their first product, a gin, to Jessica Schacht, Jeremy's wife, because of what he calls her "amazing palate." They took it to the local farmers' market, ran out of bottles quickly, then wound up leading a convoy of buyers back to the distillery where they shortly ran out of product again.

The Schacht family.

PER SE VODKA (40%)

Fans of the American Tito's Vodka are sure to enjoy this light, creamy, and sweetish spirit, highly approachable and lightly floral in nature and supremely mixable at the bar.

GIN (43.8%)

From a first impression of "London Dry," this gin opens up to a more aromatic, floral but still juniper-forward nose and a piney, forest-floor body that brightens in the second half with an almost wintergreen-ish finish. Chill, sip, repeat.

IMPERATIVE DRY VERMOUTH (18%)

Created with Island winemakers Rathjen Cellars, this extremely aromatic and bone dry light gold vermouth offers florals and woody spice on the nose and a complex citrusy, spicy body. Use in place of Lillet for a fascinating take on the Vesper.

NOCINO! (27.1%)

The nose of this deep brown liqueur is equal parts walnut, lemon zest, and brown spice, with roasty accents. On the palate it combines honey and allspice up front, sweet citrus in the middle, and bitter green walnut for an appetizing finish. A lovely local take on an Italian classic.

Since that 2014 opening, Ampersand has added a vodka and a dry vermouth to the lineup, although regulations dictate that the latter is marketed by a partner winery, Rathjen Cellars. At Christmas, a Nocino made from green walnuts is added to the lineup.

As early success led to great consumer interest, to the point that finding time to distill became difficult, tours and tastings are now available only by appointment.

Arbutus Distillery

1890 Boxwood Road, Nanaimo, BC, V9S 5Y2
(250) 714-0027
arbutusdistillery.com

Having graduated with a Master's degree in brewing and distilling from Heriot-Watt University in Edinburgh, Michael Pizzitelli says that he was somewhat reluctantly working in the craft brewing industry. Which is to say that he liked his job well enough but, of the two disciplines in which he was trained, he had a much greater interest in distillation. Problem was, there wasn't much distilling going on in Canada at the time.

Even so, around 2012 he started making plans for a distillery of his own, and the passage of the new legislation covering craft distilling in the province inspired him to put his plan into action. By the spring of 2014, he was ready to open.

Despite the difficulty in getting regular supplies of grain at the time, Pizzitelli decided to make his first product, Coven Vodka, entirely from malted barley. He followed that several months later with The Empire Gin and, several months after that, decided to indulge in one of his own interests and introduce Baba Yaga Genuine Absinthe, a spirit he freely admits he didn't expect to sell well, but which turned into a solid year-round offering.

Changes in the industry around him have made life easier for Arbutus, as well. A small Nanaimo-area maltster, Jeremy White Malting, now supplies a good deal of his malted barley, while other sources on the Island are able to keep him pretty much supplied with everything else.

THE EMPIRE GIN (40%)

The label bills this as "EPICALLY FLORAL" and it's not far from the truth. Citrusy hop notes blend with perfumy juniper and resinous herbs on the nose, while the body has a palate softness that belies its olfactory oomph. Mix with a very light tonic or use in a perfumy Gin Fizz.

CANADIAN SINGLE MALT WHISKY, BATCH #1 (43%)

Distilled in 2014, this still displays some youth, with a lightly boozy and oaky nose that otherwise offers vanilla and pear, and a soft, sweetish body that seems as much Irish as it does Canadian. A lovely warm-weather whisky.

BIRCH LIQUEUR (25%)

If you're not really familiar with the taste of birch syrup, this liqueur is a most pleasant surprise. Nutty on the aroma with something resembling fragrant walnut, the flavour is an appealing mix of maple, walnut, caramel, and woody spice. A lovely sipper.

BABA YAGA GENUINE ABSINTHE (60%)

Despite the iron teeth depicted on the label, this is, for absinthe, at least, fairly gentle, with a sweet fennel-anise nose and a flavour that is very pleasantly citrusy, along with its expected anise and wormwood notes. Serve with ice water or, for a twist, over ice, and drink slowly.

de Vine Wines & Spirits

6181B Old West Saanich Road, Victoria, BC
(250) 665-6983
devinevineyards.ca

Given its name, it should come as no surprise that de Vine was founded, and indeed still operates, as a winery. Those wines were originally fermented from off-site, purchased grapes, however, as the twenty-five or so acres that John and Catherine Windsor purchased in 2006 was fallow. Because it was part of Vancouver Island's Agricultural Land Reserve, the couple had a tax incentive to grow something, though, and the "something" they chose was grapes.

Even still, it was not until 2014 that the Windsor family, now including daughter Kirsten and son-in-law Kevin Titcomb, recognized that Vancouver Island wine would forever be the "ugly stepchild" of Okanagan wines, and turned its attention to spirits.

Distilling with ingredients at least 50 percent grown on their own land, required some inventiveness. So the rum-like Shine is made from honey rather than molasses, gins are grape-based, and the distillery's first-ever product, a vodka called Kiss, released seasonally, is distilled entirely from strawberries.

A pair of early whiskies, only one old enough to deserve the name, show great promise on the grain-based spirit front, making de Vine a definite one to watch in a crowded south Island spirits marketplace.

SILVER HONEY SHINE (42%)

An amber-hued "faux rum"—made the same way, but with honey in place of molasses—this offers a whiff of its origins on the nose but, on the palate, is more a rum-and-oaked-vodka hybrid with a medium body and dryly fruity countenance. Try it one-to-one with cola.

ANCIENT GRAINS (45%)

At just under 1 year yold, batch #3 of this unique five-grain spirit—a quartet of ancient grains plus barley—has a toasted cereal, caramel, and walnut nose and a flavour of dried and candied fruit, toasted nuts, and hints of charred wood. Complexity far beyond its age.

GLEN SAANICH SINGLE MALT (45%)

Bottled scant months before its third birthday, this almost-a-whisky offers an aroma of cooked fruit, toffee, and vanilla, and a palate that belies its youth with notes of caramelized pear, melon, cinnamon, and soft citrus. A stellar sipper!

GENEVER GIN (45%)

More so than barrel-aged gins, this provides the connection between whisky and gin with its full, round, grainy nose and gently malty-sweet, herbal, juniper-accented flavour. A lovely spirit that evokes well the Flemish origins of gin.

189

Fermentorium Distilling Co.

2010 Government Street, Victoria, BC, V8T 4P1
(250) 380-1912
fermentorium.ca

The Fermentorium, an offshoot of the long-standing Phillips Brewery, might be the only distillery in Canada that was forced into existence by the government.

As he tells the story, Matt Phillips, founder and head of his eponymous brewery, first obtained a distilling licence in 2007 with no real idea of what he was going to do with it. There were a couple of whisky runs in those days but, mostly, he just wanted to have the licence for future use. How far in the future, he wasn't sure.

Having made years of "nil" returns to the taxation branch, Phillips recalls that, in 2014, Customs and Excise threatened to pull his licence unless he started using it. Not wanting to lose the ability to create spirits, and having all the equipment and ingredients on hand, he decided to create a gin that spoke of the Island, saying that he wanted the aroma and flavour to be "like a walk in the forest." That spirit became Stump Coastal Forest Gin.

A novelty hop liqueur project came next and then, well, nothing. Phillips noted in the late fall of 2018 that the distillery had some whisky in barrels, many of which were older than the legally required three years, but also admitted that he had no schedule for when they'd be released.

"The luxury of having the distillery as part of the brewery is that we don't have to rush into anything," he says. By the time this book reaches your hands, dear reader, Phillips's whisky may have made it to market—or maybe not.

STUMP COASTAL FOREST GIN (42%)

The nose of this gin definitely speaks to the "coastal forest" aspect, with damp pine and forest-floor notes, while the body pulls back towards traditionally junipery gin, with an almost whisky-like warmth. The makings of a unique Martini.

HOP DROP ELIXIR (29%)

If you are sceptical of whether actual hops have been used, the greenish tint is the first reassurance and the grassy, herbal aroma the second. Then there's the body, lightly spicy and strongly herbaceous, yet surprisingly without bitterness. A unique product best served over ice.

SHAWN SOOLE, UNSUNG HERO OF THE BC CRAFT SPIRITS SCENE

If you've heard of Shawn Soole, it's probably in connection with his legendary commitment to the craft cocktail scene in Victoria. Under his leadership, Clive's Classic Lounge, a hotel bar in the downtown core, became one of Canada's first cocktail lounges to garner international acclaim.

Less well known, however, is the role Soole has played in the region's craft spirits industry. Not only has he championed and supported the industry at every turn, he's also consulted on several projects, including Stump Gin with Phillips's Fermentorium (see page 190), Sheringham's award-winning Aquavit (page 198) and Legend's Naramaro (page 247). The last is Soole's homage to Amer Picon, a French bitter that's a key ingredient in a few classic cocktails and hard to come by in Canada. More recent projects include a blackberry gin liqueur he worked on with Stillhead (page 200) and a solera brandy with de Vine (page 189) that we're looking forward to trying.

Why does Soole love the local craft spirits scene so much? Because it's still rife with possibility. "British Columbia is an open book ready to be written," he says. "I think so many distillers are open to trying new things is why it's dynamic. Sometimes I've been the one to pitch a project, sometimes people have come to me. But we've always ended up creating something that Canada has never seen. And I love that about distillers in this province."

Island Spirits Distillery

4605 Roburn Road, Hornby Island, BC, V0R 1Z0
(250) 335-0630
islandspirits.ca

Peter Kimmerly freely admits that he started making wine at the age of fourteen. Later, he says, when a neighbour was told by the authorities they were going to confiscate his still if it was there the next day, said still miraculously disappeared and reappeared next door and the future sea captain added distillation to his alcohol-producing repertoire.

Many years later, when Kimmerly was captain of the icebreaker *Terry Fox* in the western Arctic, a takeover of the company put him out of a job and landed him on Hornby Island, where he presided over the local ferry and built himself a hobby farm. Distilling soon followed.

Explaining that he has built "dozens of stills" in his time, Kimmerly had the thought of making his not-so-licit hobby professional and teamed up with an organic chemist friend, Naz Abdurahman. Key to the duo's fruit- and beet sugar–based spirits are what Kimmerly calls "extreme reflux rates," which means that only a very small amount of distillate is retained for every pass through the still.

Presently, Kimmerly sells his spirits only out his front door, through a couple of private liquor stores in BC, and in Alberta. So the best way to get his spirits—and the only way to try any of the over a dozen small batch releases the distillery makes—is to make your way to Hornby.

PHROG VODKA (40%)

There is not too much to the aroma of this spirit, soft graininess mostly, but there is plenty to notice, and like, in the dry, earthy, and very lightly spicy body that finishes with a glowing warmth and vague licorice rooty notes. Mix with soda for a drink with unexpected heft.

PHROG GIN (43.5%)

With fourteen botanicals included, it's no surprise that this is a hugely aromatic spirit, with floral and spice notes apparent, notably cumin and coriander. The body is thus surprising in its restraint, with lovely balance and depth. Chill and sip on its own.

GRABBA (40%)

With a faint golden hue and a nose that combines cooked fruit with hints of sandalwood, this is more reminiscent of a French marc than an Italian grappa, although not lesser for it. The body is soft, a bit woody, and slightly whisky-ish on the palate. An aperitif.

HOLUNDERBLUTEN LIQUEUR (25%)

A liqueur made with elderflower grown wild on Hornby Island, this has an unsurprisingly floral nose and impressive restraint on the palate, with hints of herbal spice on the former and a bit of lemon-lime on the latter. Serve after dinner over ice.

Merridale Cidery & Distillery

1230 Merridale Road, Cobble Hill, BC, V0R 1L0
(250) 743-4293
merridale.ca

If Rick Pipes is not the most patient man in Canadian distilling, he at least numbers among the top three or four.

A few years after Pipes and his wife, Janet Docherty, purchased the Merridale cidery in 1999, the pair went travelling through the southwest of England and north of France. During their tour, they encountered numerous spirits made from cider, notably Calvados, and thought that adding a distillery to their business might be an effective way to promote cider in their home province.

Problem was, recalls Pipes, the taxation structure of the time made selling spirits an unprofitable endeavour. So instead of releasing the spirits he was creating, he stuck them into barrels or stainless steel tanks and left them there. For years.

And so it was, that when the BC Craft designation was created in 2013, Merridale was the first to be so designated, having never used any fermentables other than BC fruit, most of it their own. Further, Pipes already had six-year-old brandies ready for bottling.

His patience has manifested itself in other ways, as well. Having decided that a couple of years of resting benefits even neutral spirits, Pipes developed a sort of "distillery solera" system in which he ages his white spirits in stainless for a couple of years before adding them to his blending tank, which he uses to make his vodka and gins.

When we spoke in early 2019, Pipes also revealed his plan to open a brewery and distillery in the Dockside Green area in downtown Victoria. Anticipated to be open sometime in the summer of 2020, the downtown distillery will be focused on distilling from grain, while the cidery will continue to work exclusively on distilling from fruit.

Merridale's Cobble Hill farm, featuring
a distillery, cidery, and an eatery.

COWICHAN VODKA (40%)

The fruit origins of this spirit are immediately evident in the perfumey, green apple–
accented nose and continue in a body that is as much an apple eau-de-vie as it is a
vodka, in a most mellow and accessible way. Delightful on its own, but feel free to mix.

COWICHAN GIN (47%)

Fruity like the vodka, yes, but with a great deal of interest added, like a piney,
floral (lavender?), and lemon-oil nose, a sweet body with grassy herbal and berry
notes, and a vaguely spicy finish. The centre of a solid fruit-based cocktail.

COWICHAN CIDER BRANDY (42%)

Light and fresh, this doesn't conform to the traditional notion of apple brandy,
with a fragrant apple nose and a light, bright, fresh body that speaks to apple,
spice, and warmth. Serve after dinner or mix with soda for a summer refresher.

COWICHAN PEAR BRANDY (40%)

Notably pear-ish in its aroma—full-on pear juice, skin, and flesh—this is a spirit that
unapologetically speaks to its source fruit, with a raw pear front, notes of peppery
spice in the middle, and a lingering dried-pear finish.
All that you could want, if you like pears.

Pacific Rim Distilling

317 Forbes Road #2, Ucluelet, BC, V0R 3A0
(250) 726-2075
facebook.com/pacificrimdistilling

Although he comes from a long line of distillers—his great-uncle Alfie ran booze to the United States during Prohibition—Luke Erridge was not considering a career in that field even as recently as a handful of years ago. Then, as a recent graduate in forestry engineering, a project he was working on near Ucluelet derailed because of toads.

"They found some toads in the area, so the whole project was put on hold because you can't cut trees where there are protected species," he recalls. The experience prompted him to reflect on his life and ask himself if he really wanted to work in a field where he could be laid off at any moment. He decided he did not.

It was a situation that might drive some people to drink, and indeed it did for Erridge, except that he was drinking in local bars to gauge the quality of the spirits being poured.

"I was tasting stuff and thinking, 'Hell, my grandfather and I make better booze than this,'" he says. So he flew his grandfather out from Ontario for six months and the duo built the distillery together. Pacific Rim opened its doors in the late winter of 2018.

Unusually, Erridge ferments his 100 percent BC barley malt spirits with a yeast he isolated from the nearby forest. He cultured up that single cell, but now treats it as a baker would a sourdough bread yeast, allowing it to develop and evolve on its own. That yeast, plus the sour mash technique he employs, enables his spirits to truly have the flavour of the Ucluelet area, he says.

Although still a very small operation—he doesn't schedule tours, he notes with a chuckle, because you can see pretty much the entire place when you walk inside—Erridge thinks constantly about how he can improve his gin and vodka and grow his business. "I don't say that I'm the best," he says, "but my goal is to be the best."

Spirits not available for tasting.

194 Kitchen Road,
Salt Spring Island,
BC, V8K 2B3
(250) 221-0728
saltspringshine.com

Salt Spring Shine Craft Distillery

After years of running Simply Bleu, one of Georgetown, Ontario's most cherished special-occasion restaurants, Cordon Bleu–trained chefs and couple Michael and Rie Papp moved west to enjoy a slightly less hectic pace on the Gulf Islands of BC.

At first, neither had any thoughts of making spirits, but a change in legislation in 2013 made the prospect of opening a distillery a lot more appealing to the Papps—as well as to a number of others who started up their stills shortly thereafter. They opened Salt Spring Shine Craft Distillery in 2016 and their first product, a vodka made from honey, was launched a year later. Since Michael liked the end result, he stuck with the base for all his spirits, a line that now includes a gin and various moonshines.

One of the biggest challenges for Papp—and anyone making honey-based spirits—is the fermentation time. It takes Papp eight weeks to ferment the honey into mead, and he can't see a way to cut this down as he believes a long fermentation is key to keeping "nasty" smells and flavours out of the mead. He sources all-BC honey for his spirits and has considered trying to make his own but, given that his first attempt saw him lose two of six hives, he thinks it's a bit of a long shot.

"I'm really an amateur beekeeper and I really don't know what I'm doing," says Papp, "but I do find it quite challenging, especially since, on Salt Spring, our problem is there just aren't enough flowers. It's just a hobby right now."

HIVE VODKA (40%)

A solid vodka with a classic flavour profile, this is clean and clear, with a good balance of fruit and spice. Meant for straight sipping in vodka Martinis, this easy-drinking spirit is arguably ever-so-slightly dangerous.

STING GIN (40%)

This mellow gin is sweet, straightforward, and incredibly light on the juniper, making it perfect for the merely gin-curious. A delicate tingly sensation takes over in the finish, making it suitable for use in classic cocktails, including the Bee's Knees.

HONEYCOMB MOONSHINE (65%)

At full-strength, this spirit will put hair on your chest. A touch of dilution and you've got a nice little after-dinner sipper with plenty of sweet heat and a touch of salinity. Probably at its best with a little soda water and citrus.

APPLE PIE MOONSHINE (30%)

No question, this spirit has captured the flavour of rich caramelized apples, with a touch of vanilla, baking spice, and sugar administered by someone with a slightly heavy hand.

Shelter Point Distillery

4650 Regent Road, Campbell River, BC, V9H 1E3
(778) 420-2200
shelterpoint.ca

Patrick Evans.

According to the distillery and farm manager at Shelter Point, Jacob Wiebe, the idea to create the distillery came about for one reason: his now-father-in-law, distillery founder, and third-generation farmer, Patrick Evans, was simply tired of working with cattle.

That was in 2006, says Wiebe, and in 2007, Evans set off with a long-time coworker and friend to tour Scotland's distilleries, placing a strong emphasis on those with farm aspects. "He wanted to make Scottish-style single malt, but he also wanted the farm distillery look and feel," Wiebe says.

Work on building the distillery began in 2008 and took two and a half years to complete, mainly because all the work was done in-house, right down to the milling of the wood used to renovate the barns on the farm. Being a carpenter by trade served Wiebe well at the time.

Spirits went into barrels in July of 2011, but it was a full five years before it was decided that the first whisky was mature enough for release.

In the meantime, a commercial raspberry farm kept the distillery afloat—although, because raspberry plants have roughly a ten-year lifespan, that element came to an end in 2019. The distillery remains concentrated on single malt, but other varieties of whisky—all made from the farm's own barley (supplemented by BC barley malt from Gambrinus in Armstrong) on the distillery's 5,000- and 4,000-litre pot stills. Even a gin and a vodka created via a new 1,000-litre column still have been added to the mix.

BARREL OF SUNSHINE (30%)

Rather intensely orangey on the nose—think Terry's Chocolate Orange, plus fruitcake—this is an appealing liqueur that is neither Grand Marnier nor Cointreau, but rather a distinct take on the orange-chocolate-spice genre.

ARTISANAL SINGLE MALT WHISKY (46%)

With a nose that reflects the very heart of the grain, this has a softly grainy and sweet aroma and a body that speaks to mellow tropical fruit, brown spice, and tobacco, with an appetizingly spicy finish. Delicious on its own or with a splash of soda.

MONTFORT DISTRICT LOT 141 (46%)

Made from barley grown entirely on the distillery farm, this whisky has a caramel/orange nose with a whisper of spice, and a flavour that is light, orangey, spicy, and lingering. For fans of Lowland malt whiskies.

DOUBLE BARRELLED SINGLE MALT WHISKY (50%)

On its own, this has a salted caramel nose and a slightly hot, dried fruit character, all of which is tempered to a lovely fruity-spicy character with just a splash of water. Sip diluted in the afternoon, straight in the evening.

Sheringham Distillery

252–6731 W Coast Road, Sooke, BC, V9Z 0S9
(778) 528-1313
sheringhamdistillery.com

Many are the challenges entrepreneurial distillers must face in Canada, from outdated tax structures to the massive marketing budgets boasted by the international brands they must compete with for shelf space. To all that, Jason and Alayne MacIssac can add another from their early days in the business: bears, who got into their pile of spent grain before local farmers could pick it up for their livestock.Such is the lot of a distillery built on a remote homestead in Shirley, British Columbia.

For years a fine dining chef, Jason MacIssac had long nursed a passion for wines and spirits, and, seeing the market developing for local spirits, spent two years researching and developing his business plan. For the brains of the operation, he brought in his wife, Alayne, possessor of considerable business savvy.

The first three years of the business from June of 2015 were, by Alayne's own account, very small scale. The couple distilled on their property, battling bears while introducing first a vodka and a white whisky, then a gin imbued with what they describe as "the smell of the sea and forest," followed by a pair of flavoured vodkas and an aquavit.

Sheringham moved to downtown Sooke in the summer of 2018 and added a new Japanese-influenced gin to the lineup. Slated for release in 2019 were a whisky made from Red Fife wheat and a very small amount of bourbon-style whisky.

RED FIFE WHISKY (45%)

Tasted a few months prior to its official release, this has a spicy toffee nose with background notes of appealing earthiness. On the palate, it has a fruity caramel front and more nutty, grainy mid-palate, finishing with a flourish of spice. A pre-dinner dram.

AKVAVIT (42%)

While boldly proclaiming its Scandinavian roots with a strong caraway and fennel seed aroma supported by hints of anise, on the palate the spice is attractively soft and balanced, finishing dry and appetizing. A Nordic aperitif, West Coast Canadian style.

SEASIDE GIN (43%)

First thing off the nose is foresty pine and spruce, followed by notes of dried seaweed. On the palate, it's surprisingly on the sweet side with soft juniper notes and barely discernable seaweed flavours in the finish. A toothsome and interesting Martini gin.

KAZUKI GIN (43%)

This light and fruity gin reduces the juniper to near-irrelevance, with fragrant berry and citrus notes on the nose and a round, fruity body with just a hint of peppery spice and a citrusy finish. Sip straight and not too cold.

BC CRAFT

It will not have escaped readers' notice that British Columbia is home to a disproportionate number of small-scale distilleries. There is a reason for this.

In many BC distillery profiles, the year 2013 features prominently—that being the year that the provincial government changed the laws governing distilling, thus enabling the opening of a slew of distilleries. That's how significant the changes were.

The main change was to establish two distinct classes of distillery: Commercial and Craft. While the former can be of any size and are allowed to make their alcohol in pretty much any way they see fit, the "Craft" designation is reserved for distilleries that produce a maximum of 100,000 litres of spirit per year—just over 11,000 cases of 750 ml bottles—and employ all-BC ingredients, save for small amounts of flavourings, such as citrus peel, that do not grow in the province. All fermentation and distillation must occur on site for a BC Craft distillery, so no NGS may be employed, and the packaged, ready-to-drink cocktails known as RTDs are verboten.

While the "Craft" designation might seem restrictive, adherence brings with it significant potential for profitability. Most importantly, it allows the distilleries to keep a much larger chunk of their sales, effectively pocketing the markup that would typically go to the province's Liquor Distribution Branch. This plus tax changes have given small-scale distillers in BC a viability that is unheard of anywhere else in Canada. Small wonder that the number of distilleries in British Columbia nearly tripled in the two years following the legislative changes.

Victoria Harbour with a view of the
BC Parliament buildings. (iStock)

Stillhead Distillery

105–5301 Chaster Road, Duncan, BC, V9L 0G4
(250) 748-6874
stillhead.ca

When Brennan Colebank talks about his distillery in the Cowichan Valley, less than an hour north of Victoria, he is adamant about its purpose: to make "great whisky."

VODKA (40%)

At the risk of sounding overly poetic, the nose of this spirit is reminiscent of a walk on the seashore, with a bit of wheat field as well, while the full and positively toothsome body is spicy and faintly citrusy with, perhaps, a touch of brine. Unusual and outstanding.

LONDON DRY GIN (43%)

Not juniper-forward on the nose, but decidedly London Dry style with its fresh and inviting, faintly citrusy aroma. On the palate, it follows suit with a dry, gently juniper, and slightly spicy and tannic flavour. The makings of a stellar Martini.

CHERRY KIRSCH (40%)

Notes of cherry pit, stem, and leaf appear on the nose of this attractive spirit, all mild in their influence, while the body is a textbook expression of kirsch, with a mix of fruit and spirit that performs admirably as aperitif and digestif.

WILD RASPBERRY GIN (36%)

While many fruited gins taste like fruit with a bit of gin character, this bright red spirit is decidedly gin-ish on the nose and in the body, with moderately spicy fruit throughout, and a dry, not-at-all liqueur-ish finish. Sip on ice before or after dinner.

"Whisky is always the focus," he says, adding that a secondary purpose is to showcase the distilling arts, which is why the distillery is designed in an open concept plan with the tasting room effectively a part of the distillery. His third goal is to create spirits that reflect the produce of the area.

Of course, for a distillery that only opened its doors in October of 2017, following a year or so of planning, having properly matured whisky to sell was still a far-off goal when we spoke in early 2019. As a result, Colebank notes that he is also enjoying "dabbling" in fruit brandies and creating other assorted spirits, including a London Dry style of gin that he says fills a gap in the Vancouver Island market. "I wanted to make something that might get people to replace the major label gin that's on their shelf," he explains.

Raised in Prince George, relocated to the Valley after university, and formerly in the technology sector, Colebank says he was happy to work hard to support his wife as she was setting up her denture pratice. Now that Erica Colebank's Beautiful Smiles Denture Clinic is a huge success, he says that she is pleased to be able to support the distillery in return.

Victoria Caledonian Distillery

761 Enterprise Crescent, Victoria, BC, V8Z 6P7
(778) 401-0410
victoriacaledonian.com

Few people in the Canadian distilling world can boast a pedigree equal to that of Graeme Macaloney. As a lad growing up in central Scotland, he got himself a job on the bottling line for Black & White Whisky and found his calling in the distillation arts, leading him to enroll at Glasgow's University of Strathclyde to study fermentation and distilling.

His fascination with research served him a bit too well, however; he graduated with a master's degree in biotech engineering and was, as he says, "overqualified for work in the brewing and distilling trades." Thus, he wound up working in pharmacology, first at Pfizer, then Eli Lilly, where he worked on a 30,000-hectolitre fermentation plant in the antibiotics division.

Eventually, work and a passion for "the great outdoors" lured him to Canada's West Coast, where he finally found his opportunity to get into brewing and distilling. The route he took to achieve his dream, however, was a rather unconventional one: instead of seeking investment from banks or finance companies, he spent two years criss-crossing the country speaking to groups of whisky aficionados, eventually signing up 325 individual investors.

Financing for the business closed in September of 2014 and the facility opened two years later. Not much interested in making vodka or gin, for the time being Macaloney has the distillery side of the operation focused solely on filling barrels, mostly re-charred red wine barriques, with new-make single malt. Meanwhile, the brewery side of the operation is going strong and improving quickly under the direction of former BrewDog brewer Nicole MacLean.

201

And brewing isn't the only area where Macaloney has invested in some impressive talent. Helping out with whisky production are Dr. Jim Swan, a bit of a legend known for his ability to squeeze maximum flavour out of a whisky in a minimum of time, and former Diageo Master Distiller Mike Nicolson, who has spent time in more than eighteen Scottish distilleries.

Easy access for tourists is another asset that the brewery and distillery boast. The building is prominently located on the highway leading from the ferry to downtown Victoria, which is why tours are run seven days a week in the summer and five days a week in the winter. In the coming years, we're sure those tours will grow even more interesting with the release of house-made whiskies to bolster the imported and vatted malt whiskies Victoria Caledonian currently offers.

Spirits still maturing at the time of writing.

Victoria Distillers

9891 Seaport Place, Sidney, BC, V8L 4X3
(250) 544-8217
victoriadistillers.com

Anyone with an interest in Canadian craft spirits will likely have heard of Victoria Gin, or "Vic Gin" as it's sometimes called. Born in 2008, a year after Valerie and Brian Murray obtained their licence and still, it quickly became one of the country's earliest and most acclaimed small-batch spirits, although the tax structure in British Columbia at the time made those early years a struggle, according to company president and head distiller since Day One, Peter Hunt.

Of course, as noted elsewhere, when the BC Craft designation came into effect in 2013, life as a distiller in British Columbia was made much more economically viable. Yet while other changes to the tax structure eased the burden for what was then Victoria Spirits, the decision was made not to go "craft," since the business would have had to be modified considerably in order to become compliant.

The next big change for one of Canada's earliest small-scale distilleries occurred in 2015 when, anxious for retirement, the Murrays sold to Grant Rogers, a businessman who also happened to own a building on the Seaport Place waterfront in Sidney. Construction of new digs for the distillery began immediately and, eight months later, in the spring of 2016,

VICTORIA GIN (42.5%)

A gin that sits somewhere between the traditional London Dry and New World botanical styles, this has a floral aroma that remains unmistakably juniper-ish, plus a body that begins fruity and perfumey and ends with a London Dry spiciness. A gin for all reasons.

EMPRESS GIN (42.5%)

Striking in its violet hue, this might be described as a more subdued version of the distillery's hallmark gin, with an even more floral nose and a soft, approachable palate that is equal parts floral, herbal, and fruity. Add tonic or citrus for Instagramability.

OAKEN GIN (42.5%)

The nose of this light gold spirit speaks to its oak barrel aging with its vanilla appeal, while the palate mixes that vanilla with notes of spice and juniper, finishing with a flourish of woody oak. A definite digestif gin.

CACAO CHOCOLATE LIQUEUR (25%)

Forget sugary and syrupy, this is pure chocolate indulgence in liqueur form, with Ecuadoran cocoa nibs and husks providing a pure chocolate nose and a body that is only faintly sweet and fully cocoa-ish. A stunning after-dinner sipper.

the renamed and relocated Victoria Distillers opened its doors.

The final—for now—major change at the distillery took place in 2017. Having had discussions about creating a signature gin for the iconic Empress Hotel in Victoria, it was decided to formulate something distinctly different and visually provocative—what we believe was the first gin in Canada made blue by the addition of butterfly pea powder. Launched, suitably enough, at the hotel, it was a near-instant hit and, as of the fall of 2018, accounted for over 90 percent of the distillery's production. The other 5 to 10 percent is composed of a variety of other spirits, including the namesake gin and other products only available at the distillery store.

Wayward Distillation House

2931 Moray Avenue, Courtenay, BC, V9N 7S7
(250) 871-0424
waywarddistillationhouse.com

When Dave Brimacombe and his wife, Andrea, decided to open a distillery a few years ago, he was aware of being relatively late to the party. Rather than play catch-up, he decided to try to so something completely different—as in, making all of Wayward's spirits with pure, unpasteurized, unfiltered BC honey.

"We're a scrappy little company so I was looking at non-traditional fermentables from the very beginning," explains Brimacombe. "I looked at milk protein, whey—since we have a large dairy producer just down the street—and raspberries and apples and grapes. I tried them all but the one that intrigued me the most was honey."

Since then, a few other distillers have joined Brimacombe in making honey spirits, but he was the first in Canada, a particularly bold move when you consider that honey is expensive

DRUNKEN HIVE RUM (42.5%)

This spirit's light, fruity, and floral aroma is plenty enticing, but can't possibly set you up for the rich, buttery, and complex flavour profile that follows. Highly suitable for lush cocktails or straight, after-dinner sipping.

WAYWARD ORDER ELIXIR 151 (75.5%)

As of this writing, it was no longer against the rules to call a honey spirit "vodka," but there's plenty of time for Wayward to change the labels and add the word "vodka," since that's what this white spirit really is—albeit over proof. It's rich, full-bodied, and has just the right amount of well-integrated funk, sweetness, and spicy notes.

BOURBON BARREL AGED CHAR #3 GIN (45%)

After six months in a charred bourbon barrel, Unruly Gin picks up a goodly amount of vanilla, also evident along with a hint of mint on the nose. A solid, warming finish leaves behind a pleasingly sweet burn.

CAESAR'S GHOST PEPPER VODKA (40%)

Made with ghost peppers, this is a seriously and pleasantly hot vodka, with little prickles of heat spreading out over the palate and into a long finish. To be used as a base spirit for a first-rate spicy Bloody Caesar.

and takes long to ferment, both factors that hike up the retail price of the spirits. When Wayward's first gin was released in late 2014, for instance, it retailed for about ten dollars more than other premium gins at the time. It was a big risk, but the company's "Unruly" spirits line quickly garnered critical acclaim and developed a loyal following.

That signature hint of floral sweetness has both challenges and rewards: Brimacombe's botanical mix for the gin took ages to concoct, since it had to work with the raw spirit's profile, but it's a natural for a rum. Encouraged by the Gold Medal with Distinction he picked up from the Canadian Artisan Spirit competition for his rum recently, he's planning on making a lot more of that.

☞ LOWER MAINLAND, FRASER VALLEY & WEST COAST

The 101 Brewhouse & Distillery

1009 Gibsons Way, Gibsons, BC, V0N 1V8
(778) 462-2011
the101.ca

With small-batch spirits, craft brewing, and elevated roadhouse fare all under one roof, there's something for everyone at The 101 Brewhouse—a distillery/brewpub that caters to the local community in Gibsons, as well as to Sunshine Coast day-trippers.

Opened in the summer of 2017, The 101 was just getting around to laying down its first whisky in May of 2019, largely because running all three parts of the business had been a challenging exercise, especially since it started with a very small still that was running overtime to make its gin and vodka. In 2019 the facility finally acquired a "a great big beautiful gleaming German still" with a 750-litre pot capacity and two columns with ten plates each. Head distiller David Longman quickly put it to work to make a white dog (see page 29) from wheat, rye, and malted barley, which is going into bourbon barrels to mature.

Operations manager Matt Cavers says they're obviously looking forward to the end result, but it's only one piece of the puzzle they're constantly working on to make sure the 101 Brewhouse grows into more and more of a community hub—through events and, of course, just day-to-day interactions.

"It's a cliché from the craft drinks world that the thing that makes them fantastic is the possibility of knowing the people who make what's in your glass and knowing exactly where that drink comes from," says Cavers. "So we put a lot of value on socializing and drinking. And it's nice to feel like we're going to places that we have some ownership over and familiarity with."

Spirits not available for tasting.

Anderson Distilleries

106–3011 Underhill Avenue, Burnaby, BC, V5A 3C2
(604) 961-0326
andersondistilleries.ca

While some distillers are drawn to their craft by a passion for spirits and others by circumstance, Ian Anderson just figured that opening a distillery made sound economic sense.

"I was graduating with a degree in physics and I decided that distilling could be a lucrative way to use my skills," he says. Of course, it didn't hurt that, around that same time, the BC government changed the laws to make small-scale distilling a more viable vocation.

By the end of 2015, Anderson Distilleries was licenced, although it took the better part of a year before he was "selling in earnest," Anderson says. Noting that distilling aligns quite nicely with physics ("It's all energy flow and mechanics"), Anderson says that he both designed and built all of his own equipment, along the way developing a few proprietary tweaks that are uniquely his, including a device with a polymer membrane that he says helps to smooth and soften his spirits in much the same way oak aging does.

Anderson's equipment isn't the only thing about his distillery that's unusual. Also quite out-of-the-ordinary is his Montague line of high-strength, unsweetened flavoured alcohols that he markets almost exclusively to bartenders. These spirits, which range from 60 to 75 percent alcohol, present the essence of their flavouring in concentrated form, which he says allows skilled mixologists to exert greater control in their drink preparations.

In addition to the five brands in the Montague line, Anderson markets seven liqueurs made, as much as possible, with all-natural ingredients like fresh mint leaves and lemon zest, and a trio of gins including a smoked Rosemary Gin and a London Dry that he sells only by special request.

Spirits not available for tasting.

Bruinwood Estate Distillery

2040 Porter Road, Roberts Creek, BC, V0N 2W5
(604) 886-1371
bruinwood.com

Given that it's located on the Sunshine Coast, it might come as a surprise to learn that Bruinwood is a distillery born in BC wine country. More to he point, it was conceived during the ilming of a television series entitled *C Wine Cellar*.

Self-described "young filmmakers unning around the Okanagan and hooting on a shoestring budget," Jeff arringer and wife Danise Lofstrom vere enjoying a meal with winemaker lex Nichol when the Nichol Vineyard wner began to wax poetic about the rt and science of distillation. The otion took hold in the minds of oth filmmakers.

Many years later, when the couple rew tired of working for others, arringer and Lofstrom decided to ake their dream a reality. Beginning 1 2014, a year of planning followed y two more for zoning and one for uilding brought them to the distil- ery's official opening day in June of 018.

GIN (40%)

A distinctly different sort of gin, this has a complex aroma that features baking spice, fennel, and, of course, juniper. On the palate, it's a spice box of allspice, nutmeg, licorice, and pepper—all judiciously balanced to a delicious whole. A refined spirit to sip chilled in your finest stemware.

NUCINO (40%)

If you're expecting a sweet walnut liqueur, this is something entirely different. Roasted walnuts and coffee on the nose, and dry coffee, nutty, clovey flavours in the body make this a spirit for mixing into an innovative cocktail or sipping as a digestif.

VANILLA VODKA (40%)

"Vodka and vanilla" is a pretty good way to describe this spirit, although the artificial-tasting and cloying impression that phrase might evoke does no service to the elegance of this very pale yellow vodka. The dry, aromatic, and lingering vanilla finish is, alone, worth the price of admission.

ADVOCAAT (17%)

Although popular in the Benelux countries, this custardy drink has failed to catch on elsewhere, which, in our view, is a tremendous pity. Creamy, rich, and only gently boozy, this sweet delight is as good as any European version. Serve instead of dessert.

Bruinwood's idyllic rural distillery.

Having made alcohol in one way or another all his adult life, and with a strong background in cooking, Barringer became the distiller, teaching himself as he progressed. "To me, distilling was not something I needed to learn," he says. "It's really just cooking."

Wheat, malted barley, and a bit of honey come together in the distillery's Aquasen Vodka, which, in turn, serves as the base for Bruinwood Gin, featuring an impressive fifteen botanicals. A pair of flavoured vodkas round out the distillery's white spirits portfolio, while its most unusual product is an Advocaat, possibly the only one made in Canada.

Crow's Nest Distillery

117–667 Sumas Way, Abbotsford, BC, V2S 7P4
(778) 251-6002
crowsnestdistillery.com

Even though the Crowsnest Highway (for which this Abbotsford distillery is named) ends about an hour's drive east of the Crow's Nest Distillery, co-owners Daniel Paolone and Ian Jarvis felt the road's historical significance outweighed any slight geographical dislocation. And that's because Crowsnest, an east–west highway that connects Alberta and British Columbia and runs roughly parallel to the Canada–US border, was an important bootlegging route during Prohibition days.

Almost everybody in the spirits industry takes an interest in the history of Prohibition, but Paolone's is especially keen, since one of his ancestors, Stefano Paolone, an Italian immigrant during the early twentieth century, was involved in the illegal liquor trade that saw spirits transported from British Columbia along Crowsnest, then down into the United States via Whisky Gap, Alberta.

Reviving the family tradition—legally this time!—has been Paolone's passion since he started building Crow's Nest Distillery with friend and business partner Ian Jarvis in 2016. Presently, its core products are vodka and rum (white and spiced), made from ingredients sourced within one hundred kilometres of the distillery.

Aside from all of this, one of the most unusual features of this distillery is its packaging, which has some of its products sold in fully reusable, stainless steel bottles and flasks. This is in keeping with its commitment to move towards a fully sustainable, zero waste facility with as small a carbon footprint as humanly possible.

Spirits not available for tasting.

VANCOUVER'S GIN CRAWL

Like gin? Then Vancouver might just become your favourite city!

We know of no other city in Canada, and possibly North America, where it is possible to sample so many different gins at the source as in Vancouver. In fact, while we were researching distilleries in British Columbia's largest city, it occurred to us that a distillery "gin crawl" might be a lot of fun.

We'd begin on Granville Island with the **Liberty Distillery**'s Endeavour Origins Gin, perhaps mixed with tonic, since our crawl is just beginning. From there, we would take the Aquabus across False Creek Inlet and walk up to the **Long Table Distillery** for a Martini made with their stellar London Dry Gin.

Resisting the lure of Long Table's other gins, we would continue our walk to **Yaletown Distilling** for a sample of their BC Gin before venturing onward to the **Red Racer Taproom**—not technically the

distillery, of course, but a **Central City Brewers & Distillers**–owned outlet—for a straight-up sip of the unusual and enchanting Queensborough Omakase Japanese Style Gin.

A taxi would be required for our next stop, **Resurrection Spirits** in the East Village, perhaps for a White Lady made with their exceptionally floral Gin. A short, four-minute walk from there would land us at our final stop and a soothing sip of the purple and fruity Salal Gin at **Odd Society Spirits**.

Mind, you, if the sprit still moved us, we wouldn't be averse to making Odd Society the penultimate stop and continuing onward via cab across the Vancouver Harbour to the **Woods Spirit Company** for a taste of their Cascadian Gin, maybe mixed with their Pacific Northwest Amaro and a guest vermouth for an end-of-the-night Negroni.

Martini mixing with Endeavour Gin at Liberty Distillery.

Central City Brewers & Distillers

11411 Bridgeview Drive, Surrey, BC, V3R 2N1
(604)-588-2337
centralcitybrewing.com

Few are the beer drinkers in BC, and increasingly across Canada, who are unfamiliar with Central City Brewers, or at least the Red Racer brand that identifies their most popular lagers and ales. Born as a downtown Surrey brewpub and helmed by Gary Lohin, a brewer of impeccable credentials, it didn't take long before ales like Red Racer Pale Ale and IPA were the talk of the BC beer scene.

Expansion seemed inevitable, and indeed expansion arrived in 2011, in a very big way. Keeping the brewpub operational, Central City opened a not-so-central production facility four kilometres away and added a distillery to the mix. For Lohin, the addition of the distillery was a no-brainer.

"For about $150,000 we could get two stills (they now operate three), whereas we were spending millions on the brewery," he recalls, "To get another revenue stream for that price just made sense."

The new facility, which Lohin describes as "brewery porn," opened in July 2013, with Heriot-Watt grad Stuart McKinnon heading the distillery side. Whiskies were the focus right from the start and have been critically well-received since their entry to the market. But the distillery's gins—made principally from NGS because Lohin found their malt-based spirit didn't provide the cleanness they wanted in their London Dry–style gin—are not to be overlooked, either.

QUEENSBOROUGH DRY GIN (43%)

There is an undeniably foresty aspect to the nose of this gin, but in a way that's soft and appealing, and the flavour follows suit with a front-palate sweetness sliding to a more juniper middle and a dry, appetizing finish. Classic and original at the same time.

QUEENSBOROUGH OMAKASE JAPANESE STYLE GIN (43%)

Yuzu and cherry blossom shine through in the aroma here, with the palate reflecting the softness and fragrance of the other Japanese botanicals. A subtly complex gin for solo sipping.

LOHIN MCKINNON SINGLE MALT WHISKY (43%)

A soft whisky with a softer nose, this light golden spirit offers fruity honey notes in its aroma and a bright, fairly round body, as buttery as it is oaky. Lovely in its youth, this has even greater promise with the passage of time.

LOHIN MCKINNON WINE BARREL FINISHED SINGLE MALT WHISKY (43%)

Extra aging in BC wine barrels adds layers of fruitiness to this already fruity malt, with oaky plum notes in the aroma and a deeper, fuller mouthfeel and flavour. A definite after-dinner dram.

Dragon Mist Distillery

213–19138 26th Avenue, Surrey, BC, V3Z 3V7
(604) 803-2226
dragonmistdistillery.com

When Sherry Jiang emigrated from China to Canada in 2004, she quickly recognized two things: (1) Her Chinese medical degree was not going to serve her especially well in her adopted country; and (2) If she wanted to be able to drink a good baijiu, the national spirit of China, she was going to have to make it herself.

Fortunately, distilling was in her family tree, with grandparents who formerly ran a distillery in China, and her medical background gave her an appreciation of the science of fermentation and distilling. So after many years of research, in 2012 she opened Dragon Mist with her baijiu and a vodka as her initial products.

Although Jiang has since expanded her distillery's lineup to include several different liqueurs, the star of the show, and the most unusual product, remains the baijiu. Without delving too far into the technical side of its production, baijiu is unique in the spirits world thanks to its unusual semi-solid fermentation, instigated by a combination of yeast, bacteria, and other organisms known as *qu*, and steam-driven distillation. Although still rare in the western world, it is the world's most consumed spirit.

Jiang says that her most popular products vary with the seasons. During the winter, and especially around Chinese New Year, the baijiu is by far the bestseller, she says, but in the summer months the fruit liqueurs take over.

VODKA (40%)

Made entirely from BC wheat, this vodka has a slight hint of stone fruitiness on the nose and a bit of an earthy character that grows as it heads towards the finish. An esoteric vodka that won't satisfy everyone, but will please some a whole lot.

BAIJIU (56%)

If you are unfamiliar with baijiu, which has an admittedly poor reputation in the west, this is a great place to start. Perfumey sesame and light soya on the nose introduces a soft palate with light lychee and more forceful herbal notes, finishing with a flourish of pepper and warmth. Outstanding.

LIMONCELLO LIQUEUR (30%)

The nose of this bright yellow spirit has a full-on lemon intensity—peel, pith, flesh, and juice. The flavour is gently sweet and offers pure lemon juice up front with more of a zest and pith character in the finish. Serve chilled before or after dinner.

COFFEE LIQUEUR (22%)

Pitch black, this has a freshly ground and heavily roasted coffee bean aroma with a sweet palate of espresso and an undercurrent of burnt raisins. Serve over or beside vanilla ice cream, or use for a White Russian or boozy iced coffee.

Deep Cove Brewers & Distillers

Unit 170, 2270 Dollarton Highway
North Vancouver, BC, V7H 1A8
(604) 770-1136
deepcovecraft.com

MEDITERRANEAN GIN (42%)

The distinctive rosemary note in the aroma of this gin speaks to its Mediterranean-ness, while its round and lightly fruity flavour references the olives also used. A unique interpretation best enjoyed straight with a platter of mezzes.

VODKA (40%)

Medium-bodied with a lightly sweet, faintly grainy nose, this begins on a fairly neutral note before growing slightly melony on the mid-palate and a bit grainier on the finish. All in all, a versatile vodka for mixing with everything from tomato juice to tonic.

AKVAVIT BARREL-AGED (42%)

A year in charred oak gives this a golden hue and a spicy, slightly soapy nose with hints of vanilla. On the palate, it speaks first of caraway, then of vanilla, and finally some oak, with a blast of caraway returning in the finish. Perhaps better before the barrel.

RED FIFE WHISKEY (42%)

Tasted prior to its official release, this mix of organic Red Fife wheat, rye, and malted barley offers a youthful mix of vanilla, oak, charred woody notes, and caramel, with a red wine barrel finish adding a bit of red fruitiness. Still young, but showing promise.

Pretty much every craft brewery or distillery likes to note how connected they are to the surrounding community, but when someone from Deep Cove makes the claim, it somehow resonates a bit more than it does with most.

For starters, the very name of the brewery and distillery is taken from the name of the scenic neighbourhood adjacent to the tasting room. Then there's the active charity sponsorship the business embraces, plus the fact that, save for the head distiller, Lucas Westhaver, all the staff hail from North Vancouver.

Founded in 2013 as a combined brewery and distillery, the road to its present state has been quite evolutionary, with its full-service lounge added only recently. Their persistence has paid off, though, with the operation now a North Vancouver drinks destination and the brewery and distillery so busy that tours are now available only by special request or through brewery tour services such as Vancouver Brewery Tours and Vine & Hops.

Gillespie's Fine Spirits

8–38918 Progress Way, Squamish, BC, V8B 0K7
(604) 390-1122
gillespiesfinespirits.com

John McLellan was well into his distillery planning when he fortuitously met Kelly Ann Woods, an experienced mixologist. Given their mutual fascination with distillation and the blending of the fruits thereof, the two hit it off and it's no surprise they ended up opening Gillespie's—although admittedly not where they had originally planned.

"A bunch of roadblocks prevented us from opening in Vancouver," recalls Woods, "but as a result, we got into Squamish just as the community was really developing."

The distillery, named after Cam Gillespie, a friend of McLellan's who died tragically in a motorcycle accident, opened its doors in September 2014 with a vodka crafted from BC wheat. Other spirits followed, including a rye-based vodka, a limoncello made from hand-rasped organic lemons, a New World–style gin, plus a line of shrubs—sipping vinegars suitable for mixing—called Boozewitch.

"I'm a descendant of witches," says Woods. "So it's in my nature to ferment. That's the source of the Boozewitch name."

In addition to the distillery, the couple operates the Squamish Gspot, an almost-hidden cocktail bar that began as an extension of their tasting room, but developed into a lounge furnished largely with repurposed furniture and through donations from grateful customers. Hit the bar on the right night, during her self-described "rock star hours," mainly Saturdays, and you may even find Woods herself behind the bar.

SIN GIN (43%)

Juniper is not meant to be the message of this gin, and it isn't. Instead, notes of elderflower lend a fruitiness, accented by plummy notes, while soft pine and spruce gently assume the mantle in the mid-palate and finish. Perfect for a Ramos Gin Fizz or a light G&T.

RASPBERRY GIN (28%)

A somewhat unusual spirit, this marries the botanical base of the distillery's gin with the bright freshness of local raspberries and a touch of sugar to produce a fruity, herbal, not-too-strong sipper ideally suited to ice cubes and summertime.

LEMONCELLO (28%)

Those who shy away from the cloying sweetness of some limoncellos have nothing to fear here. A fresh-off-the-tree lemon peel nose foretells the softly sweet body with notes of fresh lemon zest and spicy alcohol. Serve over ice or mix with soda for a boozy lemonade.

Goodridge&Williams Craft Distillers

8–7167 Vantage Way, Delta, BC, V4G 1K7
(604) 946-1713
gwdistilling.com

oodridge&Williams is, in some ways, the odd man out in BC distilling. While certainly still much smaller than the national distillers, it is seen in some circles as a "big player" in the spirits game, with almost national distribution, sales volumes that put them well outside the limits for "BC Craft" designation, and, perhaps most damning of all, a strong presence in the ready-to-drink, or RTD, market.

But despite those attributes, and more than a few unfounded suspicions, G&W crafts all of its spirits on-site at its admittedly industrial-ish distillery in Delta, with no shortcuts or NGS used, and employs all-BC ingredients, just like any smaller BC Craft–certified contender. And as for those RTDs, well, some of them are actually pretty good!

G&W was founded in 2013 by Stephen Goodridge, a product development expert who, for years, worked with the Mark Anthony Group. In 2014, Goodridge sold the company to Paul Meehan, a brewing industry veteran and, in 2015, returned to corporate product development, leaving Meehan fully in charge of the operation. It is to the latter's credit that in the four short years since, G&W has grown to be a significant presence in not just the BC spirits market, but across Canada and beyond.

SID THE HANDCRAFTED VODKA (40%)

A wheat-based, pot-distilled spirit, the aroma is sweet and soft, almost floral, with only subtle alcoholic heat. The creamy mouthfeel remains on the sweet side with a borderline caramelly smoothness that signals a vodka for sipping straight.

TEMPO RENOVO DRY GIN (40%)

Made from BC wheat, this gin reflects its West Coast origins with a juniper and pine-needle nose, supported admirably by floral notes and a soft, New World character low on London Dry and high on foresty, almost minty roundness.

WESTERN GRAINS CANADIAN WHISKY (40%)

Maturation in ex-bourbon barrels affords this spirit a gentle character with toffee and cooked peach on the nose and vanilla and caramel on the palate, accented by a light charred wood note. Mix one-to-one with ginger ale or enjoy neat before a meal.

NORTHERN GRAINS CANADIAN WHISKY (40.2%)

The wheat and barley come from BC's north, and a finish in Okanagan wine barrels, after three years in bourbon barrels, gives this a fruity richness that is evident on the nose and in the rounded, orange marmalade–ish body. Sip neat or mix in a Manhattan.

Long Table Distillery

1451 Hornby Street, Vancouver, BC, V6Z 1W8
(Moving to 1428 Granville Street in late 2019 or early 2020)
(604) 266-0177
longtabledistillery.com

The Joyce, one of Long Table's most popular cocktails, featuring their London Dry Gin.

escribing himself as a "West Coast ginsmith," Long Table co-founder and head distiller Charles Tremewen is quick to take issue with the "BC Craft" rules as they apply to the creation of gin.

"We [Tremewen and wife, Rita] want to make a damn fine gin and create damn fine diversity within the spirits segment," he says. "We are happy to not be Craft because we would find that far too limiting."

Tremewen attributes his passion for gin to his British background, but says he had no thoughts about distilling professionally until he and Rita made a trip to the craft distilling hub of Portland, Oregon, in 2010. Inspired by what he witnessed there, he enrolled in and graduated from the Artisan Distilling Program at Michigan State University and the couple opened Long Table as Vancouver's first craft distillery in 2013.

At Long Table, they are open and unrepentant about using NGS since, as Tremewen rightly points out, a large number of distillers in England, the birthplace of gin, do exactly the same thing. "For us, gin is a recipe," he says, adding that the NGS he purchases is simply the base for that recipe and, because of the technology involved in its creation, likely a more pure and honest base than he could produce himself.

His gins, which number among the best we tasted during the creation of this book, would seem to bear that out.

BARREL AGED GIN (44%)

While many barrel-aged gins come across as whisky wannabes, this is an oaked gin of a different sort, with aroma botanicals balanced by hints of caramel and vanilla and a flavour that is slightly sweet, but leaves no question as to its gin-ness. Cocktails away!

LONDON DRY GIN (44%)

The nose of this classically styled gin offers a gentle juniper, almost minty in its herbal appeal. On the palate, that same juniper mixes brilliantly with fresh citrus on the mid-palate and black peppery spice in the finish. A solid Martini or G&T gin.

CUCUMBER GIN (44%)

From the aroma of this gin, you might not expect the cucumber to follow with its spicy-floral character but, in the body, the cucumber comes through impressively, with supporting notes of pepper and juniper. Chill, strain, enjoy.

LÅNGBORD AKVAVIT (42%)

The caraway on the nose of this bright spirit is fragrant and slightly floral, while the body is more rounded with spice, rose notes, a hint of orange, and a long and warming caraway finish. Sip neat on a winter afternoon.

THE CANADIAN ARTISAN SPIRIT COMPETITION

Encouraged by the success of the BC Distilled Festival, founder Alex Hamer has gone on to establish two even more ambitious projects—an annual, cross-country craft spirits contest, the Canadian Artisan Spirit Competition (CASC), and Artisan Distillers Canada (ADC), a national association focused on building awareness of the country's artisan distilleries and promoting best practices.

For the 2019 competition, over seventy distilleries from across the country participated in the CASC, which is operated and overseen by the ADC. Each distiller selects their best spirits and sends them off to Hamer, who painstakingly re-packages every entry into tiny, numbered, and label-free bottles,

before sending them out to a panel of judges across the country. (Full disclosure: Christine served as a CASC judge in 2018 and 2019.)

Over the ensuing six-week period, judges taste, rank, and critique each individual sample, periodically sending scores and comments back to Hamer, who keeps an eye on things to make sure there are no anomalies. The CASC medals come out every January and, at the same time, Hamer sends the judges' comments back to all the distillers, although with no mention of the judges' names. Distillers enter in the hopes of winning a gold medal, of course, but many also consider the tasting notes to be valuable feedback—to the point that some have even tweaked recipes as a result.

The Liberty Distillery

1494 Old Bridge Street, Vancouver, BC, V6H 3S6
(604) 558-1998
thelibertydistillery.com

Lisa Simpson, proprietor and director of operations.

Vancouver residents and visitors alike are well familiar with the artisan culture that has thrived on the city's Granville Island for many a year. Sometimes described as an "urban oasis," the once industrial site beneath the Granville Street Bridge has long served as home to craftspeople, retailers of local goods and produce, restaurants, a famous brewery, and, since November 29, 2013, The Liberty Distillery.

Not that the distillery's creation came easily. It took founders Robert and Lisa Simpson four years of planning, approvals, meeting with government officials, and, finally, construction to make the central Island operation a reality, and another year after that to obtain the cocktail bar licence that now sees people lining up to secure a spot at the bar at busy times like Saturday afternoons.

(So confused were officials regarding the licensing of a distillery and bar that, for the first few months of its existence, Liberty's tasting room was only allowed to sell shot glasses—which came with a complimentary shot of vodka, of course!)

The result of all this work is a true destination, with gorgeous reclaimed wood used for the chairs and barstools, a two-part bar that dates from the turn of the twentieth century, and

a church pulpit for the cash register. Plus, of course, a baker's dozen of products produced on the 140- and 220-litre copper pot stills, which also provide a backdrop to the cocktail bar.

TRUST CANADIAN RYE (43%)

With a nose that speaks equally to mature barrel notes, the spiciness of rye grain, and vanilla-ish caramel, this three-year-aged spirit is sprightly and vibrant on the palate, with ample spice and a dry and warming finish. The makings of a stellar Manhattan.

TRUTH VODKA (42%)

A creamy vodka with a lightly spicy-floral nose and a soft, almost pillowy body that begins with a note of candied sweetness and finishes with a soothing and lightly spicy warmth. Room temperature for sipping or chilled with seafood.

ENDEAVOUR ORIGINS GIN (45%)

Herbs and spices dominate and define the aroma of this seasonal release, with a combination of fruit and forest showing in the palate. A pleasantly spicy finish completes the picture of this highly mixable spirit.

ENDEAVOR OLD TOM GIN (45%)

Amber hued, this has an allspice-accented aroma with less sweetness than you might expect. On the palate, however, that works to its benefit in concert with an apple-y sweetness and spicy dried apple finish. For old-school cocktails.

Lucid Spirits Distilling Co.

105B–8257 92nd Street, Delta, BC, V4G 0A4
(604) 349-3316
lucidspirits.ca

Lucid Spirits owner Kashmir Birk says, growing up on a farm "there was always a still somewhere, or at least a Mason jar of something magical that you just *had* to try." With this sort of background it's hardly surprising that, after changing jobs every few years, the self-described "jack of all trades" (and, judging by his success, master of most) finally decided to open his own distillery business.

It was in the spring of 2015 that Birk finally made the decision to go ahead with Lucid, although he says the idea had been percolating for some time. The clarity of purpose he felt, the *lucidity*, he says, was partly the inspiration for the name.

The following two years were spent licensing, organizing, and building the business, with Birk doing the architecture and construction himself, even writing up his own real estate contract. The doors finally opened in September of 2017, with the first product being a vodka made from BC winter wheat.

Birk's interest in whisky brought about the second spirit, an unaged but oak-rested wheat spirit, followed by a similar spirit made from 50 percent rye and 50 percent wheat, a gin, and what is perhaps Lucid's most unusual product, a new-make wheat whisky "watered down" to bottling strength with freshly pressed apple juice. "Everything I do is done with intent," explains Birk, "and the intent there is to let the apples shine."

NORTHERN GIN (42%)

Promoted as an "uncomplicated gin," this lives up to its billing, with gentle juniper on the nose and a softly herbal-citrus-pepper body. For people just discovering the joys of gin, this is a superb entry point.

OAKED GIN (40%)

We suspect that it was a well-charred barrel in which this relatively mild-mannered gin was rested, resulting in a sweet and vanilla-ish spirit that, again, will appeal more to non-gin drinkers than it will to gin aficionados.

APPLE SPIRIT (40%)

Sweet red apple in the aroma, this has a soft but notable caramel apple character in the body, undeniably on the apple brandy side but heading towards apple whisky or apple pie moonshine. Sip after a heavy meal to aid in digestion.

BC RYE (40%)

The nose of this youthful spirit is quite fragrant with lightly citrusy grain, while the body might be a bit too expressive of vanilla, but counters that with a dry and spicy finish. A hopeful portent of whiskies to come.

Mad Laboratory Distilling

119–618 E. Kent Avenue South
Vancouver, BC, V5X 4V6
madlabdistilling.com

In planning

The founder of almost every small distillery will tell you they never would have gotten the doors open without a lot of support from fellow distillers, the community, and family members. Over at Mad Laboratory, though, a small distillery housed in an industrial space in south Vancouver, Scott Thompson makes no bones about telling you that it was far more than just a little help from his friends that made it possible for him to fulfill his fifteen-year dream.

"We basically started with nothing as far as the budget goes," says Thompson, who established the distillery in 2015 after years of working in the bar and restaurant industry. "So all the equipment was scrounged, donated, or salvaged and fixed up with the help of good friends, including one who happens to be a welder. We're not much better off than that now, but we've slowly started adding things and I'm trying to increase productivity and efficiency."

He's also recently finally started his aging program, which sees malted barley spirit—all of which comes off the wood-fired pot still—barrelled off into casks that were used to make bourbon at the OOLA Distillery in Seattle. It will probably be ready for sampling at the tail end of 2021, which may be testing Thompson's patience a little. He's a self-proclaimed "whisky guy" and his love for that spirit was one of the chief reasons he opened Mad Lab in the first place.

While he waits for both his whisky and clearance from the city to open a tasting room, the latter of which is expected at some point in the near future, Thompson is working on a Turkish raki and a blueberry kombucha cordial in addition to his flagship vodka, gin, and white dog—all of which are made from hand-milled malted barley.

MAD DOG SINGLE MALT (45%)

Although it arrives with the damp grain aroma you'd expect from a malted barley distillate, the complex flavours are fruitier than most and it seems to finish with a light note of tea and earthiness. With potential for the future, right now it's probably more of a mixer than a sipper.

VODKA (40%)

A surprisingly sweet vodka, with flavours in the confectionary family, this vodka is great for people who want a local option suitable for straight sipping. Serve on the rocks.

223

Northwest Distilling

104–20120 Stewart Crescent
Maple Ridge, BC, V2X 0T4
(604) 818-6972
northwestdistillingco.ca

In
planning

F ittingly enough, the partnership behind Northwest Distilling was born at a liquor store.

Both Kyle Gurniak and Kameron Price had backgrounds in hospitality when they met while working in liquor retailing and, finding that they had similar entrepreneurial ambitions, almost immediately began plotting their way out. The first plan, not surprisingly, was to open a bar—but not just any bar. The prospective partners wanted to feature unusual spirits, and so began searching for unique creations.

The first one they discovered, a black vodka from the UK called Blavod, turned out to be unavailable in BC but, in doing their research, the pair found out that it wasn't too difficult to set themselves up as importers. So out the window went the bar idea and their focus turned to bringing brands like Blavod, Ukrainian vodka Nemiroff, and the American Black Roberts Spiced Rum into Canada.

That, recalls Gurniak, was when the Canadian dollar was at its strongest point in years and the currency exchange made the importing game profitable. When the dollar dropped back down to its traditional level, however, the partners started thinking about other careers, and the idea of making their own spirits came immediately to mind.

"We did it sort of backwards," says Gurniak. "We got our location first, signed the lease, and then started getting together all the rest of the business." That was in the middle of 2015; a year later, they were open for business.

For two and a half years, the Polish still they installed in their distillery has been working flat out making a single spirit, the ten times distilled Northwest Vodka. At the start of 2019, however, they bought a second, more efficient still and were looking to expand into a gin and maybe a premium vodka before the end of the year. For now, their priority is to get their tasting room and cocktail bar open and begin offering tours, all of which was expected to have happened by the end of summer 2019. Still, visitors are advised to call ahead just to be certain.

Spirits not available for tasting.

Odd Society

1725 Powell Street, Vancouver, BC, V5L 1H6
(604) 559-6745
oddsocietyspirits.com

Bartender Mia Glanz at the Odd Society cocktail bar. (Photo by R. D. Cane.)

While all spirits get their start as water, Odd Society may be the only distillery in Canada that owes its origins at least in part to water. We should explain.

Growing up the son of Eastern European immigrants in Edmonton, Gordon Glanz first developed an interest in distilling when, fearing that something was wrong with the local tap water, his mother insisted the family distill every drop consumed. This triggered fascination in both Glanz and his brother and it wasn't long before the pair were homebrewing beer and indulging in a little subversive distillation.

Later travels in Germany cemented the young Glanz's fascination and led him to pursue a master's in brewing and distilling from the Heriot-Watt University in Edinburgh. Returning to Canada and settling in Vancouver, he began planning for the opening of his own distillery.

Although provincial laws governing craft distilling were in flux in the early 2010s, Glanz decided to go ahead with his project in the hope the changes would be beneficial, even building a large tasting room that he might eventually be allowed to convert into a cocktail bar.

The distillery opened in 2013 and quickly became a local favourite. Among the many projects undertaken is a peated whisky currently aging, for which peated malt was used like a botanical rather than as an ingredient.

MIA AMATA AMARO (30%)

A modern amaro that bursts forth from the glass in a flurry of spice, orange peel, and sandalwood notes, it continues into a complex and boldly spicy body that culminates in cocoa nib and orange brandy notes. A robust digestif.

PROSPECTOR CANADIAN RYE WHISKY (46%)

Distilled entirely from rye, this shows its pedigree well on the nose, with notes of clove, allspice, and fennel seed, but is surprisingly light and fresh in the body, with most of its spiciness saved for the long and languorous finish. A sipping whisky.

CANADIAN SINGLE MALT CASK WHISKY, BATCH #3 (40%)

One of the distillery's occasional releases, this spirit aged in small (30-litre) barrels sports plenty of wood notes along with cinnamon and vanilla spiciness. A youthful whisky that demonstrates potential for the future.

SALAL GIN (30%)

A seasonal release made with salal berries in the style of a sloe gin, this deep purple and earthily fruity gin has a warming and fruity front with a spicier, more junipery mid-palate. The fruit surprisingly makes a return appearance in the finish, making this a lovely digestif.

THE
HOTEL GEORGIA
AND OTHER
CANADIAN COCKTAILS

If you visit either of the two fabulous bars at Vancouver's Rosewood Hotel Georgia (Prohibition and Hawksworth, both highly recommended), you might spot a frothy little cocktail called the Hotel Georgia. Invented, circa 1951, at this very hotel (where else?), it's one of Canada's oldest classic cocktails. We list it here, along with a few of the country's other most notable drinks—national treasures that can all be made with Canadian craft spirits.

HOTEL GEORGIA (CIRCA 1951)

2 oz. gin
½ oz. orgeat
½ oz. lemon juice
6 drops orange flower water
1 egg white

Shake well without ice, then add ice and shake again. Strain into chilled coupe.

THE HABITANT (CIRCA 1951)

We can't say for certain when this drink was invented, but like the Hotel Georgia, its first recorded reference is in Ted Saucier's 1951 cocktail book, *Bottoms Up*. According to Saucier, it was created by Larry Denis, head bartender at the Seigniory Club of The Log Chateau, or as it's now known, the Fairmont Le Château Montebello.

2 ½ oz. Canadian whisky
1 oz. fresh lemon juice
1 oz. maple syrup
Dash bitters

Shake over ice and strain into a chilled coupe.

Note: Modern craft cocktail drinkers with a preference for drier cocktails might do well to cut a half ounce off each of the three main ingredients.

TORONTO COCKTAIL (CIRCA 1922)

Since Ontario was deep into prohibition when this cocktail was invented, it was probably concocted elsewhere—most likely in London, England, where barman/cocktail chronicler Robert Vermeire first wrote about it in 1922. Although not on a lot of menus in its namesake city, most good bartenders know how to make it.

2 oz. Canadian whisky
¼ oz. Fernet-Branca
¼ oz. simple syrup

Stir all ingredients together in an ice-filled mixing glass. Strain into a chilled glass and garnish with an orange twist.

OLD PAL (CIRCA 1930)

First mentioned in 1930's *The Savoy Cocktail Book*, the Old Pal probably wasn't born in Canada, either. It's included here, though, because of the way Canada's bartenders have enthusiastically adopted it on the grounds that it's one of the most approachable classics to specifically call for Canadian rye whisky. Much like a Boulevardier, it's a Negroni variant that sees gin swapped out for whisky and dry vermouth .

1 oz. Canadian rye whisky
1 oz. Campari
1 oz. dry vermouth

Stir all ingredients together in an ice-filled mixing glass. Strain into a chilled glass or, if you prefer, serve on the rocks.

MONTRÉAL COCKTAIL (2017)

This modern classic was created by fifteen A-list Montréal bartenders in 2017 to commemorate the city's 375th birthday, a collaborative effort that's proof you *can* rule by committee.

1 oz. London Dry gin
1 oz. Canadian rye whisky
1 oz. aperitivo (like Campari)
1 oz. Gentian liqueur (like Suze)
Grapefruit twist, for garnish

Stir all ingredients (except the twist) together in an ice-filled mixing glass. Strain into a chilled coupe and garnish with grapefruit twist.

One Foot Crow Craft Distillery

1050 Venture Way, Gibsons, BC, V0N 1V7
(604) 220-0550
onefootcrow.com

It would be perhaps a bit harsh to say that Bob Botteri and his wife, LaVonne Girard, stumbled into the distilling business, but neither would it be entirely inaccurate. Both were employed in the film industry, and when not travelling, they made their home on a property in the Okanagan Valley that also just happened to be home to some grape vines. A *lot* of grape vines.

MINERAL INFUSED VODKA (50%)

Yes, it's a black vodka, and whether it's fact or a trick of perception (we strongly suspect the former) this has a full and rich aroma and flavour, a distinct minerality, and viscous body. A Vodka Soda like no other, but more fun served chilled and neat.

GUNPOWDER GIN (50%)

Mineral-infused, like the vodka, but here the richness somewhat obscures the aromatics lurking beneath, releasing only hints of peppery juniper and herbs, while the body seems like an aromatized version of the vodka. Chill well and serve on its own.

LAVONNE'S LAVENDER GIN (40%)

Dare we call this the "white sheep" in the line? Crystal clear and hugely perfumey with—what else?—lavender, this is a soft and fragrant gin that is much more approachable than the aroma suggests. Use in an Aviation or any other floral gin cocktail.

Wanting to make use of their agricultural bounty, they tried making wine one year and jelly the next, but neither worked out. In year three, Bottieri tried his hand at grappa and found the results were, in his words, "not bad."

Musing over drinks one evening, the couple began to wonder what it would take to become professional distillers and, after a bit of investigation, discovered that it was fairly easy. So, as Bottieri tells it, one day they were working in film and the next they found themselves distillers.

After taking a distilling course, plus a little trial-and-error education, they wound up on a five-acre farm on the Sunshine Coast. Unfortunately, Agricultural Land Reserve rules meant that they would need to grow at least 50 percent of their ingredients on the farm if they wanted their distillery there. They couldn't do that, so an alternate premises was found in nearby Gibsons.

The couple still grow some of their botanicals on the farm, but the more significant aspect of their vodka and gin is the colour—pitch black. This comes from the "mineral infused" aspect of the spirits, said minerals being humic and fulvic acids.

Pemberton Distillery

1954 Venture Place, Pemberton, BC, V0N 2L0
(604) 894-0222
pembertondistillery.ca

Although the "Pemberton potato" may not be a household name outside of agricultural circles, it's pretty famous among food historians who have championed its quality for generations. These potatoes owe their world-class flavour largely to "Spud Valley's" rich soil, which is why master distiller Tyler Schramm thought it important to try to capture the region's unique *terroir* with organic, additive-free potato spirits.

With that in mind, Schramm set off for Edinburgh to get his masters in brewing and distilling at Heriot-Watt, following a degree in environmental sciences. Upon his return, he and brothers Jake and Jonathan built their distillery in 2008 and were in production with one 1,000-litre and one 500-litre German-made copper pot still.

"There are several challenges with potatoes," explains Schramm. "One is the fact that your typical potato is about 90 percent water and 10 percent starch, whereas your typical grain kernel is the opposite. So, with potatoes, you just have much more raw material

SCHRAMM ORGANIC GIN (44.8%)

This potato-based gin is strongly herbal and seems to draw much aromatic muscle from its most unconventional ingredient, hops. The flavour is dry, herbal-grassy, and medium-bodied, making it a solid mixing gin.

KARTOFFELSCHNAPS (34%)

The honey and herbs used to accent this schnaps are immediately apparent on the nose, with a softly field honey–accented aroma. The body is definitely sweet, though not cloying, and speaks to honey, grassy herbs, and a modicum of potato-y earthiness.

SCHRAMM ORGANIC POTATO VODKA (40%)

The earthiness of the aroma borders on pungent but, in fact, merely highlights the character of the potatoes used, which also yield a full and toothsome body with mineral and truffle notes accented by a hint of overripe pear. A definite sipper.

APPLE BRANDY (42%)

The aroma of this apple spirit speaks to the orchard—earthy and fruity—while the flavour is a rustic mix of fresh and dried apple with some phenolic notes and a very dry finish. Save this for after dinner.

The beautiful *terroir* of Pemberton, BC. (iStock)

going into it."

Worse, potatoes don't store well, so Schramm can only make his spirits during and shortly after potato season, which starts in August. Having developed a taste for single malts in Scotland, however, when the potatoes run out in mid-May he turns his attention to grain spirits and, over the years, has played around with making Canadian single malts in almost every regional Scottish style. His first 10 year old will be released in early 2020 and, like everything else at this family-run distillery, it's certified organic and BC Craft.

Resurrection Spirits

1672 Franklin Street, Vancouver, BC, V5L 1P4
(604) 253-0059
resurrectionspirits.ca

It's safe to say that Brian Grant had no idea what he was getting himself into when, as a bartender-partner in a bar in Vancouver's Gastown neighbourhood, he became interested in making his own cocktail bitters.

As drinks aficionados will know, the first step in making bitters is obtaining a high-proof spirit to use as the solution for the flavouring herbs and spices. But rather than purchase NGS, Grant decided he wanted to make his own base spirit so he bought himself a small still. The first realization that followed that purchase, he says, was that he didn't know what he was doing.

And that might have been the end of the story, but for Grant's meeting and befriending a French master distiller who taught him the basics of distillation. Intrigued, Grant next travelled to Spokane, Washington's Dry Fly Distilling Consultation Program and Distilling School to learn more, then returned to Vancouver to open Resurrection.

The idea of his distillery, says Grant, is to explore the flavours found in rye. As such, following his November 2017 opening in East Vancouver, Grant launched two products: a white rye (a.k.a.

new-make whisky) and a gin. (Since our visit in late 2018, Resurrection has added a rosé gin to its lineup.) Unsurprisingly, Grant is also laying down rye spirit in barrels with the initial release of his whisky expected to occur on December 5, 2020.

Inside the Ressurection Spirits cocktail bar.

WHITE RYE (45%)

Although distilled to 90 percent alcohol, there remains enough of the characteristic rye grain spiciness on the nose of this spirit to keep it interesting, with a pillowy palate hinting at cotton candy up front and black pepper in back. A characterful alternative to vodka for cocktails.

GIN (45%)

Lemon and juniper are both evident in the aroma of this New World–style gin, but the real star of the show is the floral notes contributed by rose. Even so, the body is less floral than it is juniper, with plenty of lemon zest in the finish. The makings of a unique G&T or floral White Lady.

Roots and Wings Distillery

7897 240 Street, Langley City, BC, V1M 3P9
(604) 371-2268
rootsandwingsdistillery.ca

When we asked Rebekah Crowley if she had ever envisioned herself as a distiller, the answer came quickly: "No, not at all!" Having said that, Crowley quickly added that, while her vocation might have been unplanned, she wouldn't have it any other way.

A Canadian working in the tech sector, Crowley was temporarily based in North Carolina when she travelled back to BC to visit with a friend and, in so doing, met Rob Rindt. The two hit it off and, after Crowley's work brought her back to Victoria, Rindt enticed her to downsize to consulting work and come live with him on his family's Western Turf Farm in Langley.

An interest in spirits soon had the couple wondering if they might try distilling on their own, which led Crowley to take the distilling course offered at Urban Distilleries in Kelowna (see page 257). Licensing and equipment followed, and by February of 2017 the distillery was open.

As a true farm distillery, Roots and Wings uses the farm's own potatoes and mostly their own corn, with the rye used in Crowley's maturing whisky coming from area farms. A new-in-2019 lounge licence allowed the couple to add a cocktail bar to the mix, and a 150-person capacity event venue will become a focus going forward.

(Photo by Kathy Mak)

VITAL VODKA (40%)

The potato (and corn) base of this vodka is immediately apparent in its earthy aroma, reminiscent of washing and peeling potatoes. The body follows suit with a more gentle earthiness and a dash of sweetness in the finish. Meant for mixing.

REBEL (40%)

A corn whisky released too young to go by that name, this nonetheless shows a considerable amount of woodiness in both its aroma and flavour, and leaves one hoping that further maturation will round out the edges. In the meantime, mix with ginger ale.

SIDEKICK (40%)

A cinnamon- and honey-accented spirit for fans of Fireball who aren't fond of that spirit's sweetness and spice, this shows both of its flavourings well on the nose. In the body, the cinnamon becomes more dominant, with a soft sweetness that complements it well.

RENEGADE (40%)

This horseradish vodka announces itself with its namesake aroma and a hint of singed wood. The body continues the theme with a modest and earthy, really umami-ish horseradish flavour and a dry finish. Ideal for a Caesar made, obviously, without horseradish.

Sons of Vancouver Distillery

1431 Crown Street, North Vancouver, BC, V7J 1G4
(778) 340-5388
sonsofvancouver.ca

ons of Vancouver bills itself as a "really, really small batch" distillery—and they're not kidding around. Founded in 2016 by friends James Lester and Richard Kraus, the North Vancouver operation is really not that much more than a hole-in-the-wall with parking spaces to match. Yet what gets done there almost defies its size.

In addition to operating the distillery and what must be one of the city's smallest cocktail bars (a mere twelve-person capacity), several times a year, Sons offers a five-day Distillery School that helps train other would-be small batch distillers. It might not be the sleekest of training centres but, judging from the number of distillers we've spoken with who reference Sons, it apparently gets the job done.

Back to the partners: their goal at Sons is to eventually become a whisky distillery but, of course, that takes time. While they continue to distill 100 percent rye spirit for barrel maturation, the two pursue their interim business plan, which is to have one base spirit (their vodka), something sweet (the amaretto), and "something else" (the chili-flavoured vodka). All are based on a 50–50 mix of BC–grown barley and wheat.

Inside the "really, really small batch" distillery.

The trainer/distillers were, themselves, trained at 2bar Spirits in Washington state and they remain on friendly terms with the Seattle operation. (In fact, the samples they used to promote themselves prior to opening were all distilled at 2bar.) And despite the relative smallness of their business, and the somewhat shambolic appearance of the cocktail bar and tasting room, the background both partners have in process control and automation seems to serve them quite well in their current vocations— all of which bodes well for whiskies to come.

Sons of Vancouver's casual-cool tasting room.

VODKA VODKA VODKA (40%)

The pre-distillation fermentation with a Champagne yeast seems to favour this spirit with a soft sweetness on the nose and a sprightly character, lively and faintly fruity. A pleasing return of sweetness on the finish makes this a solo sipper.

NO. 82 AMARETTO (26%)

The sweet mix of fruity, almondy, and vanilla notes in this not overly sweet liqueur come from the apricot kernels, vanilla beans, and orange peels used. The end result is an amaretto that is delightfully quite unlike mass-market versions. An even richer bourbon barrel–aged version is released every Christmas.

CHILI VODKA (40%)

This fiery vodka, made hot by bird's eye chilies, which also contribute some of its orange colour, is not for the timid. (For stability, some colouring is now added.) This is all about the spice and so sits well in a Bloody Caesar or, a bit surprisingly, with pineapple juice.

Stealth Distilleries

3–20 Orwell Street
North Vancouver, BC, V7J 2G1
stealthvodka.com

Trying to locate the Stealth distillery, particularly after sunset, may lead you to conclude that the business is extremely well-named. Those who persist and eventually find the entrance, at the rear of an industrial building in the southeast end of North Vancouver, are rewarded with a thorough tour and a tasting of a pair of very impressive vodkas.

That shouldn't come as a surprise, considering that Stealth was conceived from the beginning as a vodka-only distillery.

WHEAT VODKA (40%)

By a significant margin the more neutral of the two vodkas, this offers faint notes of sweet grain on the nose and a slightly sweet start that segues quickly to a crisper body that stimulates the salivary glands with its dryness. Mixes with almost anything.

CORN VODKA (40%)

The sweeter and rounder of the pair, this has a nose that is vaguely evocative of candy floss, although nowhere near as sweet, and a creamy body that boasts a slight cornflakes character before an appealingly dry finish. Chill and serve straight.

The concept of Stealth took shape in 2006, when small business consultant John Pocekovic was, as he says, "drifting from contract to contract and in search of something new." A friend suggested developing a spirits cooler, an idea that eventually morphed into creating the Stealth Vodka brand and having it distilled under contract in Chicago and imported to the Canadian market.

It was an arrangement that served Pocekovic well for six years, except for one fact: it wasn't making any money. So, heading back to the drawing board, he began raising capital from friends and family and eventually leased his current premises and bought his equipment in 2016. Along the way, he met his now-distiller Randy Poulin, who was dating Pocekovic's daughter at the time, and the two men took turns training at Moonshine University in Kentucky.

As an ex-banker, Pocekovic knew before he opened who his customers were going to be and how much vodka he would need to sell. He says he's on track in that regard, which could mean that Stealth Vodka won't be quite so stealthy in the very near future.

The Woods Spirit Co.

1450 Rupert Street, North Vancouver, BC, V7J 1E9
(604) 787-1735
thewoodsspiritco.com

One of Fabio Martini's childhood memories was descending to the family home's basement in the fall, blackening out the windows with garbage bags to ensure privacy, and distilling with his father the pomace left over from the latter's home winemaking. As such, he was perhaps predestined to someday wind up running his own legal distillery.

That distilling experience, plus his love of "making things," led him to first contract the use of the Sons of Vancouver Distillery in the middle of the night, then sign a seven-year lease on his own premises in 2016. All to make one product, an amaro.

Intending to create something that "was not *like* Campari, but could be used *in place of* Campari," Martini arrived at the idea of first macerating then vacuum distilling his botanicals, a seemingly complicated but actually quite simple process that allows the distillation to take place at about 30° C rather than conventionally much hotter temperatures. (The idea was suggested by Martini's business partner, who just happens to be a scientist.) This allows Martini to individually distill each delicate ingredient without needing to cook it, then blend all the botanicals together and marry the mix into the base spirit.

Other products have since been added to the raison d'être amaro including, logically, a gin. And with a lounge licence in hand as of early 2019, no doubt yet others will eventually populate the new cocktail bar.

PACIFIC NORTHWEST AMARO (28%)

A different sort of amaro, this offers a complex mix of aromas including orange peel, floral herbs, and a bit of earthy spice, with a body that trends from lightly sweet to bittersweet to a piney-herbal finish. Aperitif, digestif, Negroni—you choose!

BARREL-AGED AMARO (28%)

Two years of bourbon-barrel aging adds vanilla and a hint of oak to the nose and creates a thicker, richer palate-coating body that finishes in bitter vanilla. Reserve for after mealtime.

DRY CASCADIAN GIN (47%)

The vacuum distillation of Cascade hops ads a citrusy element to this juniper-forward dry gin, with a peppery-fruity-citrusy nose and a mix of juniper, grapefruit, and black pepper in the body. Bold enough to mix with tonic and sufficiently gentle to sip on its own.

LIMONCELLO ITALIAN LIQUEUR (30%)

With a distinct lemon meringue on the nose, though neither too sweet nor creamy, this is a traditional limoncello that is sweet without being confectionary and offers a light and peppery bite at the finish. Enjoy after dinner.

Yaletown Distilling Company

1132 Hamilton Street, Vancouver, BC, V6B 2S2
(604) 669-2266
yaletowndistillingco.com

Craft beer drinkers in the lower mainland area will be well familiar with Yaletown Distilling's sister operation, Yaletown Brewing. The savvier among them will even be aware of the parent company, the Mark James Group, but only the true veterans of the Vancouver beer scene will recall that both operations, as well as the other Mark James Group brewpubs and Red Truck Ale production brewery, grew out of a menswear shop back in the 1990s.

The store on Broadway in the Kitsilano neighbourhood is long gone, but its legacy lives on in plenty of beer, and at least one gin and one vodka.

The distillery operates alongside the Distillery Bar + Kitchen and also produces a more recently released single malt whisky plus several seasonal specialties that depend on what local ingredients they can get their hands on. All three core products, the gin, vodka, and whisky, are made from British Columbia barley malt and the gin features eight botanicals. All are the products of brewer-turned-distiller Tariq Kahn.

Spirits not available for tasting.

After Dark Distillery

1201 Shuswap Avenue, Sicamous, BC, V0E 2V0
(250) 836-5187
afterdarkdistillery.com

After Dark is a community-minded little distillery that, as often as not, is involved in hosting local concerts, charity barbecues, and big tasting events. Opened in 2017 by Dean and Louise Perry, the couple even polled their neighbours in Sicamous so that they might produce a gin in line with local taste preferences. The end result was citrusy, with more emphasis on haskap berries than juniper. In the Kootenays, it would appear, most people don't like the evergreen forest flavour profile that's popular elsewhere.

In addition, the family-run distillery makes a vodka from corn and malted barley that won silver at the 2019 Canadian Artisan Spirit Competition, over ten flavours of moonshine, and a young whisky they call "Loudmouth Soup." The fully aged, and hopefully slightly quieter, whisky is coming soon. While we wait, we can listen to the After Dark Distillery song by Seal Skull Hammer, a hillbilly band from nearby Salmon Arm. There's surely another distillery out there, somewhere, with its own theme song, but After Dark is the only one of which we're aware.

MONASHEE MOUNTAIN VODKA (40%)

If it weren't for subtle vegetal and herbaceous aromas and flavours, this spirit would conform well to the classic vodka profile. It has a gorgeous pepper finish, though, which, with its can't-put-my-finger-on-it, esoteric flavour, creates an intriguing vodka that will have you going back for seconds.

COPPER ISLAND GIN (40%)

This light-bodied, aromatic gin is gentle with the juniper pine, which is well-balanced against a light perfume. It tastes slightly sweet, with citrus and lemongrass brightening it up, making for a lovely G&T gin when combined with a low-sugar, natural tonic water.

Bohemian Spirits

215 Mark Street, Kimberley, BC, V1A 2B2
(250) 427-5430
bohemianspirits.com

When Wade Jarvis moved to the southern Okanagan Valley to pursue a career in forestry, becoming a full-time distiller was the last thing he expected. But when the financial crisis hit in 2008, he started first brewing beer, and then fermenting wine at home as ways to save money, graduating shortly thereafter to hobby distilling.

In the back of his mind, he says, he figured there was a potential future business in spirits production, but the laws of the time offered little incentive to the budding craft distiller. So he shared his vodka and gin with family and friends and had some "really great parties," he recalls, but kept those entrepreneurial dreams on the back burner.

Until, that is, the laws finally did change in 2013. By February of 2014, Jarvis and his wife, Erryn Turcon, had incorporated Bohemian Spirits and begun production—although, owing to the very small scale at which he was operating, actual retail sales didn't commence until over a year later.

By the start of 2019, having long since outgrown the distillery's original, non-walk-in-friendly space, Jarvis began searching for a new locale, which he found in the spring and occupied in the summer. Much more central and accessible to the local tourist trade, the new location is not only close to both the local golf course and ski resort, but also features, for the first time in Bohemian's history, a proper tasting bar.

COLOSSAL PINK GIN (40%)

Decidedly pink, as billed, this has a fruity, junipery nose that is as appealing as it is enigmatic, with a body that follows suit with bold juniper flavours mixed with dried berry notes and a citrusy finish. Not at all reticent, this is London Dry with a fruity twist.

HEARTH CHERRY BRANDY (30%)

No clear, wood-finished distillate this, its cloudy countenance is your first sign that it's a different sort of brandy, with sour cherry notes on the nose and a berry-ish, gently boozy body and finish. A satisfying sipper, well-suited to winter.

HARMONY HERBAL LIQUEUR (28%)

Pale pink in colour, this has a nose of cherry and cinnamon, allspice and strawberry, with a sweet and fruity body that saves its herbal notes for the mid- and back-palate, finishing bittersweet. Midway between a fruit liqueur and an amaro, serve it after dinner.

Dubh Glas Distillery

8486 Gallagher Lake Frontage Road, Oliver, BC, V0H 1T2
(778) 439-3580
thedubhglasdistillery.com

It was not by accident that Grant Stevely set up his distillery in Oliver, British Columbia. To start, the property he chose has a well that is connected to an underground aquifer, the source of all the distillery's water. Secondly, Oliver is one of the warmest places in the Okanagan, meaning that Stevely's whiskies can benefit from accelerated aging. And thirdly, the presence of about a hundred wineries within a half-hour drive of his front door, he says, means that he has a fairly constant stream of visitors during the busy tourist season of June through September.

Of course, none of that would matter if Stevely weren't passionate about and skilled in the production of whisky. Five minutes spent in his company, however, and you're absolutely certain about the former and pretty confident in the latter.

Stevely moved to Oliver after quitting his job of eighteen years in Alberta and selling most of what he owned. Training in the United States followed and enlisting the consultancy of master distiller Mike Nicolson helped him get the business up and running. The re-cooperage of ex-bourbon barrels into smaller sizes

(along with that accelerated aging in the hot Oliver summer) means that his whiskies were coming along quite nicely when we visited near the end of 2018. While he waits on future releases to follow his summer of 2019 whisky launch, gin and a new-make single malt ensure some income.

As for the name, it is pronounced, more or less, "Douglas" and is both Stevely's middle name and Gaelic for "from the dark water," a reference to the distillery's water source.

Grant Stevely. (Photo by Lionel Trudel.)

VIRGIN SPIRITS–BARLEY (50.8%)

The same spirit that is aging in the back of Dubh Glas, this new-make single malt has a soft, pillowy nose with light melon notes and a hint of caramel, and a somewhat yeasty, banana-ish body that grows more whisky-like when reduced in strength with water. Which is how it deserves to be enjoyed.

NOTEWORTHY GIN (43%)

Juniper and herbal notes combine to form a quality that is almost menthol on the nose, while the body goes from orange and coriander to spicy vanilla to a juniper-accented finish. An assertive gin for cocktailing.

Elder Bros. Farms

3121 Mission Wycliffe Road, Cranbrook, BC, V1C 7C8
(250) 581-2300
elderbrosfarms.com

Attila Lepsis didn't move from Hungary to Canada with the intent of owning North America's largest elderberry farm—it just worked out that way.

Arriving as a trained chef in 2000, Lepsis worked at a couple of restaurants before finally opening his own place, The Hun, in downtown Barrie, Ontario. That is where he and his young family might have stayed were it not for the fire that roared through the city's historic district in December of 2007, causing enough smoke damage to the restaurant that the business became unsalvageable. Fortunately, Lepsis had a friend in the construction industry who was willing to give him a job—work that eventually took him to Cranbrook, BC, where he and his wife fell in love with the countryside.

Deciding to settle in the province's interior, Lepsis thought back to his youth in Hungary, where his grandmother's elderflower syrup was a staple at breakfast. Recognizing that elderberries are only minimally farmed in Canada, he bought eighty-five acres in the fall of 2016 and set about establishing a farm he envisions as, one day, being home to twenty thousand elderberry plants, roughly ten times what he currently farms.

While he and his family were readying the farm for planting in 2017, Lepsis applied for his distillery licence, which he received in 2018. Distilling began in the fall of that year, using cherry juice from nearby Creston as a base fermentable. After testing seventeen recipes of various strengths with friends, he decided on a strength of 30 percent alcohol ("not too strong or too weak, a happy medium") and three flavour combinations.

ELDERFLOWER & HONEY SCHNAPPS (30%)

Honey may be listed on the label, but this moderately sweet schnapps is all elderflower, and rather spectacularly so, from the dense perfume of the aroma to the slightly syrupy body with its generously floral nature. Lovely on its own or in cocktails.

ELDERFLOWER & CHERRY SCHNAPPS (30%)

Light pink in colour, this presents a fascinating mix of its two ingredients on the nose, alternating between alcohol-steeped cherries and fresh elderflower. The flavour is a bit more tangled, but still shows well as a digestif.

CHERRY & HONEY SCHNAPPS (30%)

Not as bold a representation of cherry as the Elderflower & Honey is of its main ingredient, this red spirit has a soft, perfumy, and natural cherry nose, with a flavour that introduces honey notes alongside cherry juice and spicy alcohol. The base of a lovely Cherry Fizz.

Fernie Distillers

531 1st Avenue, Fernie, BC, V0B 1M0
(250) 278-0365
ferniedistillers.com

While it might be a bit of a stretch to say that opening Fernie Distillers was Andrew Hayden's and Jillian Rutherford's way of rationalizing a move from Calgary to their long-time weekend getaway destination, there is an element of truth to it. The couple was in search of a business that, as Rutherford says, "would fit with Fernie in a complementary way."

With Hayden's history in the beverage alcohol business and Rutherford's engineering background, distilling was a fit, not just with the town and surrounding region, but for the entrepreneurs themselves. A distilling course in nearby Kelowna was enough to start the interest growing, and a week-long stint training at the Sons of Vancouver Distillery (see page 234) helped seal the deal.

"The Sons people were incredibly generous," recalls Rutherford, Fernie's head distiller. "They really did everything they could to help us."

Meanwhile, the local Legion in Fernie was struggling, and hearing that a potential distillery was scouting for space in town, the Legion president suggested splitting the space, with the distillery occupying the disused event hall. He didn't have to ask twice.

"They said, 'This is the price and it's only for sale to you,'" says Rutherford. "So we bought it."

The distillery opened on Canada Day in 2018 with a 75 percent white wheat, 25 percent malted barley vodka and an Earl Grey tea–infused liqueur called Fernie's Fog. (All the product names evoke some aspect of Fernie's history or geography, says Rutherford.) A gin soon followed and, in the spring of 2019, the first of a line of seasonal spirits appeared, 5th and Park Damson Gin, named for the intersection in town where 35 kilograms of damsons were picked.

NO. 9 MINE VODKA (40%)

A wheat-based vodka that strays into new-make wheat whisky territory, the nose has some peach pit fruitiness while the body has a slightly rough fruitiness with a sweetish, berry-ish finish. An unusual take on the category, suitable for mixing.

PROSPECTOR GIN (40%)

The nose has a lovely and very perfumey mix of citrus and juniper and gentle spice, while the body mixes juniper and citrus to its advantage, with the almost Christmassy spice left to the finish. Perfect for a G&T.

FERNIE FOG LIQUEUR (40%)

The nose of this amber liqueur shows well-steeped Earl Grey tea, while the very sweet body affords a mix of Earl Grey and baking spices with brown sugar, ending with something close to a black tea finish. Definitely for after dinner.

Forbidden Spirits Distilling Co.

4400 Wallace Hill Road, Kelowna, BC, V1W 4C3
(250) 764-6011
forbiddenspirits.ca

Blair Wilson is yet another member of the ranks of individuals who thought they were retiring to a bucolic existence, only to wind up building a distillery.

The former restaurateur and North Vancouver MP bought a parcel of land in the Okanagan with the intent of moving his family to the fields and becoming a gentleman farmer of sorts. Once resettled, however, he started thinking about what he could do with his twenty acres of apple orchards, outside of simply selling his harvest to local processors. The first plan of attack was to begin making cider but, after he happened upon a New York state distillery that was using apples to make its spirits, he quickly changed course.

The first item on the agenda was to build the distillery and tasting room, which he did using wood reclaimed from the property's century-old barn. Stained glass elements added by the distillery's general manager, Marisa Vardabasso, completed the dramatic look and added a reverential ambiance to the building.

The church-like effect is deliberate. Forbidden Spirits styles all of its graphic elements on the Garden of Eden theme, from the "fallen angel" that adorns its Rebel Vodka to the stylized inverted cross that serves as the distillery's emblem.

As of summer 2019, only two products were in production: Rebel Vodka, made from sourced apple juice, and Forbidden Vodka, made entirely from the juice of apples grown on the farm, while Adam's Spiced Rum and Eve's Original Gin are expected to eventually follow.

REBEL VODKA (40%)

A most unusual vodka, this bright spirit has a slightly sweet and subdued aroma—is that a whiff of apple skin?—and a flavour profile that is as much eau-de-vie as it is vodka: fruity sweetness, a bit yeasty, drying to an almost raisiny finish. Brightens with a drop of soda.

Jones Distilling

616 Third Street West, Revelstoke
BC, V0E 2S1
jonesdistilling.com

In planning

The Jones Distilling Tasting (Class)Room.

In researching this book, we have come across distilleries built in the most unusual of locations, from garages to legion halls to hockey arenas. Jones Distilling, however, is the only BC distillery we know of that is located in a school.

That would be the Mountain View School, a century-old building in old Revelstoke that had sat unused for years. The man behind the transformation is Gareth Jones, an Englishman with some distilling in his family history—a fanciful story on the distillery website tells the tale—who arrived in Revelstoke via the British army and a stint living in Salmon Arm.

Anxious to add spirits to the area's other small-scale alcohol offerings, Jones trained in distilling in Kelowna before spotting the potential in the historic school. When the Revelstoke School District put the building up for sale in early 2016, Jones submitted a proposal and, in August of that year, won the right to buy and redevelop it, subject to his signing a Heritage Revitalization Agreement that would guarantee maintenance of the school's character.

The distillery opened in May of 2018 with not Jones himself, but rather twenty-five-year-old Megan Moore in charge of distilling. Described by Jones as "a unicorn," Moore was discovered chatting about distilling in a bar by the company's marketing manager. With a background in brewing and distilling, Moore was, Jones decided, a perfect match for the company after a job interview in which, as he puts it, "It quickly became apparent I wasn't interviewing her; she was interviewing me."

The first product was Mr. Jones Premium Vodka, which was winning awards almost before it was even widely for sale. It was followed in 2019 by a series of Revelstoke Premium Gins, and in the summer of 2019, the first of the Revelstoke Collection (what Moore describes as a set of "alcoholic botanical cordials" intended to be mixed with tonic or lemonade): a fruit- and botanical-fuelled, 20-percent-alcohol creation called Sweet Spot.

Spirits not available for tasting.

245

Kootenay Country Craft Distillery

7263 Gustafson Road, Winlaw, BC, V0G 2J0
(250) 355-2702
kootenaycountry.ca

s Kevin Goodwin puts it, when you're a farmer you're always doing something other than just farming. Even so, his and wife Lora's trajectory from organic produce farmers in Montana to distillers just across the border in Winlaw is a bit unusual.

An American by birth—now with dual citizenship, married to a Canadian—Goodwin describes himself as having been a bit of a jack-of-all-trades when he and Lora were commercially farming strawberries and vegetables in the US. As his trade frequently included heavy equipment operation, once the couple decided the Kootenays would be a fine place to raise their family, he decided to start a construction company in BC rather than continue with their farming ways.

At the time, being homebrewers and winemakers, the couple was more than familiar with the science of fermentation and had watched with interest the growth of the local craft brewing scene. While travelling in the early 2010s, however, they noticed a corresponding surge in the number of small-scale distilleries and, interested in transitioning careers again, decided that a craft distillery would be a good fit for their area.

The decision to explore the field further led Goodwin to a distilling course in Seattle and a friendship with a consulting Master Distiller. That was followed by two years of licensing, construction, and further education. Two years later, in March of 2014, the Kootenay Country Craft Distillery opened with a wheat-based vodka. That was followed by a gin and a broad series of flavoured vodkas, including one made purely from honey.

Now, with their feet under them, as Goodwin describes it, the pair is beginning to move into brown spirits—the first being a rye whisky. With the clear spirits still selling well, however, the challenge is finding the time to get the barrel program going.

Spirits not available for tasting.

Legend Distilling

3005 Naramata Road, Naramata, BC, V0H 1N0
(778) 514-1010
legenddistilling.com

If there is a prettier view from a distillery than that from Legend Distilling, perched on a forested ridge overlooking Okanagan Lake, we are not sure where it might be. Which is why when the husband and wife team of Doug and Dawn Lennie were looking for a place for their distillery, they knew from the outset that it would have to be somewhere in Naramata.

Entrepreneurs feeling the effects of the financial crisis in 2009, the Lennies were looking for a business that might prove somewhat recession-proof and landed on brewing as a possibility. Having seen how the industry was growing, however, they became more attracted to the less-populated distilling field, although they were daunted by the laws in place at the time.

When those laws changed in 2013, however, the couple was ready to forge full speed ahead and had their distillery up and running by the summer of 2014 in a building that, for thirty years, housed a doctor's office.

Legend opened with a vodka and a gin, but the Lennies soon decided the focus they wanted for their business was on making spirits that spoke of their locale. So vodkas flavoured with local berries, liqueurs made with locally roasted coffee or hand-harvested sumac, and gins juiced with local herbs and botanicals, including smoked rosemary, were added to the lineup. A wheat- and rye-based whisky was primed for release when we visited in late 2018.

HARVEST MOON GIN (28%)

A foraged fruit riff on sloe gin, this attractive pinkish-purple gin has an aroma equal parts berries, brambles, and juniper and a body that mixes complex fruit notes with distinctive gin botanicals. For sipping over ice in the waning months of summer.

NARAMARO (30%)

An Okanagan take on on France's Amer Picon, this offers an herbal-fruity, almost medicinal aroma and, like many a classic amaro, begins sweetly and finishes bitter, with orange and leafy herbal notes in between. An afternoon pick-me-up or evening digestif.

MANITOU ORANGE & SUMAC LIQUEUR (30%)

This pale orange liqueur combines local sumac berries with orange to produce a terrifically perfumy orange-lemon aroma and a not-overly sweet body that is lighter and less oily than most orange liqueurs. Combine with gin or sip straight.

BLACK MOON GIN (40%)

The smoked rosemary shows itself first in a smoky aroma, then in the perfumey rosemary. This relationship is inverted in the body, with rosemary and juniper more immediately evident and soft smokiness following. A sensational campfire gin.

Maple Leaf Spirits

948 Naramata Road, Penticton, BC, V2A 8V1
(250) 493-0180
mapleleafspirits.ca

M aple Leaf is the oldest BC craft distillery still operating under its original owner, Jorg Engel. Considering its early history, that might be an even greater achievement than it at first appears.

PEAR WILLIAMS (40%)

The aroma of this clear fruit brandy is an appetizing mix of fresh pear and spicy bread dough, while the palate is more digestif than aperitif, with a light Bartlett pear-y sweetness up front and a spicy, soothing strength in the middle and finish.

LADY OF THE CASK FINE BRANDY (42%)

Don't call it cognac, because that's not allowed, but the character of this brandy may well remind you of the French classic. The nose speaks to fine oak while the palate shows a maturity beyond its youth. Lovely for after dinner or in cocktails.

CHERRY LIQUEUR (25%)

Made from fruit both distilled and infused, the aroma and flavour of this Montmorency cherry–based liqueur is equal parts sweet and tart, with a tremendous balance between the two. Enjoy with minimum 70 percent cocoa–content chocolate.

MAPLE LIQUEUR (25%)

Organic maple syrup is added to the distillery's kirsch to create a liqueur that, while sweet, is not as sweet as you might expect. Instead, there is a very pure maple flavour layered over softly warming alcohol, with a slightly fruity finish. Enjoy after dinner or over ice cream.

After emigrating from Germany in 2001, Engel set himself up in the Okanagan Valley where, as all good Canadians know, a lot of fruit is grown. Having been raised in a country where small-scale distilling is fairly commonplace, he couldn't understand why some of this fruit was not being turned into spirits, and so, from 2002 to 2004, he worked towards getting himself a distillery licence.

He finally succeeded in 2005, but found the law required him to establish his business in an area zoned as industrial land, which, in his case, meant a rather poorly trafficked area of Penticton.

"No one knew I was there," he now says, and it showed in his first-year sales—a whole 450 bottles. Thankfully, he was able to hang in until the laws were changed in 2013 and he moved the business to the heart of the Naramata wine region. With hundreds of thousands of tourists following the local winery trail each summer, being noticed is no longer an issue.

Monashee Spirits Craft Distillery

307 Mackenzie Avenue, Revelstoke, BC, V0E 2S0
250 463-5678
monasheespirits.com

n 2014, when underwater welder and deep-sea diver Josh Lafferty was thirty-three years old, his entire life changed.

"I had a really bad accident; not diving, it was riding motocross and being a dumbass," says Lafferty. "I chased a really big jump and missed. Shattered everything in my legs from my knees down. I spent about four or five months in a wheelchair, had a dozen surgeries, and had to learn how to walk again. So my career as an underwater welder was done."

He's remarkably upbeat when telling the story of that life-changing, painful, and possibly traumatic experience. And that was before he got ripped off by a Kootenay moonshiner who paid him for a spot of welding work with a bucket of molasses. Annoyed at first, the avid make-your-own-wine-and-beer guy decided that, when life gives you molasses, your only option is to make rum. That was his first experiment in making spirits, but obviously not his last. Along with his wife, Jennifer, Lafferty opened Monashee on Revelstoke's main drag in 2017.

ETHOS GIN (43%)

An outstanding Martini gin that draws you in with an herbaceous and spearmint-y aroma and keeps you happy with a gorgeous balance of juniper and delicate herbs. A lovely dry and peppery finish immediately makes you want more.

VODKA (40%)

We love that so many vodkas are breaking from neutral territory. This one, made from triticale, announces its iconoclasm with a floral and spicy nose and a bright mixture of subtle mint, light fruit, and pepper. Serve on the rocks.

BARREL AGED GIN (43%)

Eight months in a used Scotch whisky barrel has imparted some surprising notes to this triticale-based gin, detectable right off the bat in its distinctly gingery and vanilla-ish aroma. An intriguing spicy-sweet, medium-to-light-bodied experimental release.

VULCAN'S FIRE CINNAMON LIQUEUR (30%)

There are a lot of craft cinnamon liqueurs on the market these days, but few mixed as well as this one, which is an artful balance of pepper and sweet. Après-ski fodder, for sure.

THE RICH GET RICHER IN BRITISH COLUMBIA

With already far more distilleries than any other province, at the time of publication BC is poised to gain even more. With thanks to *The Alchemist* magazine, the following are either opening up as we type these words or expected to appear sometime in late 2019 or 2020:

VANCOUVER ISLAND & THE GULF ISLANDS

Copper Kettle Spirits in Ladysmith; James Bay Distillers in Victoria; Western Red Distilling Company in Victoria; Wild Coast Distilling in Cobble Hill.

LOWER MAINLAND, FRASER VALLEY & WEST COAST

Copper Spirit Distillery in Snug Cove; Montis Distilling in Whistler; New Wave Distilling in Abbotsford; Tallant Distillery in Vancouver.

OKANAGAN, KOOTENAYS & THE INTERIOR

Alchemist Distillery in Summerland; Distillery 95 in Radium Hot Springs; Lost Boys Distillery in Fernie; Mount 7 Spirits Craft Distillery in Golden; Trench Brewing & Distilling in Prince George; Wiseacre Farm Distillery in Kelowna.

The Monashee cocktail bar. (Photo by Cole Hofstra Photography)

Since it's a small space with relatively low ceilings that couldn't support a tall column still, Lafferty had to engineer a special design workaround that involves a hybrid with two shorter columns, which he uses to turn triticale into vodka, young whisky, and a gin that scooped Best in Class Canadian Gin and Spirit of the Year at the 2019 Canadian Artisan Spirit Competition. He's been pretty busy filling orders since the results were announced—not that business wasn't brisk before, given seasonal tourists flocking to Monashee's next-level cocktail bar.

Perhaps everything does happen for a reason.

Okanagan Spirits Craft Distillery

5204 24th Street, Vernon, BC, V1T 8X2
& 267 Bernard Avenue, Kelowna, BC, V1Y 6N2
(250) 549-3120; (778) 484-5174 (Kelowna)
okanaganspirits.com

Before there was a distillery boom in British Columbia—or anywhere else in Canada, for that matter—there was Okanagan Spirits.

Established in 2004, Okanagan was born of a desire to create brandies, originally using a wood-fired still in very small quantities, from the orchards that surround Vernon. In order to get the business off the ground, founder Frank Dieter brought in a group of investors, including local residents, the Dyck family.

According to present-day Okanagan CEO Tyler Dyck, "investor attrition" didn't take long to creep in. With no framework for craft distilling in place at the time, recalls Dyck, the going was extremely tough in those early years and some of the investors began to drop out as early as 2007, with the Dyck family picking up the slack.

By 2010, now owning most of the business, the formerly silent Dycks had begun to take on an operational role, beginning with the formation of the Craft Distillers Guild of BC,

GIN (40%)

This is a gin broadly in the London Dry model, although with more than a cursory nod to New World aromatics. Decidedly juniper-forward, it nevertheless has a gentle palate entry and a peppery-floral finish. For Martinis more than for mixing.

BRBN (40%)

Despite the name, don't expect something typically bourbon-ish here. Rather, appreciate it for its roundness, almost pillowy soft aromatics, and sweet, sippable character. Consider it aged corn whisky with a Canadian accent.

LAIRD OF FINTRY SINGLE MALT WHISKY (42%)

Produced in limited quantities and sold via a lottery system, this hotly anticipated annual release is light and balanced on the nose, with dry notes of caramel and lemon peel and faintly sweet, gently oaky, and vanilla-ish on the palate. A gentle sipper.

BLACKCURRANT LIQUEUR (24%)

A perennial winner at the World Spirits Awards, this *crème de cassis* presents a pure, tart blackberry nose and a mouth-filling, slightly puckering body of highly concentrated fruit. Use sparingly in a Kir Royale or enjoy neat before or after dinner.

The Okanagan Spirits family. (Photo by Jeremie Dyk)

of which Dyck remains president, and the construction of a second location "in front of more people" in downtown Kelowna.

With Kelowna operational and the Guild's lobbying successful in convincing the provincial government to establish the "BC Craft" designation, Dyck decided that the distillery could use some more space in Vernon, so he spent two years finding and building their current location, which opened in early 2015. Around that same time, the distillery's whisky program reached full stride and Okanagan completed its transformation from a fruit-focussed distillery to one with a wide range of products spanning everything from fruit liqueurs to gin, single malt, and absinthe.

Old Order Distilling Co.

270 Martin Street, Penticton, BC, V2A 5K3
(778) 476-2210
oldorderdistilling.ca

Oddly enough, given that the distillery ferments and distills exclusively grain, Old Order was born of an interest Graham Martens had in making use of the fruit from his family farm in nearby Summerland. Initially, his idea was to open a cidery, but that plan was shelved for lack of sufficient proper cider apples.

Settling on a distillery instead, Martens faced his second hurdle, namely, the law prohibiting him from setting up on the farmland. So a premises was found in downtown Penticton and he began the process of establishing his distillery, with a tasting bar up front.

Midway through construction, however, the laws were changed to allow distilleries lounge licences, so another shift was made and a cocktail bar was added to the plan. That bar is now open five days a week during the busy summer season (closed Mondays and Tuesdays) and on the weekends the rest of the year.

After opening in 2014, Martens became increasingly interested in whisky and eventually shifted all his production to grain spirits. "The end game is whisky," he now says, with ten barrels aging in the back of the distillery and more planned for the future. A small barrel purchase program allows people to customize the aging of their own whisky.

HERITAGE VODKA (40%)

Round, smooth, and soft in both aroma and body, this pot-distilled vodka comes across as equal parts neutral spirit and new-make whisky, with hints of vanilla and grain husk on the nose and an herbal, peppery character. A sipping vodka.

BLACK GOAT VODKA (43%)

Martens adds a proprietary mix of plant-sourced minerals when watering this down to proof, giving it a deep brown hue and adding earthy, minerally notes to the nose. The body seems chewier and there are distinct slate notes on the finish. More than a novelty.

LEGACY GIN (43%)

Not shy with the juniper on the nose, this is a fairly full-bodied gin with peppery anise and floral notes in its aroma and balanced juniper, citrus fruit, and black pepper in the body. Sip on its own at any temperature or mix into a Vesper or Martini.

BLESSED BEAN LIQUEUR (24%)

The cold-brew coffee blended into this liqueur shows in the fresh coffee bean aroma with perhaps a hint of vanilla. That vanilla is more apparent at the start of the taste, although it fades quickly behind sweet coffee flavours. A clever cocktail ingredient.

Taynton Bay Spirits

1701 B 6th Avenue, Invermere, BC, V0A 1K4
778-526-5205
tayntonbayspirits.com

When you think of spirits from the Kootenays, the last thing that comes to mind is tequila.

But when Justin Atterbury and partners Jason Powers and Paul Christie were playing around with a wheat-barley spirit, the flavour profile seemed similar to Mexico's signature liquid. So they christened it "Tequil-Eh," a name that worked well until Mexico's Tequila Regulatory Council (CRT) got wind of it. We guess they didn't think the name was very funny and, after a little legal consultation, Taynton Bay realized it'd be better off changing the name. It's now called "Gringo's Revenge."

When not fighting it out with the CRT, Taynton Bay is busy churning out a lot of spirit for a small-town distillery that's just over two years old, as well as running The Station Neighbourhood Pub, a lakefront bar and restaurant replete with an awesome patio in downtown Invermere. The distillery's ambitious production schedule calls for running the still 24/7 to make a vodka, a gin, and a line of "tea" spirits—low-proof (14 percent) drinks meant to be enjoyed with a splash of soda, like an aperitif made with loose leaf tea instead of bitter herbs and roots.

Unlike many modern Canadian distilleries, no whisky production is planned. It was, mind you, but that was before a chance conversation with a liquor store manager in Vancouver.

"I was telling him how excited we were to start making whisky and he kind of sarcastically said to me, 'I can hardly wait 'til all you craft distillers flood the market with your whiskey in about two to three years' time'," Atterbury recalls. "That really resonated with me. And right then, I realized that we do better when we're different."

GINGER MATCHA (14%)

The aroma suggests ginger and plum, which follows through on the lightly sweet, kombucha-esque palate, with a fair degree of light heat on the tail. Would make a fine aperitif, ideally served over rocks with a splash of soda.

STRAWBERRY HERBAL (14%)

Jolly Rancher candy on the nose, followed by sour cherry and citrus on the palate, this is a liqueur for people with acidic palates. Since the sweetness is restrained, this low-alcohol tea spirit would probably appeal most to people with a soft spot for limoncello.

True North Distilleries

1460 Central Avenue, Grand Forks, BC, V0H 1H0
(778) 879-4420
truenorthdistilleries.com

If you look at the True North website, at least in its early 2019 version, you'll find that "it all started with bees." Which, according to Scot Stewart, the principal partner and distiller, is technically true. But while the bees did play their part in the establishment of the distillery in the early days, Stewart says the ultimate goal was always whisky.

Said bees resided on a parcel of land the True North partners purchased in 2012, shortly after which they applied for their combination distillery and winery licence, the first such licence awarded by the province, according to Stewart. Mead production followed—technically wine, under BC regulations—but, when a change in law required a significant increase in the number of hives on the property, that plan was abandoned and a renewed emphasis was placed on spirits, particularly whisky.

While the company's first whiskies were made entirely from rye grown on the farm, Stewart says he quickly came to the realization that he was not a farmer, so he now buys local grain for his conspicuously low-oak whiskies. That novel approach to whisky-making was developed when he discovered that his four sisters disliked oak,

rather than disliking whisky, and they quite enjoyed whiskies made without undue oak influence.

Uniquely, because his wife, Heather, is a fan of rum, Stewart grows his own sugar cane in what he describes as a "grow-op," presses the cane on an old sorghum press, and distills the boiled-down juice to make a pair of 100 percent Canadian rums. As he's not a big fan of spiced rum, the True North version is flavoured entirely with locally grown and organic chilli peppers.

A hodgepodge of other products, including a Scottish-style whisky made with barley malt kilned over local peat, and the company's bestseller, a new-make rye called Black Dog After Dark, round out the company's portfolio.

Spirits not available for tasting.

Tumbleweed Spirits

7–6001 Lakeshore Drive, Osoyoos, BC
(778) 437-2221
tumbleweedspirits.com

Tumbleweed's Cherry Moonshine. (Photo by Over Ocean Media)

When they were still but children, Mike Green and his future wife, Andrea Zaradic, loved Osoyoos. So when life in North Vancouver grew too congested and frenetic, the couple looked eastward for a lifestyle change.

VODKA (40%)

Bright and clean with a nose that hints at overproof spirit, even though it isn't, this lightly fruity (stone fruit and melon) vodka has a fresh taste with just a hint of slightly spicy herbals on the finish. Chill lightly and enjoy neat.

GIN (40%)

A very aggressive nose introduces a gin that's surprisingly mellow on the palate, with notes of resinous herbs, citrus, and juniper, and finishes with a dash of spicy heat. Combine with a good dose of tonic on a hot summer day.

CHERRY MOONSHINE (40%)

Although it is Bing cherry red in colour, this is not overly evocative of its signature fruit in either aroma or flavour, with a vegetal, cherry compote nose and a spicy, boozy palate that hints at cherry in the start and finish. Sip slowly after a meal or mix with soda.

NINE MILE CREEK SHINE (40%)

A whisky wannabe, this is a youthful spirit that speaks heavily of the barrels in which it was aged and less of the grain from which it spawned. Perhaps something that shall improve with time.

Since they already had what Green terms a "recreational property" in Osoyoos, it seemed the natural place for the pair to settle full-time. Winemaking was considered as an occupation, but Green says they abandoned that idea when they realized the region was replete with wineries. So perhaps distilling instead.

With Malcolm Bucholtz of Saskatchewan's Prohibition University as consultant, Tumbleweed embarked upon what Green describes as a "steep learning curve" before finally opening on the May long weekend in 2016. Fortunately, a local farmer made deciding upon their first spirit a proverbial slam dunk.

"A farmer from Rock Creek, who still provides us with almost all our grain, showed up one day with a big bucket of rye," recalls Green. "It was terrible to work with, sticky and awkward, but we were really happy with the results." That result was Rock Creek Rye.

With what amounts to a new-make whisky in production, it will come as no surprise that Tumbleweed has several grain spirits in the barrel aging, from a bourbon-style recipe to straight rye and triticale whisky. While they age quietly, a vodka, gin, and various flavoured and unflavoured moonshines keep the tourists happy in the summer and the locals content year-round.

Urban Distilleries

402–1979 Old Okanagan Highway
West Kelowna, BC, V4T 3A4
(778) 478-0939
urbandistilleries.ca

Mike Urban was already a hobby distiller, brewer, and home winemaker when he and some friends arrived in the French city of Cognac during a trip to France. Intrigued by the possibility of exploring a working distillery, they took the tour and a question was planted in Urban's mind: could I do this in Kelowna?

As time has long since proved, he could and did. Urban Distilleries opened in January 2011 as one of the pioneers of British Columbia's now explosive craft distilling scene. More than a pioneer, in fact. Through Urban's Canadian Craft Distilling Institute training school, delivered in co-operation with Prohibition University founder Malcolm Bucholtz, Urban's distillery has also served as the launching pad for countless other Canadian and American distilleries.

Working on a German-made still with all-BC ingredients, the Urban distillery is an impressively diverse operation, making everything from Okanagan fruit liqueurs to eaux-de-vie and whiskies. As per the "+ Winery" part of the sign outside the distillery, Urban makes two types of mead as well.

One of the distillery's charitable projects is support for the Save a Spirit Bear initiative, which promotes the protection and preservation of endangered species in British Columbia. Partial proceeds of every Spirit Bear brand go toward the Great Bear Education & Research Project.

SPIRIT BEAR GIN (40%)

Flavoured with ten botanicals including Okanagan-grown lavender and apple, this boldly announces the former in its aroma while a bit of peppery juniper at the start of the taste precedes a floral body with a lightly spicy finish. A gin for those who think they don't like gin.

SINGLE MALT WHISKY (40%)

Uniquely packaged with a piece of a French oak cask in every bottle, this has a rather oaky character that speaks to its youth. The distillery claims that every week of bottle aging is equivalent to six months in cask, though, so it's an issue that could work itself out fairly quickly.

URBAN BURBAN (42.5%)

Although aged in new charred American oak, just like bourbon, this shows more sweet creamy corn than it does charred wood and vanilla, with a soft and sweet nose and smooth and creamy finish. For sipping all on its own.

RASPBERRY LIQUEUR (24%)

Made with locally grown black and red raspberries, this has a depth that eludes many such fruit liqueurs, with elements of the juice and skin and even a hint of the vine present. Suitable for after-dinner sipping or mixology.

Vernon Craft Distilleries

1C–4601 23rd Street, Vernon, BC, V1T 4K9
(778) 930-1011
vernoncraftdistilleries.com

Kyle Watts and Ben Drodge definitely count among the more unusual distillery owners we have encountered.

Both highly successful businessmen in stressful occupations, Drodge with clothing manufacturing and Watts a trial lawyer, the friends were looking for a supplemental business that was, in Drodge's words, "more relaxing." When we suggested that few of the distillery owners we've spoken with would rush to describe their business as relaxing, he pauses, then chuckles. "I suppose that if you were counting on it to pay the bills, it wouldn't be a terribly relaxing business," he says, "but we already have businesses for that, so we're able to focus on the fun and passion of the distillery."

Explaining that both he and Watts had been hobby distilling and visiting distilleries for years prior to opening Vernon Craft, Drodge says the partners really just wanted to mine the traditions of the business. As such, they concentrated on making the cleanest vodka they could from local grains, mostly wheat, and made a "moonshine"—really more a new-make whisky, says Drodge—out of a mix of barley and wheat.

With no on-site sales or tasting bar, the pair are able to work to their own schedule. "Sometimes we'll go in for four or five days and get three months of work done," says Drodge. And if packaging becomes an issue, Drodge says they sometimes borrow workers from his clothing factory next door.

The bottom line for the partners is more the love of distilling than its commercial aspects. Concludes Drodge, "We want this to be our family business for many years to come."

Spirits not available for tasting.

Wynndel Craft Distilleries

1331 Channel Road, Wynndel, BC, V0B 2N1
(705) 271-5567
wynndelcraftdistilleries.ca

When husband and wife Wilhelm and Jeanette Meerholz emigrated to Canada from South Africa, they landed first on the Prairies, where, among other enterprises, they ran a saskatoon berry farm for a time. Although they didn't know it then, it was experience that would serve them well when Wilhelm announced they needed to live somewhere warmer and they crossed the Rockies to settle in British Columbia's Creston Valley.

Arriving in Wynndel, they found a saskatoon berry farm that Jeanette says nobody was quite sure what to do with. "We said, 'We know what to do with it!'" she recalls, and the couple purchased the Duck Lake farm in 2013.

At first, the Meerholzes shipped much of their production west, but as transportation costs began to rise they considered other ways to make money from their berries. Distilling, they decided, was the best option, so Wilhelm, who also goes by the name Pat, took courses in both Canada and the United States and planning for the distillery began in earnest in 2016.

The first Wynndel Craft Distilleries spirits became available at the local farmers' market in November of 2017. Brandies, liqueurs, and schnapps are made from saskatoon and other berries grown on the farm, supplemented by fruit and juice they buy from other Creston Valley producers, while locally grown apples are the base of their gins.

The Meerholzes still operate the farm on a commercial basis, but the distillery is thriving despite the limits its rural setting place upon its efficiency. Says Jeanette with a smile, "It's very small, but I think that we're doing pretty well."

OLD TOM APPLE GIN (40%)

Crystal clear, this has a bright and herbal juniper aroma that presents surprisingly little in the way of fruitiness or classic Old Tom character. On the palate, It offers a touch of sweetness on a spicy-fruity body with a lingering pepper finish. Martini or mixing, your choice.

CAPE BRANDY (40%)

Light amber with a faint haze, this youthful brandy sports a grapy, almost blueberry-ish nose and a sweet, borderline sugary body with flavours that evoke white port wine and a slightly spicy, definitely hot finish. Enjoyable, but something that should improve with the years.

SASKATOON LIQUEUR (25%)

With a colour midway between pink and purple, and a nose of dried berries accented by a whiff of petrol, this is a sweet and very saskatoon-ish liqueur that balances the fruit with a light spiciness in the second half. Sip after a heavy meal or cut with soda and lemon.

Yukon Spirits

102 Copper Road, Whitehorse, YT, Y1A 2Z6
(867) 668-4183
twobrewerswhisky.com

When it first opened in 1997 as the Chilkoot Brewing Company, Yukon Brewing became not the first brewery to open in Canada's north, but the first to survive and, indeed, thrive. So perhaps it wasn't really so much of a surprise a dozen years later when its founders, Bob Baxter and Alan Hansen, decided to add distilling to their alcohol production resumés.

"Alan, being a chemical engineer, has always had a fascination with distilling," says Baxter. "So after for years joking about how we should buy a still, we finally went ahead and did it."

It helped that the brewery was profitable by that point, so the partners didn't need to rely too heavily upon spirits sales. "It's much more fun when we don't have to depend on spirits to keep the lights on," says Baxter.

Although the original intent was to produce clear spirits, that approach changed in the two years between the commencement of planning and the actual purchase of a still. Recognizing that what was most popular on the brewery side were bigger, fuller-flavoured ales, the pair figured the same would be true for the distillery side and so switched to a whisky focus.

RELEASE NO. 13: CLASSIC (43%)

The nose of this golden whisky offers caramel, melon, plum, and five spice powder, while the body is nectar-ish and softly fruity with notes of tropical fruit and golden apple. Evocative of Speyside single malts and a stellar Canadian whisky.

RELEASE NO. 15: SPECIAL FINISHES (43%)

The aroma is rich with the sherry notes its barrel imparted, while the body seems not to have had quite enough time to absorb them. Expect spice and cotton candy smoothness, with a jumble of spice in the finish.

RELEASE NO. 11: INNOVATIVE (43%)

The use of a brewer's Munich malt shows in the rich, toasted grain nose with soft roasted apple notes. The body demonstrates its brewery roots with a rich, amber ale–like maltiness and a hint of ash in the finish. A successful and enjoyable experiment.

RELEASE NO. 12: PEATED (43%)

The whiff of smoke on the first nosing becomes a mix of peat and campfire once it opens up, while the body begins with a bit of citrus before growing smokier with plummy fruit in the mid-palate. A clean, breath-of-smoke finish seals the deal.

Northern lights over downtown Whitehorse. (iStock)

While distilling got under way in 2009, the first Two Brewers Whisky was not released until 2016. Others have since followed, but because the roughly one-thousand-bottle batch sizes aren't large enough to allow for blending for consistency, Yukon Spirits makes an asset of that limitation by labelling each as a numbered release, divided into four categories: Classic, Special Finishes, Peated, and Innovative. Once each release is sold out, it is gone forever.

While a team of distillers works on the whiskies, as well as the company's "Concepts" line of white spirits and liqueurs, Hansen is the person at the helm of the distillery, in part because of his engineering background, but also, according to Baxter, thanks to his "remarkable palate."

Distillery
COCKTAILS

⁕ 🍁 🍁 🍁 ⁕

With the growth in the variety of products many Canadian distillers are making, it is increasingly possible to create several classic cocktails using the products of only a single distillery. Here are a few that we found during our research.

AMPERSAND VESPER

3 oz. Gin
1 oz. Per Se Vodka
½ oz. Imperative Dry Vermouth

Stir over ice and strain into a cocktail glass. Garnish with an orange twist.

DRAGON MIST BLACK RUSSIAN

1 oz. Vodka
1 oz. Coffee Liqueur

Pour over ice in a rocks glass and stir before serving.

JDD SOCIETY AMERICANO

1 ½ oz. Mia Amata Amaro
1 ½ oz. Barrel-Aged Vermouth
2–3 oz. soda to taste

Combine Amaro and Vermouth over ice in a tall glass and stir. Top with soda and stir again gently before serving.

LEGEND WHITE LADY

1 ½ oz. Doctor's Orders Gin
1 oz. Manitou Orange & Sumac Liqueur
¾ oz. lemon juice

Shake over ice and strain into a cocktail glass.

TAWSE MARTINI

3 oz. Dry Gin
¾ oz. Vermouth

Stir over ice and strain into a cocktail glass. Garnish with an olive or lemon twist.

DILLON'S MANHATTAN

3 oz. Rye Whisky
1 ½ oz. Vermouth
3 dashes DSB Bitters

Combine over ice and stir. Serve on the rocks or strain into a cocktail glass, garnished with a quality maraschino cherry.

GLOSSARY

ABSINTHE   An anise- and worm-wood-flavoured spirit once hugely popular in France, particularly so in Paris. Suspicions that its wormwood ingredient was poisonous led to it being banned, however, although such fears were ultimately proved incorrect around the start of this century.

ABV (ALCOHOL BY VOLUME) Unlike "proof," the ABV measurement of any spirit is simply the percentage of ethanol in the liquid. It's the universal standard by which the "strength" of alcohol is measured.

ADVOCAAT   An egg liqueur traditionally made with a brandy base, commonly sold in Belgium or the Netherlands. It's pretty rare in Canada, which is actually our loss.

AGE STATEMENT   Simply, the number of years a spirit has been aged. Some marketers mislead consumers by putting a number on a label so that it appears older than it is, but this is a more common problem with big brands (especially rum producers) than it is with craft spirits.

ALEMBIC   The oldest still design, an alembic is a simple, three-part piece of equipment: a pot, which gets heated, a receiver, and a tube that connects the two and collects all the vapours.

Some version of that rudimentary design is still used for the production of many spirits, notably traditionally distilled tequila.

AMARO   A category of usually lower strength spirits defined by their flavouring with bitter herbs.

AQUAVIT (AKVAVIT) A Scandinavian white spirit not entirely dissimilar to gin, except with juniper swapped out for caraway. Regional traditions dictate whether the base spirit is made from potatoes or grain, whether or not it's aged, and which other botanicals are also employed.

ARAK   A grape-based anise-flavoured distillate common in Syria, Iraq, Lebanon, Turkey, Jordan, and other countries in the surrounding region. Not to be confused with Arrack from Indonesia.

BAIJIU   The world's most consumed spirit, this Chinese liquor is wildly complex, thanks to the fact that there are many styles, all produced according to regional traditions and preferences. Unique in that its source ingredient—often sorghum or rice, but it can also be made with wheat, corn, or other grains—is fermented in a solid or semi-solid state.

BASE SPIRIT   To a cocktail lover, the base spirit might refer to the main ingredient. In craft spirits lingo, this refers to the distillate used in liqueurs, gins, aquavits, or arak, which see botanicals or fruits added to a "base spirit," such as a vodka.

BLENDED WHISKY   *See* "Scotch."

BOURBON   A specific type of American whiskey produced according to a strict set of rules governing ingredients—at least 51 percent corn—distilled and barrelling proofs, and aging requirements. Despite what a lot of people think, it can be made anywhere in the United States, but it needs to be unadulterated—meaning no charcoal aging as with Tennessee whiskeys like Jack Daniel's—and aging must take place in new, charred oak barrels.

BRANDY   Spirits distilled from fruit wine, usually made from grapes, and generally aged in wooden barrels. Although brandies may be made any-where, the most famous come from France.

CALVADOS   A type of French brandy made from apples (and occasionally pears), the production of which is limited to specific regions in north-western France. When Canadians try their hand on this style, they have to come up with a new name for it.

CANADIAN WHISKY   Although commonly referred to as "rye," there are no regulations governing the grain composition of a Canadian whisky, although it is required to be aged for a minimum of three years. (For more information, see the "The Large Legacy Distillers" section beginning on p. 21.)

COGNAC   A distilled and aged grape brandy that can only be made in one region of France: Cognac. Canadian producers mimicking this style have to come up with new nomenclature.

COLUMN STILL (COFFEY STILL)   Vastly more efficient than the pot still, a column still consists of two cylinders that sit side-by-side and work continuously and in harmony to create a high-proof spirit.

DISTILLATE   The spirit that comes off the still before dilution or aging. Always water-clear, the alcohol con-tent can range from a high of 96 per-cent for a vodka to below 80 percent, sometimes well below, for whiskies.

EAU-DE-VIE   A white spirit made from fruit, and bottled without the addition of juice or sugar.

FERMENTABLES   The material that is fermented to produce alcohol prior to distillation.

GENEVER (GENEVA) The precursor to gin, genever was immensely popular in the low countries—what is now Belgium and the Netherlands—during the nineteenth century. It is generally fuller and richer than gin, and although juniper is a required ingredient, it need not show its presence in the aroma or taste.

GIN A white spirit defined by the addition of botanical flavourings, especially, and, in theory at least, predominantly juniper.

GIN, BARREL-AGED Simply, gin that has been aged in a barrel of some sort.

GIN, LONDON DRY A style of gin native to England; it must be distilled "in a traditional still" to not more than 70 percent alcohol, by European standards. In Canada, its only requirement is that no sweetening agents be added.

GIN, NEW WORLD (AKA BOTANICAL, AROMATIC, NEW AMERICAN) A poorly defined style of gin that, in the broadest of definitions, puts aroma and non-juniper flavours ahead of the peppery, spicy character of the juniper berry.

GRAPPA A protected term specific to Italy, this is usually a white spirit made from the seeds, skins, and stems (known as "pomace") left over after winemaking. Unique to grappa, only steam may be used in the distilling process.

HYBRID STILL A still designed to act as both a pot and a column still, changing between the two via the addition or removal of piping or the simple shifting of a few valves.

LIMONCELLO A lemon liqueur that's wildly popular in southern Italy, often made according to family recipes from household to household. The Amalfi coast is famous for making some of the best commercial expressions.

LIQUEUR A sweet spirit of moderate to low strength, usually fruit- or cream-based.

LOUCHE The absinthe louche is a cherished part of the drinking traditions associated with *la fée verte*, or "the green fairy." If you slowly add water from an absinthe drip to the clear spirit, the water will swirl around and turn the beverage opaque.

MAILLARD REACTION A culinary term that describes the chemical reaction between sugars and amino acids when they're exposed to heat. Browning meat, caramelizing onions, or deeply roasting malt for beer and spirits are all examples of the Maillard Reaction. After years spent wondering why nobody has used it for a band name, we're happy to report that some enterprising musicians in Kalamazoo have finally fixed that.

MARC   The French equivalent to the Italian grappa, marc has fewer restrictions in its production methods—water may be used, for example—and is often barrel-aged prior to bottling.

MASH   The grains that are fermented to create a "wash" or "beer" that will be distilled into a spirit, usually to be aged and bottled as whisky.

MASH BILL   Distillers sometimes talk about a mash bill (especially in the United States), which is really just the recipe—as in, say, 70 percent corn, 16 percent wheat, 14 percent barley. In Canada, distillers sometimes use the term, but not always, since it's common for Canadian whisky to be distilled separately and then blended together.

NOCINO (NUCINO)   A sticky, rich, and indulgent northern Italian liqueur made from green, unripe walnuts and often enjoyed around the holidays.

PÀLINKA   Similar to a rakia, this is a fruit brandy distilled mainly in Hungary. Several provinces in Austria are also designated pàlinka producers.

PASTIS   A French anise-flavoured spirit that became popular around the time that absinthe was banned.

PEATED   A peated whisky is one that's been made with malt dried with peat smoke. This is a common practice in Scotland, where peat, a fuel, was used to heat most buildings until recently. The smoke affects the flavour of the spirit, even though it's been distilled.

POT STILL   A more modern take on the alembic, the pot still distills in batches via two separate chambers connected by a swan's neck–like piece of piping.

PROOF   Somewhat confusingly, people still sometimes refer to alcohol's "proof" instead of ABV (Alcohol By Volume). It derives from a ritual developed in the British Royal Navy in which sailors would pour spirits over gunpowder. If the soaked gunpowder still ignited, that was "proof" that it hadn't been watered down. The "proof" number is simply double the spirit's ABV.

RAKIA   Fruit brandy from central Europe. Although the one most commonly available in Canada (Slivovitz) is made from a specific variety of plums, rakia can be created out of any stone fruit, as well as pomace, grapes, figs, or berries.

RED FIFE   A heritage grain (Canada's first wheat, actually) that's been revived of late by bakers and distillers looking to pre-modern ingredients for fresh inspiration. This reddish-hued grain is said to have a more complex flavour profile and low gluten levels.

RUM A spirit distilled from molasses or, less commonly, sugar cane juice. Under present Canadian law, it must be aged in wood for a minimum of one year, which is why many Canadian molasses-based spirits are known as "rhumb" or some other variation on the name.

SCOTCH Whisky distilled in Scotland and subject to the category rules there. Generally, Scotch fits into one of three categories: Blended, which is a mix of grain spirit with barley malt–based whisky; Blended Malt, which is a mix of barley malt–based whiskies from different distilleries; and Single Malt, which is made entirely from malted barley at a single distillery.

SINGLE MALT When not used with "Scotch" or "Scottish," this denotes a whisky made entirely from malted barley at a single distillery, and in Canadian terms, aged in wood, usually oak, for a minimum of three years.

TANNIC A tannic, or astringent taste in a spirit (or wine, for that matter) derives from tannins, which are biomolecules in a wide range of plants. You hear a lot about it in tea culture, the wine world, and the spirits world, since we experience it as a sensation of drying out the tongue.

TERPENES Organic compounds produced by many different plants that are responsible for a lot of a plant's odours—pine, citrus, and even the skunky smell of cannabis. Like tannins, these are actually part of the defense mechanism of a lot of plants, since they're designed to ward off certain animals.

TRITICALE A hybrid grain that's a cross between rye and wheat. It's starting to generate interest thanks to its hardy and drought-resistant properties. A lot of distillers are starting to experiment with it, since it also has a unique flavour profile.

VODKA A clear spirit distilled to high proof, still bafflingly defined in the United States as "to be without distinctive character, aroma, taste or color [sic]." We respectfully disagree. (See "Legal Definitions of Spirits in Canada" on p. 131.)

V.S., V.S.O.P., X.O., ETC. A system of classifying cognacs and brandies according to age and composition. When applied to other spirits, their use is simply clever marketing.

WHISKY (WHISKEY) Simply, a spirit made from grain and typically aged, often to conform with legal labelling requirements. By convention, the "e" is used in the United States and Ireland, while the e-less spelling is applied in Canada, Scotland, and elsewhere.

BIBLIOGRAPHICAL SOURCES & SUGGESTIONS FOR FURTHER READING

BOOKS

Abou-Ganim, Tony. *Vodka Distilled.* Chicago: Surrey Books, 2013.

Bitterman, Mark. *Bitterman's Field Guide to Bitters and Amari.* Kansas City: Andrews McMeel Publishing, 2015.

Broom, Dave. *Gin—The Manual.* London: Mitchell Beazley, 2015.

Broom, Dave. *The World Atlas of Whisky* (Second Edition). London: Mitchell Beazley, 2014.

Bryson, Lew. *Tasting Whisky.* North Adams: Storey Publishing, 2014.

De Kergommeaux, Davin. *Canadian Whisky: The New Portable Expert* (Second Edition). Toronto: Random House, 2017.

Francis, Daniel. *Closing Time: Prohibition, Rum-Runners and Border Wars.* Madeira: Douglas & McIntyre, 2014.

Heron, Craig. *Booze: A Distilled History.* Toronto: Between the Lines Press, 2003

Malleck, Dan. *Try to Control Yourself: The Regulation of Public Drinking in Post-Prohibition* Ontario, 1927–1944. Vancouver: UBC, 2012.

MacKinnon, Tanya Lynn. *The Historical Geography of the Distilling Industry of Ontario, 1850-1900.* Wilfrid Laurier University, 2000 (Thesis).

McCallum, Scott and Victoria Walsh. *A Field Guide to Canadian Cocktails.* Toronto: Random House, 2015.

Pashley, Nick. *Cheers! An Intemperate History of Beer in Canada.* Toronto: Harper Collins, 2009.

Roberts, Julia. *In Mixed Company: Taverns and Public Life in Upper Canada.* Vancouver: UBC, 2009.

Rogers, Adam. *Proof: The Science of Booze.* Boston: Mariner Books, 2014.

Sismondo, Christine. *America Walks into a Bar: A Spirited History of Taverns and Saloons, Speakeasies and Grog Shops.* New York: Oxford University Press, 2011.

Soole, Shawn and Nate Caudle. *Cocktail Culture: Recipes and Techniques from Behind the Bar.* Vancouver: TouchWood Editions, 2013.

ARTICLES

Gillman, Gary. "Special Regulatory Report: Canadian Whisky, Its History, Taste, Legal Regulation" Lawgill.com, 2012.

WEBSITES

albertacraftdistillers.com
bcdistilled.ca
canadianwhisky.org
flaviar.com
sawsa.ca
whisky.com

MAGAZINES

The Alchemist, Glacier Media Group, Vancouver.

ACKNOWLEDGEMENTS

Many people have assisted in the creation of this book and our sincere thanks go out to each of them, particularly all the distillers, distillery owners, and managers who took the time to speak with us and, in many cases, to offer or send along samples of what they produce.

In addition to all of those distinguished professionals, we would like to thank the following: Whitney Moran, our wonderful editor at Nimbus, whose patience and understanding was nothing less than remarkable; Lexi Harrington and Ian Gibb, our two excellent photo researchers at Nimbus; Spirits Canada in general and CJ Helie in particular for helping us to catalogue Canada's craft distillers; Craig Heron for allowing us to reproduce his Prohibition chart from *Booze: A Distilled History*; Alex Hamer of Artisan Distillers Canada for all of his help in sorting out who distills what and Shawn Soole for his assistance with the same; Kate Boushel, bartender extraordinaire in Montréal who helped us to get a handle on that scene; Craig Pinhey, who offered an assist in the Maritimes; and last but in no way least, our agent, Clare Pelino, who believed in and supported this project from start to finish.

We would be remiss if we did not also mention the two people in our lives who not only stoically endure the vagaries of life with freelance writers and authors, but also support us in all our crazy endeavours, including the creation of this book. Thank you, Maggie and Al. You're both stars!

INDEX OF DISTILLERIES

ABOUT THE AUTHORS

MAGGIE BEAUMONT

Stephen Beaumont is a globally recognized writer specializing in beer and spirits. The author or co-author of thirteen books, including two editions of the international bestseller *The World Atlas of Beer*, and his latest, *Will Travel for Beer*, he is also a columnist for a variety of publications from *Whisky Advocate* magazine to the website just-drinks.com. He documents his incessant world travels online at beaumontdrinks.com and on Twitter and Instagram at @BeaumontDrinks. He lives with his wife in downtown Toronto.

JESSICA BLAINE SMITH

Christine Sismondo is a Toronto writer, historian, and the author of *America Walks into a Bar* and *Mondo Cocktail: A Shaken and Stirred History*. She's a National Magazine Award winner, a columnist for the *Toronto Star* and *Quench*, as well as a regular contributor to the *Globe and Mail* and *Maclean's*. Most recently, Sismondo wrote a six-part podcast series on Prohibition for Wondery's American History Tellers.